Hermeticism

Its Relevance to the Teachings of the Warrior, Scholar and Sage

By Jim Moltzan

Disclaimer

This book is intended for information purposes only. The author does not promise or imply any results to those using this information, nor are they responsible for any adverse results brought about by the usage of the information contained herein. Use the information provided at your own risk. Furthermore, the author does not guarantee that the holder of this information will improve his or her health from the information contained herein.

The author of this book has used his/her best efforts in preparing this book. The author makes no representation of warranties with respect to the accuracy, applicability, or completeness of the contents of this book.

This book is © copyrighted by CAD Graphics, Inc. No part of this may be copied, or changed in any form, sold, or used in any way other than what is outlined within this book under any circumstances. No part of this book may be reproduced or transferred in any form or by any means, graphic, electronic, or mechanical, including photocopying, recording, taping, or by any information storage retrieval system, without the written permission of the author.

© 2025 CAD Graphics, Inc.

ISBN: 978-1-958837-50-4

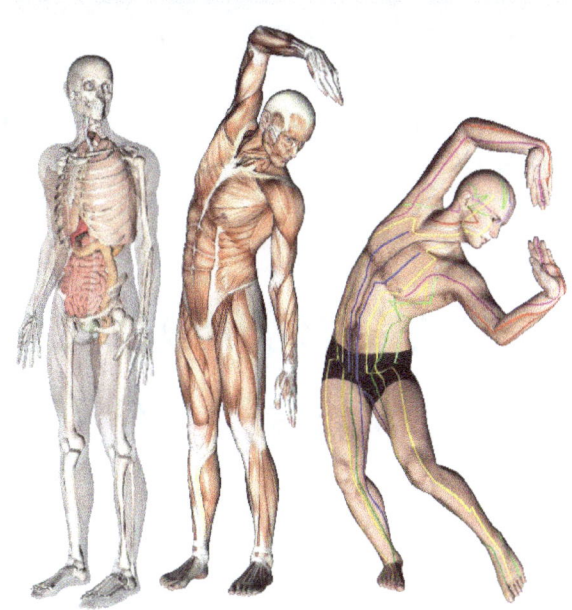

We are the architect of our own health, happiness, destiny, or fate.

Table of Contents

Preface 1
Acknowledgments 2
Author's Note 3

Part I — The Hermetic Foundation 4
1. Origins of Hermeticism 5
2. The Seven Hermetic Principles 11
3. Trauma, Conditioning and Search for Wholeness 16
4. The Eighth Principle 21

Part II — The Warrior–Scholar–Sage Path 28
5. The Warrior (Jing) 29
6. The Scholar (Qi) 34
7. The Sage (Shen) 40

Part III — The Somatic & Psychological Great Work 46
8. Breath, Posture and Nervous System Mastery 47
9. Practical Methods of Self-Regulation 62
10 Emotional Alchemy 78
11. Discernment and Boundaries in a Manipulative Age 85
12. Meaning-making, Purpose and Personal Integration 93

PART IV — Expanded Consciousness & Creative Self 100
13. Expanded Consciousness 101
14. Co-creation and Hermetic Art of Shaping Reality 108
15. The Hermetic Adept in Society 116
16. Conflict, Shadow Dynamics and the Hermetic Approach to Resolution 123

PART V — Destiny, Virtue & Cosmic Principle at Work 130
17. Service, Contribution and the Hermetic Role in Collective Evolution 131
18. Destiny, Freewill and the Unfolding of the Hermetic Path 139
19. The Principle of Rhythm 147
20. The Principle of Gender 157
21. Ethics, Moral Discernment and the Responsibilities of the Hermetic Adept 166

PART VI — The Final Transmutation 174
22. Suffering, Adversity and the Alchemy of Meaning 175

   23. Becoming a Luminous Presence 183

   24. Integration and Completion 191

Part VII – Appendices & Resources 198

   Appendix A – Concept of Kan and Li 199

   Appendix B – Nervous Systems 202

   Appendix C - Qigong 204

   Appendix D – Small Circulation Exercises 208

   Appendix E – Other Breathing Patterns 213

   Appendix F – 8 Pieces of Brocade 216

   Appendix G – 5 Element Qigong 220

   Appendix H – Chamsa Meditation 222

   Appendix I – 8 Vessels Matrix of Exercises 228

   Appendix J – Emotional Energetics: Energy Vampires & Energy Suns 230

   Epilogue - The Journey Continues 235

   References 240

   Glossary of Terms 245

   Glossary - Graphic 262

   About the Instructor, Author & Artist - Jim Moltzan 266

   Books Available Through Amazon 268

   Contacts 270

Preface

Human life moves through physical, emotional, mental, and spiritual layers that often become fragmented by stress, distraction, and the pace of modern culture. Yet beneath the surface of everyday experience, there is an underlying order. A pattern of meaning that ancient traditions recognized and modern psychology and neuroscience increasingly acknowledge. This book draws from more than four decades of study and practice across martial arts, holistic health, somatic awareness, and contemplative disciplines. It approaches Hermeticism not as an archaic philosophy, but as a practical lens for understanding how human beings grow, heal, and mature.

Hermetic principles describe universal dynamics that remain visible today in cognition, emotional regulation, trauma responses, decision-making, interpersonal behavior, and the search for purpose. When the classical teachings speak of mind, vibration, polarity, or correspondence, these principles parallel what contemporary research reveals about perception, neuroplasticity, autonomic patterns, and the interplay between inner states and outward behavior. This work examines those relationships in a grounded, applicable way, showing how age-old ideas can support clarity, stability, and transformation in daily life.

Woven throughout the book is the developmental model of the **Warrior, Scholar, and Sage.** These archetypes represent three essential capacities: embodied strength and grounding (*Jing*), refined understanding and discernment (*Qi*), and ethical, integrated wisdom (*Shen*). Together, they form a structure for personal evolution that aligns with both Hermetic teaching and Taoist (Daoist) internal cultivation. They also speak directly to modern challenges such as identity confusion, emotional volatility, chronic stress, and the need for ethical clarity in an increasingly complex world.

This book does not promote a belief system, nor does it ask the reader to accept any tradition uncritically. Hermeticism encourages inquiry, experimentation, and self-honesty. Its value arises not from doctrine, but from application through breath, posture, attention, decision-making, personal boundaries, and the willingness to refine one's inner life. Readers are invited to test these principles in their own experience, using them to make sense of adversity, to cultivate resilience, and to deepen their understanding of themselves and others.

My hope is that this work serves as a guide for those who seek coherence amid fragmentation and meaning amid uncertainty. Hermeticism, viewed through a modern lens, offers not just a philosophy but a practice in a way of aligning thought, emotion, and action with deeper purpose. The Great Work begins wherever one stands and continues through the choices made day by day.

Acknowledgments

This book would not exist without the wisdom, guidance, and resilience of countless individuals who have contributed directly and indirectly to its creation. Gratitude is extended to the teachers, mentors, and colleagues who preserved Hermetic, Taoist, philosophical, and psychological wisdom across generations. Their commitment to truth and integrity forms the foundation upon which this work stands. Their teachings, whether shared in formal settings, private conversations, or quiet gestures, have shaped the lens through which this manuscript was conceived and refined.

Acknowledgment is also due to the authors, researchers, and practitioners whose scholarship illuminates the intersections between ancient knowledge and modern science. Their dedication to understanding the human mind, body, and spirit has profoundly influenced the integrative approach taken in this work. Each study, insight, and theoretical contribution represented a stepping-stone toward a more coherent and comprehensive synthesis of Hermeticism, psychology, neuroscience, and embodied practice.

Deep appreciation is extended to the readers, as students, seekers, practitioners, scholars, clinicians, and everyday individuals who continue to embody courage, curiosity, and compassion. Their struggles, triumphs, insights, and questions have shaped the clarity and direction of this book. Many have shared their personal journeys of healing, transformation, and self-understanding, reminding the author that the Great Work is not an abstract philosophy but a lived experience unfolding within real human lives.

I am indebted as well to those who have walked paths of hardship, trauma, and profound change. Their resilience is a testament to the human spirit. Their stories echo the core message of this book: that suffering can refine, adversity can illuminate, and self-discovery can lead to service. The courage of these individuals continues to inspire the ongoing work of integrating ancient wisdom with contemporary insight, and their presence, often anonymous yet deeply felt, rests at the heart of these pages.

Finally, my gratitude extends to the friends, family members, and supportive communities who have encouraged my projects of writing through seasons of growth, reflection, and renewal. Their belief in the value of meaningful work, their willingness to listen, and their commitment to the deeper dimensions of human life provided steady ground beneath the creative process. This book is, in many ways, a collaborative accomplishment made possible by every conversation, challenge, inspiration, and shared moment of human connection.

Author's Note

The material in this book represents the convergence of many paths I have walked throughout my life of martial arts training, holistic health education, contemplative study, personal introspection, and decades of teaching others. Although these influences are diverse in origin, they share an underlying aim: understanding what it means to become a more integrated human being. This manuscript is not the result of a single realization or sudden insight, but the gradual refinement of questions I have asked repeatedly: *What helps people grow? What sustains them? What undermines them? And what universal principles remain steady across the many systems that seek to answer these questions?*

Hermeticism emerged as a natural framework through which to organize these inquiries. Its principles mirror patterns I have observed for years in my own practice, in students, and in the broader arc of human behavior. I did not set out to write a "Hermetic" book. Rather, Hermetic logic became the most coherent language for describing the processes I had already been witnessing how people build stability, how thought shapes perception, how inner states influence outward action, and how transformation unfolds when a person commits to their own development. These principles offered a container large enough to hold the complexity of real-life growth without reducing it to motivational slogans or overly simplified self-help concepts.

Although I have spent many years teaching and learning in structured settings, much of what appears in these pages comes from lived experience in my own mistakes, corrections, quiet observations, private discipline, and long periods of study outside the spotlight. I write this not as an authority removed from real struggles but as someone who has navigated confusion, adversity, reinvention, and the difficulties of discerning truth from illusion. The tools that were most meaningful to me are the ones I share here, not as prescriptions but as offerings.

This book is meant to serve as a companion for readers traveling their own path of refinement. Whether you are drawn to martial arts, philosophy, psychology, or spiritual inquiry, the goal is the same: to provide a structure for understanding yourself more clearly and acting from a place of integrity. The principles explored here are not reserved for practitioners of any one tradition. They apply to anyone seeking to live with greater awareness, coherence, and purpose.

My hope is that readers approach this material with curiosity and patience, taking what resonates, questioning what does not, and allowing the process of reflection to unfold naturally. The Great Work belongs to each of us individually, yet its effects ripple outward into every relationship, choice, and moment of everyday life.

— *Jim Moltzan*

Part I — The Hermetic Foundation

1. Origins of Hermeticism

Historical Setting

Hermeticism did not originate solely from Egypt or Greece; rather, it emerged within the multicultural environment of Hellenistic Egypt, particularly Alexandria, between the 1st and 3rd centuries CE (Copenhaver, 1992). Alexandria was a center of intellectual syncretism where Egyptian priestly traditions, Greek philosophical schools, Jewish mysticism, and nascent Gnosticism interacted. Within this environment, a body of writings arose under the name *Hermes Trismegistus*, a syncretic figure combining the Greek god Hermes with the Egyptian god Thoth, both associated with writing, wisdom, and esoteric knowledge (Fowden, 1993).

The *Corpus Hermeticum*, a collection of Greek philosophical dialogues, and the *Asclepius*, a Latin treatise, serve as the foundational texts. These writings were preserved through Byzantine scholars and later rediscovered during the Renaissance. Their translation by Marsilio Ficino in 1463 fueled a major intellectual shift, influencing figures such as Giordano Bruno, Paracelsus, and Johannes Kepler (Yates, 1964).

Religious and Philosophical Influences

Hermeticism is often described as an amalgamation of:

- **Platonic metaphysics:** ideas of emanation, the cosmic hierarchy, and the ascent of the soul.

- **Egyptian temple theology:** concepts of divine mind, cosmic order (*ma'at*), and ritual purity.

- **Stoicism:** the immanent presence of Logos as a rational divine principle.

- **Gnostic and mystical thought:** emphasis on inner knowledge (*gnosis*) as salvific.

These threads, woven together, created a tradition devoted to the study of divine reality, the nature of the cosmos, and the transformation of the human being.

Core Principles of Hermeticism

While Hermeticism encompasses a wide spectrum of texts and practices, scholars routinely identify seven foundational principles, largely derived from the *Kybalion* (1908) and corroborated by themes in the classical *Hermetica*. Although the *Kybalion* is not ancient, its principles reflect the philosophical structure present in the original texts

(Godwin, 2017). Classical Hermetic concepts are synthesized with these widely taught principles to create a comprehensive and historically grounded overview.

The "philosopher's stone"

Hermetic Practices and Applications

1. Alchemy
Alchemy is both a physical and psychological discipline. While medieval alchemists sought to transmute metals, Hermetic alchemy is primarily inner transformation, of purifying the soul, refining consciousness, and awakening divine potential (Principe, 2013). The *"philosopher's stone"* symbolizes perfected awareness.

2. Astrology and Cosmic Sympathy
Hermetic astrology interprets celestial patterns as mirrors of terrestrial and psychological processes. The cosmos is a living organism; planetary movements reflect intelligible principles operating within the human being (Campion, 2008).

3. Theurgy and Contemplation
Theurgy, the ritual invocation of divine intelligences, appears in later Hermetic streams influenced by Neoplatonism. In contrast, the *Corpus Hermeticum* emphasizes inner illumination through meditation, purification, moral virtue, and contemplation of the divine (Fowden, 1993).

4. Ethical Transformation
Ethics lie at the heart of Hermetic self-cultivation. The *Poimandres* dialogue emphasizes compassion, self-restraint, truthfulness, and purification of the passions as prerequisites for spiritual ascent (Copenhaver, 1992). These virtues enable the soul to rise beyond material identification toward union with the divine.

Hermeticism's Continuing Influence

Hermeticism influenced:

- **Renaissance magic and science**, contributing to early models of cosmology and natural philosophy.

- **Christian mysticism**, including Johann Arndt and Jacob Böhme.

- **Modern esotericism**, such as the Rosicrucians, Golden Dawn, and contemporary occult communities.

- **Psychology**, including Jung's symbolic interpretation of alchemy as a map of individuation (Jung, 1968).

Today, Hermetic principles echo through mindfulness, energy practices, somatic awareness, and integrative models of consciousness, areas closely aligned with holistic mind-body-spirit research.

Hermeticism represents a profound synthesis of metaphysics, psychology, cosmology, and ethical transformation. Emerging from the intellectual ferment of Hellenistic Egypt, it forged a worldview in which mind, cosmos, and divinity are integrally connected. Its principles of mentalism, correspondence, vibration, polarity, rhythm, causality, and gender, provide a philosophical framework for understanding the universe as a dynamic, intelligent whole.

More than a historical curiosity, Hermeticism continues to inspire modern discussions on consciousness, holistic health, energy systems, and the synergy between science and spirituality. For practitioners committed to inner refinement, ethical living, and expanded awareness, Hermeticism offers a perennial path toward wisdom.

The Return of Hermeticism in a Fractured World

Humanity is living through a period of profound fragmentation. The modern world is technologically advanced yet psychologically strained, socially networked yet emotionally disconnected, and intellectually saturated yet spiritually malnourished. Rates of anxiety, depression, loneliness, and attention dysregulation have climbed to unprecedented levels, particularly among younger generations shaped by digital environments (Haidt, 2024). Stress physiology has become chronically activated, with many living in states of sympathetic overdrive, an internal turbulence that often goes unnoticed until it manifests through illness, exhaustion, or emotional collapse (van der Kolk, 2014).

In an era marked by overstimulation, shrinking attention spans, and weakened interpersonal skills, individuals increasingly struggle to regulate their emotions, understand their inner world, or maintain a coherent sense of identity (Lissak, 2018). Technology has not merely altered the pace of life; it has rewired the very neurological structures that underlie perception, motivation, and social development (Crum et al., 2013). What once required human interaction is now simulated by screens. What once required personal discipline is now outsourced to algorithms. What once required community is now attempted in isolation.

It is in this context that ancient Hermetic philosophy has quietly reemerged. Not as an esoteric curiosity, but as a deeply relevant psychological framework for restoring personal wholeness.

Hermeticism as a Universal Model of Human Functioning

Hermeticism, often caricatured as mystical, occult, or symbolic, contains within its core seven principles that operate as a compact, universal psychology of human experience. These principles, articulated in texts attributed to Hermes Trismegistus, describe predictable patterns in cognition, emotion, behavior, and consciousness. When examined through the lens of modern research, they map astonishingly well onto contemporary psychological and neurological understandings.

- **Mentalism** teaches that the mind shapes perception and experience. This parallels predictive processing theory, in which the brain constructs reality through internal models (Clark, 2013).

- **Correspondence** captures the repeating patterns between inner and outer worlds, similar to how cognitive schemas shape external relationships and behavior (Beck, 1976).

- **Vibration** reflects emotional and physiological oscillations—breath, heart rate, neural rhythms—recognized today in neuroscience and somatic psychology (Porges, 2011).

- **Polarity** mirrors cognitive reframing and emotional transformation, demonstrating how states such as fear and courage exist on the same continuum (Tversky & Kahneman, 1974).

- **Rhythm** corresponds to circadian biology, hormonal cycles, emotional waves, and the natural oscillations of human energy (Czeisler, 1999).

- **Cause and Effect** align with behavioral conditioning and the habit-loop research popularized in modern psychology (Duhigg, 2012).

- **Gender** symbolizes the balance of active and receptive forces—the integration of logic and intuition, structure and empathy—that contemporary psychology associates with emotional intelligence and developmental maturity (Jung, 1959).

Far from outdated metaphysics, Hermeticism offers a remarkably adaptive framework for modern human development, one that integrates cognitive, emotional, somatic, ethical, and spiritual dimensions into a single, coherent philosophy.

A Path Forward in a Time of Disconnection

Modern people struggle not because they lack access to information, but because they lack a unifying structure that connects:

- body
- mind
- emotions
- ethics
- identity
- purpose
- consciousness

Hermeticism provides precisely that structure. Its principles do not require belief or dogma; they require only observation, reflection, and practice. They function as "laws of inner physics" that operate whether one knows them or not.

Psychologists note that a central feature of modern distress is fragmentation, or a disconnection between internal states, external behavior, and the deeper sense of self (Herman, 1992). Hermeticism, by contrast, teaches correspondence and coherence: the alignment of inner and outer worlds, the integration of body and mind, and the harmonization of thought and action.

Its emphasis on self-responsibility, ethical clarity, emotional transmutation, and embodied presence makes Hermeticism uniquely suited for a time when individuals are overwhelmed by external influence and lacking internal sovereignty.

The Need for Embodied Wisdom

What distinguishes this modern interpretation of Hermeticism from other philosophical approaches is its integration with **embodied practice**. Contemporary research in psychology and neuroscience confirms what Hermetic and Taoist traditions taught centuries ago:

- Posture influences emotional state (Peper et al., 2022)
- Breath regulates the nervous system (Zaccaro et al., 2018)
- Embodiment is essential for trauma recovery (van der Kolk, 2014)
- Meaning-making is central to psychological resilience (Frankl, 2006)

In this book, Hermetic principles are paired with modern breathwork, somatic grounding, cognitive reframing, and ethical development to form a complete model of human flourishing. This is Hermeticism not as myth or metaphor, but as a practical blueprint for living.

A New Hermeticism for a New Era

The modern revival of Hermetic thought is not accidental but rathe it is adaptive. The Seven Principles fill a void left by fragmented educational systems, digital overstimulation, weakened community, and declining physical health. They offer what contemporary society lacks:

- a grounding philosophy rooted in wisdom
- a model for emotional and psychological coherence
- a framework for personal sovereignty
- tools for regulating stress
- guidance for ethical living
- a pathway to meaning and integration

The world is changing rapidly, and individuals increasingly struggle to keep pace. Hermeticism does not promise escape from modern life; it offers tools to navigate it with strength, discernment, and purpose.

By uniting ancient wisdom with modern science, embodied practice, and ethical clarity, Hermeticism becomes not a historical artifact but a living system capable of guiding modern individuals toward resilience, maturity, and wholeness.

This is the foundation on which the rest of this book is built.

2. The Seven Hermetic Principles

A Universal Psychology

Although often regarded as mystical axioms originating in antiquity, the Seven Hermetic Principles form a remarkably cohesive psychological and philosophical system. When interpreted through a contemporary lens, they describe the fundamental mechanisms by which humans perceive, interpret, and interact with the world. Each principle corresponds not only to spiritual insight, but also to modern findings in neuroscience, behavioral science, physiology, and cognitive psychology.

These principles endure because they reflect structural truths about human experience. They reveal how individuals shape their internal world and how the internal world, in turn, influences behavior, relationships, and subjective reality. Properly applied, they offer a foundation for personal transformation, resilience, ethical development, and conscious living.

The Seven Principles are presented below in their traditional order, followed by interpretive commentary bridging ancient insight and modern science.

1. The Principle of Mentalism

"All is Mind; the Universe is Mental."

The **Principle of Mentalism** asserts that reality is shaped by the mind's interpretive processes. It does not claim that the external world is imaginary, but rather that experience of the world is inherently filtered, constructed, and influenced by cognitive and perceptual mechanisms.

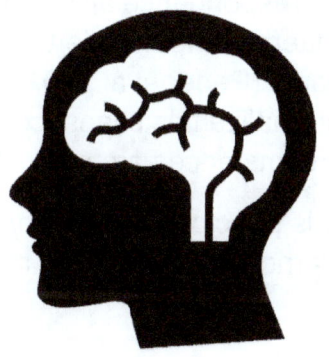

Modern neuroscience supports this perspective. Research in predictive processing theory shows that the brain does not passively receive information; instead, it actively constructs reality by predicting and interpreting sensory input (Clark, 2013). Cognitive schemas, or deep mental frameworks formed by early experiences and reinforced through repetition, shape how individuals interpret events, relationships, and challenges (Beck, 1976).

Mentalism thus describes a psychological truth:
the mind conditions perception, and perception conditions experience.

In practical terms, this means that two individuals can face the same situation and yet encounter vastly different realities based on their interpretive lens. Trauma, belief systems, cultural conditioning, and habitual emotional states all influence this mental construction of the world (van der Kolk, 2014).

Mentalism therefore underscores the importance of mental hygiene, cognitive awareness, and the capacity to question one's own assumptions. Without such awareness, individuals become prisoners of their own unexamined patterns of thought.

2. The Principle of Correspondence

"As above, so below; as below, so above."

Perhaps the most widely cited Hermetic maxim, the **Principle of Correspondence** indicates that patterns repeat across levels of reality. In modern terms, this principle mirrors systemic thinking and the recognition that internal states influence outward behavior, while external environments shape the internal world.

Psychology refers to this as *reciprocal determinism,* a continuous interplay between cognition, behavior, and environment (Bandura, 1986). Cognitive-behavioral science likewise affirms that internal beliefs shape behavior, and behavior reinforces beliefs (Williams et al., 1997).

Correspondence also aligns with somatic psychology, where bodily posture, breath patterns, and muscle tension influence emotional states, self-image, and cognitive clarity (Peper et al., 2016). When the outer world is disordered, individuals often internalize this chaos; conversely, when the inner world is regulated, external circumstances are navigated with increased clarity and agency.

This principle forms a conceptual bridge to later chapters that explore embodiment, the Warrior–Scholar–Sage model, trauma integration, and ethical development.

3. The Principle of Vibration

"Nothing rests; everything moves; everything vibrates."

In Hermetic terms, vibration refers to the energetic, emotional, and psychological motions that underlie all aspects of existence. Nothing is static. Thoughts, emotions, physiological states, and even identity fluctuate.

Physiology affirms this principle through the study of neural oscillations, heart-rate variability, respiratory rhythms, and hormonal cycles (Czeisler, 1999). Emotional states also move in waves; they arise, peak, and pass as part of the nervous system's natural ebb and flow (Porges, 2011).

Hermeticism recognized long ago what modern somatic therapies now emphasize:
to influence emotion, one must influence vibration.

Breathwork, posture adjustments, mindful movement, and grounding practices all shift the nervous system's vibratory state (Zaccaro et al., 2018). This is why individuals who struggle with chronic anxiety, anger, or depression often benefit from physical as much as psychological interventions.

Vibration is also central to transmutation, the process by which undesirable states are transformed into constructive ones, an idea echoed in cognitive reframing and emotion regulation research (Tversky & Kahneman, 1974).

4. The Principle of Polarity

"Everything is dual; everything has poles."

Polarity teaches that opposites are not separate forces but rather *different degrees on a single continuum*. Cold and heat are variations of temperature; fear and courage are variations of emotional activation; pessimism and optimism are variations of interpretation.

Psychology demonstrates this principle in cognitive reframing techniques, which help individuals shift interpretation along the same continuum of meaning (Beck, 1976). The same event may be perceived as a catastrophe or an opportunity depending on cognitive framing.

Polarity also illuminates trauma responses: hypoarousal and hyperarousal exist on the same physiological spectrum, reflecting the nervous system's adaptive but often maladaptive responses to overwhelming experience (Herman, 1992).

Hermetic polarity is not merely descriptive, it is prescriptive. It suggests that transformation does not occur by fighting an opposite, but by shifting along the continuum toward a more constructive expression. This concept will later inform emotional alchemy, personal development, and spiritual integration.

5. The Principle of Rhythm

"Everything flows, out and in; everything has its tides."

Rhythm acknowledges the cyclical nature of all phenomena. Human biology is governed by circadian rhythms, ultradian rhythms, hormonal cycles, and sleep-wake patterns (Czeisler, 1999). Emotional states rise and fall; motivation fluctuates; relationships shift; societies expand and contract.

Understanding rhythm helps individuals navigate adversity with patience and resilience. It reveals that downturns are not failures but aspects of natural cycles. Individuals caught in emotional or cognitive extremes often suffer because they resist these natural oscillations rather than working with them.

Modern stress research supports this view. Chronic stress results not from isolated events but from the loss of recovery cycles, or the body's inability to return to baseline (Porges, 2011). Hermetic rhythm encourages the restoration of these natural patterns through rest, breath regulation, mindful living, and conscious pacing.

6. The Principle of Cause and Effect

"Every cause has its effect; every effect has its cause."

This principle forms the backbone of both Hermeticism and modern behavioral science. Hermeticism teaches that nothing occurs by chance; events are born from patterns, choices, actions, and conditions.

Behavioral psychology similarly asserts that behavior is shaped by antecedents and consequences. Habits are created through cues, routines, and rewards (Duhigg, 2012). Cognitive science further demonstrates that thought patterns influence emotional states, which in turn shape actions (Beck, 1976).

Cause and Effect underscore the importance of personal responsibility. Individuals cannot control all external circumstances, but they can influence the causes they generate internally, such as habits, thoughts, breath patterns, decisions, boundaries, and moral choices.

Understanding Cause and Effect also protects individuals from manipulation. By recognizing causal chains, they become less vulnerable to coercion, gaslighting, or emotional exploitation (Tversky & Kahneman, 1974).

7. The Principle of Gender

"Gender is in everything; everything has its masculine and feminine principles."

Gender in Hermeticism refers not to biological sex, but to complementary forces:

- active and receptive
- logical and intuitive

- structured and fluid
- expressive and reflective
- analytic and empathetic

Modern psychology recognizes these as complementary cognitive and emotional capacities that support maturity, adaptability, and resilience (Jung, 1959). Healthy development requires a balance of these forces.

In many cultural systems, including Taoist philosophy, these are reflected as *yang* (active, penetrating, directive) and *yin* (receptive, nourishing, integrating). Integrating both allows individuals to think clearly, relate compassionately, act effectively, and maintain inner balance.

Gender as a principle becomes especially important when exploring leadership, ethics, boundaries, and emotional regulation in later chapters.

Conclusion: A Timeless Framework Reinterpreted for Modern Life

The Seven Hermetic Principles form a psychological architecture that remains relevant across time and culture. Rather than mystical abstractions, they describe universal patterns of cognition, emotion, physiology, and consciousness. Their modern interpretation bridges ancient wisdom with contemporary science, offering individuals a coherent roadmap for personal development and spiritual integration.

These principles are the foundation upon which the Warrior–Scholar–Sage model, trauma-informed insights, and embodied practices of this book will build. Together, they create a holistic path toward self-awareness, sovereignty, and inner mastery.

3. Trauma, Conditioning and Search for Wholeness

Modern Hermeticism cannot be approached merely as an intellectual or philosophical system. It must also be understood as a psychology of transformation, a framework for healing fragmentation and restoring coherence to the human experience. Among the most significant sources of fragmentation are trauma, psychological conditioning, and prolonged exposure to systems or environments that distort perception, weaken boundaries, and undermine autonomy.

In contemporary society, trauma is no longer confined to overt catastrophe. Individuals experience trauma through chronic stress, emotional invalidation, coercive social dynamics, digital overstimulation, neglect, and environments that steadily erode self-trust and clarity of perception (van der Kolk, 2014). Many suffer not from singular events but from the slow accumulation of experiences that separate them from themselves, a process that Hermeticism, interpreted through modern psychology, helps illuminate.

As people lose connection to their body's signals, emotional intelligence, cognitive discernment, and deeper sense of meaning, they begin to internalize the very forces that disempower them. This chapter explores trauma and conditioning through the lens of the Hermetic principles introduced earlier, while integrating contemporary research on stress, the nervous system, identity formation, and recovery.

Trauma as a Disruption of Inner Correspondence

Trauma is not defined by the event itself but by the impact the event leaves on the nervous system and the sense of self (Herman, 1992). What is often called trauma is better understood as a rupture in internal correspondence, a breakdown in the coherence between:

- thoughts and emotions
- body and mind
- memory and identity
- self-perception and lived experience

The Hermetic **Principle of Correspondence**, traditionally stated as *"As above, so below,"* can be reinterpreted as a psychological insight: *internal fragmentation manifests as external confusion,* and external chaos amplifies internal instability.

Trauma survivors often live with this mismatch. The outside world may appear calm while the internal world remains turbulent. Alternatively, the external environment may be unpredictable while the individual's inner life becomes numb, disconnected, or shut down. This dissociation reflects precisely the kind of divided experience that Hermetic philosophy warns against.

Contemporary research supports this understanding. Alterations in the autonomic nervous system, including dysregulated sympathetic and parasympathetic responses, impair the feeling of safety and connection within oneself (Porges, 2011). Over time, this prevents the natural flow of the **Principle of Rhythm**, freezing individuals in protective states that once served a purpose but later become maladaptive.

Hermeticism offers a countercurrent: coherence, integration, and the restoration of alignment between inner and outer worlds.

Conditioning and the Principle of Mentalism

Traumatic environments, whether abusive households, manipulative organizations, dysfunctional relationships, or coercive educational or martial structures, operate through systematic conditioning. They disrupt the **Principle of Mentalism** by shaping perceptual frameworks in ways that limit autonomy and distort reality.

Modern psychology recognizes this as *cognitive conditioning,* where repeated exposure to emotional pressure, fear, social coercion, or authoritarian dynamics creates predictable patterns of thought and behavior (Beck, 1976). Individuals adopt beliefs that are not their own, often gradually and imperceptibly, until they no longer trust their instincts or interpretations.

Cults, high-control groups, manipulative leaders, and abusive mentors often function through principles parallel to Milgram's obedience paradigm or Zimbardo's Prison Experiment, demonstrating how social pressure and perceived authority can override personal judgment and moral intuition (Haidt, 2024). This is not merely philosophical distortion, it is neurological conditioning reinforced through stress, hierarchy, and emotional dependence.

Hermeticism anticipates this problem: If the mind is the medium through which reality is processed, then whoever shapes the mind shapes the reality.
Healing thus requires reclaiming one's interpretive sovereignty.

Fragmentation of the Body: Trauma Through the Lens of Vibration

Trauma is fundamentally embodied. Long after the event or environment has passed, the body continues to respond as though danger persists. This occurs because the nervous system becomes locked into maladaptive vibratory states, hyperarousal (anxiety, tension, vigilance) or hypoarousal (numbness, withdrawal, collapse).

The Hermetic **Principle of Vibration** mirrors this understanding: *everything is movement.* Trauma interrupts healthy internal oscillations. Breath becomes shallow, posture collapses or rigidifies, muscles tighten, and the mind echoes these patterns.

Somatic research confirms that trauma alters neural rhythms, breath cycles, and muscular tone, creating a vibratory imprint that affects behavior, emotion, and thought (van der Kolk, 2014). Recovery requires restoring these natural oscillations through breathwork, movement, grounding, and safe interpersonal connection (Zaccaro et al., 2018).

> Thus, the Wisdom of Vibration becomes a core therapeutic insight:
> *to change the emotional state, one must change the physiological rhythm.*

Polarity, Identity, and Emotional Confusion

Traumatic conditioning often amplifies the Principle of Polarity in unhealthy ways. Individuals who have lived under coercive or unstable conditions frequently oscillate between:

- confidence and self-doubt
- overcompliance and rebellion
- hypervigilance and exhaustion
- emotional flooding and emotional numbness

These are not separate states but extremes on the same continuum. Polarity reveals that transformation occurs not by attacking one extreme but by moving inward toward equilibrium.

Modern emotion regulation research confirms this: developing awareness of emotional range and shifting toward neutral ground leads to more stable self-regulation (Teasdale et al., 2000). Trauma often restricts this range, freezing individuals in polarized states. Hermetic polarity encourages the opposite of restoring fluidity, adaptability, and the capacity to move along emotional spectrums rather than being trapped within them.

Rhythm and the Loss of Natural Cycles

Trauma disrupts natural rhythms: sleep, hunger, motivation, circadian cycles, and emotional waves are all affected. People living in chronic stress adapt to a world of hyperarousal and tension, losing access to rest, creativity, exploration, and connection (Czeisler, 1999).

The Principle of Rhythm teaches that cycles are foundational to life, and that healing requires the restoration of:

- daily rituals
- consistent breathwork

- somatic grounding
- sleep hygiene
- meaningful social contact
- time in nature
- reflective practices
- healthy work-rest patterns

Without rhythm, the psyche cannot integrate. Without integration, meaning collapses. Without meaning, life becomes reactive, fragmented, and hollow.

Cause and Effect: Breaking the Chains of Manipulation

Trauma survivors often struggle with the Principle of Cause and Effect. When people are conditioned in environments where consequences are unpredictable, punishment or reward is inconsistent, emotional responses are volatile, or social structures are coercive, they develop *learned helplessness* and lose the ability to predict or influence results (Seligman, 1975).

Hermeticism counters this by restoring agency. Cause and Effect teaches that personal actions, thoughts, and boundaries directly shape outcomes. Trauma breaks this link; healing reestablishes it. Modern therapeutic models emphasize precisely this restoration of agency as essential for recovery (Herman, 1992).

The Hermetic Path as a Response to Fragmentation

The human search for wholeness emerges from the body's innate drive toward integration. Trauma interrupts this drive; Hermeticism reorients it. The Seven Principles provide a framework for understanding trauma not as an endpoint, but as the beginning of a new form of self-awareness.

When individuals apply Hermetic principles to their healing process, they learn to:

- restore coherence between body and mind (Correspondence)
- reclaim cognitive sovereignty (Mentalism)
- regulate the nervous system (Vibration & Rhythm)
- shift emotional patterns constructively (Polarity)
- take ownership of their behaviors and decisions (Cause & Effect)
- balance internal forces and capacities (Gender)

Trauma becomes the catalyst for transformation, not the limiter of it. This is the essence of the **Hermetic Great Work** (M*agnum Opus*), or the alchemical process of turning unconscious suffering into conscious growth.

4. The Eighth Principle

Virtue and Ethical Alignment

While the Seven Hermetic Principles describe the structure of reality and consciousness, they do not explicitly dictate how a person ought to live. They offer laws, patterns, relationships, and mechanisms, but they do not prescribe moral orientation. This omission is not a flaw; the Hermetic authors assumed that wisdom naturally leads to ethical behavior. Yet in the modern world, understanding alone is often insufficient. Intelligence without ethics can lead to manipulation; insight without compassion can cause harm; and spiritual development without grounding can lead to grandiosity or delusion.

For this reason, contemporary Hermetic practice requires an **Eighth Principle: Virtue and Ethical Alignment.**

This principle functions as the moral center of the Great Work, a stabilizing force that guides the Warrior, directs the Scholar, and clarifies the Sage. Ethical alignment represents the coherent integration of thought, emotion, action, and impact. It transforms knowledge into wisdom, strength into service, and insight into integrity.

In a world marked by ethical confusion, social fragmentation, and widespread disembodiment, virtue becomes not a religious construct but a practical necessity for human flourishing.

Why Hermeticism Needs an Eighth Principle Today

Classical Hermetic texts such as the *Corpus Hermeticum* assume a worldview in which the pursuit of truth inherently aligns one with the divine mind (Copenhaver, 1992). In that context, morality was seen as a natural consequence of spiritual insight. The modern world, however, is saturated with information without wisdom, influence without responsibility, and power without accountability.

Psychologists note that ethical behavior does not automatically emerge from intelligence. Rather, it emerges from *integration*, or the alignment of internal structures and moral sensitivity (Haidt, 2024). Trauma, conditioning, and cultural forces can distort moral intuitions, disconnect individuals from empathy, or create ethical blind spots (Herman, 1992).

Thus, for Hermeticism to function as a complete developmental system in contemporary society, it must include an explicit ethical dimension.

Virtue is not an external rule imposed on behavior; it is an internal coherence between:

- intention
- action
- impact
- responsibility
- awareness

This internal coherence represents the apex of the Hermetic Principle of Correspondence:
as the inner world aligns ethically, the outer world becomes more harmonious.

Ethics as a Developmental Achievement

Ethical alignment is not merely a set of external behaviors; it is an internal developmental state. Research on moral psychology shows that ethical reasoning evolves through identifiable stages, moving from external obedience to internalized principles grounded in empathy, autonomy, and reflective judgment (Kohlberg, 1984).

The Warrior, Scholar, and Sage each contribute to this development:

1. The Warrior (*Jing*) → Ethical Strength

The Warrior cultivates boundaries, discipline, courage, and integrity. Ethical behavior begins with the ability to resist impulses, withstand pressure, and act with restraint. Without physical and emotional stability, ethical clarity collapses under stress.

2. The Scholar (*Qi*) → Ethical Clarity

The Scholar refines discernment, critical thinking, emotional intelligence, and cognitive sovereignty. Ethical decisions require the ability to evaluate consequences, detect manipulation, and differentiate truth from distortion.

3. The Sage (*Shen*) → Ethical Compassion

The Sage embodies empathy, presence, intuition, and moral insight. Here ethics become spontaneous, arising from a lived sense of interconnectedness and an integrative understanding of human experience.

These three capacities converge into *virtuous action*, the ultimate expression of the Eighth Principle.

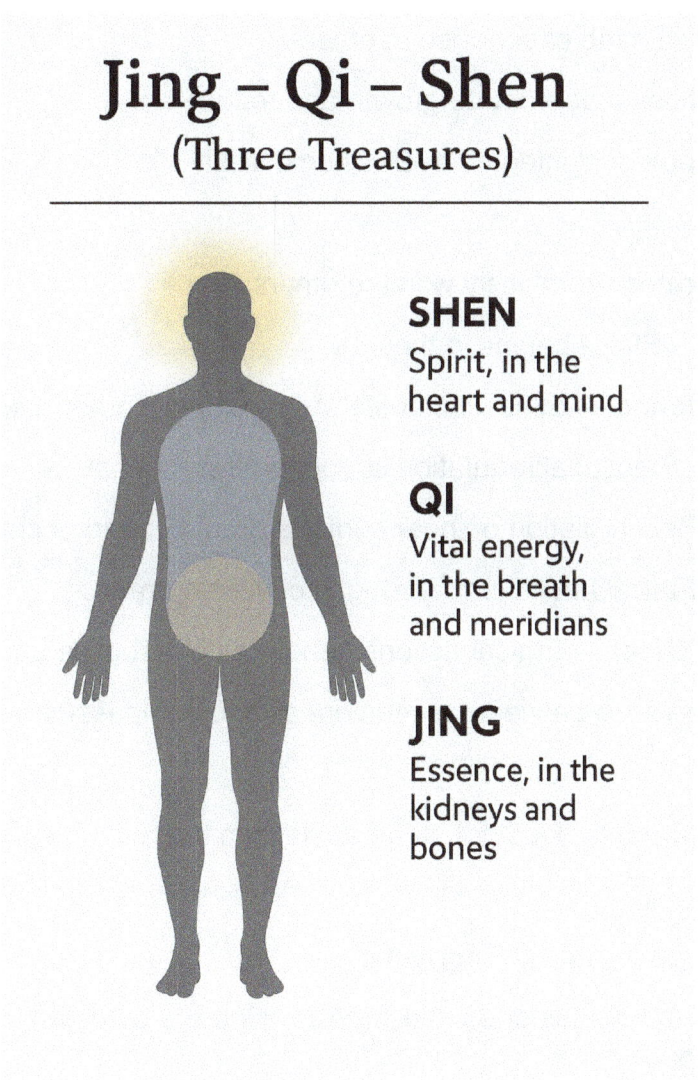

The Eighth Principle Defined: Virtue and Ethical Alignment

The Eighth Principle states:
"True mastery arises when knowledge, intention, and action are aligned ethically for the benefit of self and others."

In practice, this means:
- refusing to use insight manipulatively
- regulating emotions before acting
- evaluating the consequences of one's behavior
- accepting responsibility for impact, not just intention
- empathizing with the experience of others
- choosing actions that promote growth and reduce harm
- maintaining personal integrity even when difficult

This Principle integrates seamlessly with the others:
- **Mentalism** → Ethics begins in thought
- **Correspondence** → Ethical inner life shapes ethical outer action
- **Vibration** → Emotional regulation supports ethical behavior
- **Polarity** → Reconciliation of inner conflicts produces moral clarity
- **Rhythm** → Ethical habits form through consistent practice
- **Cause and Effect** → Ethical actions generate constructive outcomes
- **Gender** → Balance between assertiveness and compassion

Thus, the Eighth Principle does not stand apart from the rest - it synthesizes them.

Ethical Alignment and Trauma Recovery

For individuals with trauma histories, the Eighth Principle takes on special significance. Trauma often disrupts:
- trust

- boundaries
- self-worth
- intuition
- interpersonal judgment
- the ability to perceive motives clearly

Survivors may have internalized distorted messages about their value, responsibility, or rights. Ethical alignment becomes part of the healing process when individuals learn to:

- differentiate fear from intuition
- recognize manipulation and coercion
- assert boundaries without guilt
- honor their own needs
- act from clarity rather than appeasement
- reject exploitative dynamics

These changes represent the integration of Shen, where compassion pairs with discernment and strength.

Virtue as Embodied Wisdom

Virtue, in this context, is not a moral commandment; it is *the natural expression of an integrated system*. When Jing, Qi, and Shen are aligned, virtuous behavior arises spontaneously because:

- the body is grounded and stable
- the emotions are regulated
- the mind is clear
- the conscience is attuned
- the intentions are aligned with truth
- the individual is aware of the impact of their actions

This matches findings in interpersonal neurobiology, where integration leads to increased empathy, reduced reactivity, and more responsible behavior (Siegel, 2012).

Virtue is therefore not imposed from outside. It is the flowering of the Great Work.

The Eighth Principle and the Modern Crisis of Integrity

Contemporary society faces a moral crisis rooted in fragmentation:

- identity without responsibility
- influence without conscience
- spirituality without grounding
- power without empathy
- knowledge without wisdom

Hermeticism, updated with the **Eighth Principle**, offers a corrective. It demands that personal development include:

- ethical consistency
- humility
- reflective judgment
- accountability
- compassion
- integrity

These qualities restore balance to a world destabilized by individualism, digital anonymity, and overstimulation.

The **Eighth Principle** is the stabilizing axis around which the Seven Principles revolve.

Conclusion: Virtue as the Completion of the Great Work

The Hermetic path is incomplete without virtue. The Warrior provides strength; the Scholar provides clarity; the Sage provides compassion and insight. But the **Eighth Principle** ensures that all of these capacities are directed toward constructive, ethical, and meaningful action.

Virtue transforms:

- strength into service
- knowledge into wisdom
- insight into integrity
- power into responsibility

- understanding into compassion

Through the **Eighth Principle**, the Great Work becomes not merely personal evolution but ethical participation in the world, contributing to stability, harmony, and consciousness on a broader scale.

Part II — The Warrior–Scholar–Sage Path

5. The Warrior (Jing)

Strength, Boundaries and Grounding

Across cultures and throughout history, the Warrior archetype represents the foundational stage of human development, the cultivation of strength, discipline, groundedness, and embodied presence. In Hermeticism, as in Taoist internal practice, this corresponds to *Jing*, the essential physical vitality that underlies all higher functions. Without Jing, neither intellectual clarity nor spiritual insight can be sustained. Without the Warrior, neither the Scholar nor the Sage can emerge.

In the modern world, physicality is often neglected or fragmented. Sedentary lifestyles, chronic stress, poor posture, disrupted sleep, and digital overconsumption weaken the very capacities that support psychological resilience and spiritual maturity (Ratey, et al., 2008). The Warrior stage restores these lost foundations, anchoring the entire developmental process in the body, in the locus of intuition, nervous system regulation, emotional processing, and embodied knowledge.

The Warrior is not defined by aggression, competition, or conflict. Rather, the Warrior embodies **competence, stability, and sovereignty**. This chapter explores the attributes and practices that cultivate Jing in the contemporary context, integrating Hermetic principles, Taoist energetics, physiological research, and psychological resilience into a unified model of grounded living.

Jing as the Foundation of Development

In classical Taoist alchemy, Jing represents the body's stored vitality, the essence that supports physical strength, reproductive energy, immune function, and longevity. Jing is both literal and metaphorical: it corresponds to hormones, cellular integrity, musculoskeletal strength, and the instinct for survival, but also to foundational character traits such as discipline, courage, and stability.

From a modern perspective, Jing captures what physiology calls *allostatic resilience,* or the body's capacity to adapt to stress and maintain equilibrium (Sapolsky, 2004). Individuals with strong Jing demonstrate:

- physical robustness
- healthy stress-response cycles
- stable circadian rhythms
- muscular and postural integrity

- emotional steadiness
- clarity under pressure
- natural presence and groundedness

These qualities align with the Hermetic **Principles of Rhythm**, **Vibration**, and **Cause and Effect**, which together describe how physical patterns influence all aspects of human functioning.

In trauma psychology, Jing parallels what van der Kolk (2014) identifies as "embodied safety," the felt sense of groundedness necessary for emotional regulation, memory integration, and relational attunement. When Jing is depleted, the body becomes reactive, the mind becomes scattered, and the emotions become unstable.

Rebuilding Jing is therefore the first step of the Great Work.

Embodiment: The Warrior's First Task

Embodiment refers to the integration of physical awareness, posture, breath, and movement into conscious living. In Hermetic terms, embodiment reconnects the "below" with the "above," restoring the **Principle of Correspondence**.

Modern research affirms this: posture directly influences emotional regulation, memory, confidence, and cognitive performance (Peper et al., 2016). Breath influences heart-rate variability, vagal tone, and sensory processing (Zaccaro et al., 2018). Movement enhances neurogenesis, mood regulation, and executive functioning (Ratey, 2008).

The Warrior trains embodiment through:

- intentional posture
- aligned structure
- stable rooting through the feet
- conscious breathing
- martial or yogic stances and slow movement
- strength training or resistance work
- somatic awareness practices

These are not abstract or symbolic. They are physiological interventions that restore Jing and regulate the nervous system.

When individuals embody themselves, they cease living "from the neck up" and reconnect to the instinctive intelligence that trauma, conditioning, and modern overstimulation often suppress.

Boundaries as the Warrior's Ethical Structure

The Warrior is the archetype responsible for establishing and maintaining boundaries whether physical, emotional, psychological, and relational. Boundaries are the structure through which Jing is conserved. Without boundaries, vitality leaks. Without boundaries, vulnerabilities expand. Without boundaries, individuals become susceptible to manipulation, coercion, and emotional exploitation.

Modern psychology aligns with this Hermetic insight: boundary setting is central to trauma recovery, identity formation, and relational health (Herman, 1992). Weak boundaries stem from chronic stress, developmental trauma, abusive authority figures, or environments where autonomy was punished or discouraged.

The Principle of Cause and Effect underscores boundary work. When individuals set clear boundaries, they change the causal structure of their relationships, decisions, and environments. This leads to more predictable outcomes and psychological safety (Duhigg, 2012).

The Warrior practices boundaries through:

- saying no with clarity
- protecting time and energy
- maintaining physical presence
- creating structured routines
- disengaging from coercive influences
- aligning actions with personal values
- regulating emotional susceptibility

Boundaries preserve Jing, allowing higher development to occur.

Strength: More Than Muscles

Strength in the Warrior phase extends beyond physical capability. It encompasses:

1. Physical Strength

Necessary for hormonal balance, metabolic health, and nervous system stability.

2. Emotional Strength

The ability to tolerate discomfort, regulate affect, and remain present under stress (Porges, 2011).

3. Cognitive Strength

The discipline to sustain focus, resist distraction, and challenge distorted thoughts.

4. Ethical Strength

The courage to maintain integrity, even when pressured.

5. Relational Strength

The capacity to hold one's own perspective without aggression or collapse.

Hermeticism frames strength as a function of **Vibration** and **Polarity,** in the ability to direct one's internal state rather than being swept away by extremes. Taoist alchemy frames it as stabilizing Jing, the foundation upon which higher energies refine.

Strength cultivated in this phase becomes the anchor for the Scholar and the Sage.

Grounding: The Warrior's Method for Stabilizing Consciousness

Grounding means establishing a strong connection to the present moment through the body. It is the antidote to dissociation, anxiety, rumination, and emotional volatility.

Grounding practices include:
- sitting, standing and moving meditations
- deep diaphragmatic breathing
- rooting through the feet
- slow, intentional walking
- structured yogic or martial stances
- sensory awareness exercises
- cold and/or heat exposure or controlled stress stimuli
- tension and release cycles

Grounding restores the Principle of Rhythm, bringing the body back into natural oscillations. It counters modern overstimulation, which fragments attention and dysregulates the nervous system (Lissak, 2018). In trauma contexts, grounding is essential for reestablishing internal safety (van der Kolk, 2014).

For the Warrior, grounding is not optional. It is the daily discipline that transforms scattered energy into directed intention.

The Warrior and the Restoration of Sovereignty

At its essence, the Warrior archetype restores sovereignty, or the ability to inhabit one's life fully, respond instead of reacting, and act from strength instead of fear.

Sovereignty reflects the integration of multiple Hermetic principles:

- **Mentalism** (clear thinking)
- **Vibration** (regulated emotion)
- **Rhythm** (cyclical balance)
- **Cause and Effect** (disciplined action)
- **Gender** (balanced internal energies)

In Taoist frameworks, sovereignty arises when Jing is stable; only then can Qi and Shen refine upward without leaking or collapsing.

Sovereignty also protects individuals from manipulation, coercive authority, and environments that exploit psychological vulnerabilities. The Warrior is the part of the psyche that refuses to outsource judgment or identity to external forces.

Conclusion: The Warrior as the First Stage of the Great Work

The Warrior stage establishes the embodied, disciplined, grounded foundation necessary for all subsequent development. Without Jing, the Scholar becomes unrooted, and the Sage becomes unstructured. Without embodiment, insight lacks substance. Without boundaries, compassion becomes self-neglect. Without sovereignty, spirituality becomes escapism.

The Warrior is therefore not an archaic archetype, but rather it is a necessary condition for modern life. In a world of disembodiment, distraction, overstimulation, and psychological fragmentation, the Warrior restores the physical and somatic integrity that allows the human being to reenter the world with clarity, strength, and aligned intention.

The Great Work begins in the body. The Warrior makes the body a suitable vessel for transformation. Through Jing, the human being becomes grounded, stable, and ready for the next phase: **the Scholar**, where Qi, as in mental energy, clarity, and discernment takes shape.

6. The Scholar (Qi)

Clarity, Discernment and Cognitive Sovereignty

If the Warrior establishes stability in the body, then the Scholar develops clarity in the mind. This stage corresponds to the cultivation of *Qi*, the animating force associated with cognition, perception, emotion, breath, and the subtle movements of consciousness. In Taoist internal alchemy, Qi is both energy and information, the medium through which experience is interpreted and understanding is formed.

In modern psychological terms, Qi maps onto executive functioning, emotional intelligence, cognitive flexibility, and the ability to regulate attention and thought patterns. It is the stage where individuals reclaim the sovereignty of their inner dialogue, refine their discernment, and cultivate the internal order that makes higher insight possible.

The Scholar is not merely a thinker; the Scholar is **one who learns how to think**, how to evaluate, how to perceive, and how to differentiate truth from distortion. In a world flooded with information and misinformation, the Scholar's role has never been more essential.

Qi as the Energy of Perception and Insight

Qi is the bridge between the concrete and the abstract. In Taoist physiology, Qi circulates through the meridians, animating organs and modulating emotional states. In psychological terms, Qi parallels the flow of attention and affect, how mental energy is allocated, how thoughts are sequenced, and how emotions rise, move, and resolve (Siegel, 2012).

Healthy Qi manifests as:

- mental clarity
- stable attention
- curiosity
- emotional fluidity
- cognitive coherence
- creativity
- problem-solving ability
- insight

Disrupted Qi, by contrast, appears as:

- rumination
- anxiety
- emotional rigidity
- impulsive thinking
- cognitive fragmentation
- poor decision-making
- susceptibility to manipulation
- confusion or mental fog

Understanding Qi through this modern Hermetic lens allows individuals to recognize that thoughts are not merely random occurrences. They are energetic patterns influenced by physiology, emotion, environment, and habit (Beck, 1976).

The Scholar learns to direct Qi consciously, shaping the internal landscape of the mind.

Discernment: The Central Task of the Scholar

Among all intellectual capacities, none are more essential to Hermetic development than discernment. Discernment is the ability to distinguish:

- truth from distortion
- insight from impulse
- intuition from anxiety
- influence from manipulation
- wisdom from mere information
- principles from preferences

In an age of cognitive overload, discernment is both rare and revolutionary. Neuroscientists note that the prefrontal cortex, the area of the brain responsible for judgment, foresight, and impulse control, is easily overridden by emotional reactivity and digital overstimulation (Haidt, 2024). Without conscious development, individuals default to cognitive biases and habitual reactions (Tversky & Kahneman, 1974).

In Hermeticism, discernment corresponds to **Polarity** and **Cause and Effect**:

- Polarity teaches that truth often lies between extremes.

- Cause and Effect reveals that choices, once made, produce specific internal and external outcomes.

Discernment allows individuals to hover between poles, evaluate causes, predict effects, and act with clarity rather than confusion.

Cognitive Sovereignty: Reclaiming the Inner Voice

Cognitive sovereignty refers to the ability to think for oneself, free from coercion, conditioning, or distorted internal narratives. It is the Scholar's version of the Warrior's physical sovereignty and the Sage's spiritual sovereignty.

Psychologists observe that individuals shaped by trauma, high-control groups, or authoritarian environments often internalize the voices of past authorities, mistaking them for their own thoughts (Herman, 1992). This produces:

- self-doubt
- indecision
- excessive guilt
- dependency
- intellectual rigidity
- emotional instability

The Scholar's task is to disentangle the **authentic internal voice** from conditioned patterns.

Mentalism plays a crucial role here: if the mind shapes reality, then it must be freed from inherited distortions. Mental freedom requires:

- questioning automatic thoughts
- challenging internalized authority
- recognizing cognitive distortions
- identifying learned emotional responses
- evaluating beliefs through evidence
- developing metacognition (thinking about thinking)

By doing so, individuals reclaim their capacity to interpret the world without distortion.

Breath and the Flow of Qi: The Scholar's Physiological Foundation

Although the Scholar is primarily associated with the mind, its foundation is deeply physiological. Breath is the most accessible pathway for regulating Qi, influencing both emotional state and cognitive performance (Zaccaro et al., 2018). Slow, diaphragmatic breathing enhances vagal tone, reduces amygdala activation, and improves executive functioning (Porges, 2011).

The Scholar therefore trains attention through breath-based practices:

- deep abdominal breathing
- lengthened exhalations
- paced respiration (4–6 breaths per minute)
- coherent breathing for emotional balance
- breath holds for focus and stability

By regulating breath, individuals regulate Qi; by regulating Qi, they regulate thought.

This aligns with the Hermetic **Principles of Vibration and Rhythm**. Breath becomes the oscillatory motion that stabilizes cognition.

Emotional Intelligence: Qi as the Movement of Feeling

Emotion and cognition are inseparable. Emotional states influence perception, memory, decision-making, and meaning-making (Siegel, 2012). The Scholar develops **emotional intelligence**, the ability to:

- identify emotions
- understand their origins
- regulate their intensity
- express them constructively
- recognize emotional patterns in others

In Hermetic terms, emotional intelligence expresses the **Principle of Gender**, balancing active and receptive modes. Active energy provides clarity and structure; receptive energy allows empathy and attunement.

Through emotional intelligence, Qi becomes refined. Instead of being chaotic or reactive, Qi flows smoothly, integrating emotional experience into mature understanding.

Critical Thinking as a Hermetic Skill

Critical thinking is not skepticism; it is structured evaluation. It is the Scholar's method for distinguishing between appearance and essence, narrative and truth, influence and autonomy.

This involves:

1. Identifying assumptions
2. Evaluating evidence
3. Recognizing cognitive biases
4. Testing interpretations
5. Differentiating emotion from fact
6. Maintaining intellectual humility

Hermeticism encourages critical thinking through the **Principle of Cause and Effect:** actions and ideas generate outcomes. Understanding those outcomes requires logical analysis. Mentalism also reinforces this skill: the mind is powerful, but only when clean of distortion.

Critical thinking protects individuals from manipulation, misinformation, and emotional impulsiveness.

The Scholar and the Integration of Trauma

For trauma survivors, the Scholar represents the stage where understanding emerges from experience. Once the Warrior establishes grounding and safety, the Scholar can analyze past events without being overwhelmed.

This stage often includes:

- identifying old belief systems
- recognizing emotional conditioning
- examining past power dynamics
- understanding psychological manipulation
- integrating new skills of discernment
- reframing traumatic memories
- reauthoring personal narratives

This aligns with Herman's (1992) three-stage trauma model:

safety → remembrance and mourning → reconnection.

The Scholar's cognitive clarity allows memories and meanings to reorganize.

Hermetic polarity becomes a powerful tool here: trauma can be reframed not as a defining identity but as a degree on a continuum of human experience, a place from which movement is possible.

Curiosity, the Scholar's Primary Virtue

Curiosity is the antidote to intellectual stagnation, emotional rigidity, and spiritual dogmatism. It opens the mind to new ideas, dissolves fear-based thinking, and fuels lifelong growth.

Curiosity aligns with:

- **Mentalism** (expanding mental horizons)
- **Vibration** (adaptive emotional energy)
- **Gender** (balancing logic with intuition)
- **Cause and Effect** (exploring consequences)

Curiosity is the Qi-driven force that propels individuals toward knowledge, wisdom, and eventual transcendence.

The Scholar as the Architect of Inner Clarity

The Scholar transforms raw experience into meaning, turning embodied stability into intellectual freedom. This stage refines Qi by directing it, shaping it, and using it as fuel for insight. Through discernment, cognitive sovereignty, emotional intelligence, and breath-based regulation, the Scholar builds the mental and emotional structure necessary for the emergence of the Sage.

The Scholar frees the mind from conditioning.
The Scholar clarifies the inner world.
The Scholar illuminates the pathways of truth.

And with Qi aligned, the individual becomes ready for the next stage: **the Sage**, where insight becomes wisdom and consciousness expands toward integration.

7. The Sage (Shen)

Compassion, Integration and Spiritual Maturity

In Taoist internal alchemy, **Shen** represents the highest expression of human development. This is the radiance of consciousness, clarity, intuition, and moral alignment that emerges when Jing (body) and Qi (mind) have been refined and integrated. Shen is not merely spiritual insight; it is the embodiment of **wisdom, compassion, presence, and ethical maturity**.

In Hermetic philosophy, Shen corresponds to the higher aspects of consciousness described through the Principles of Mentalism, Correspondence, and Gender; principles that govern the development of intuition, insight, and moral discernment. Where the Warrior builds strength and the Scholar builds clarity, the Sage builds *coherence*, the unified field of body, mind, and spirit functioning in harmony.

This coherence expresses itself through compassion, ethical responsibility, creative insight, and a deep understanding of one's place within the larger web of existence. Modern psychology affirms that such integration represents the pinnacle of human development, associated with emotional regulation, reflective functioning, empathy, meaning-making, and prosocial behavior (Siegel, 2012; Leiberg et al., 2011).

The Sage is not an abstract ideal but a real developmental possibility, a mode of being available to any individual who engages in the Great Work with sincerity and discipline.

Shen as the Emergence of Integrated Consciousness

Shen, in Taoist alchemy, is often depicted as the "spirit" or "radiant mind," but this concept does not imply supernaturalism. Rather, Shen is the culmination of:

- stabilized physiology (Jing)
- regulated emotion (Qi)
- refined perception (Qi)
- integrated memory
- balanced internal energies
- ethical alignment
- relational attunement
- meaning-making capacity

In modern terms, Shen reflects the integration of the prefrontal cortex (executive functioning), limbic system (emotional regulation), and brainstem (somatic grounding), forming what interpersonal neurobiology calls the **integrated self** (Siegel, 2012).

Integration produces:

- inner peace
- clarity of purpose
- emotional balance
- compassion
- intuition
- resilience
- ethical clarity
- creativity
- a sense of interconnectedness

Shen is not perfection, but rather it is *wholeness*, the ability to experience life with presence rather than fragmentation.

Compassion as the Sage's Natural Expression

Compassion is not a sentimental or passive emotion. It is an active, grounded capacity to understand suffering, one's own and others', and respond with insight and integrity. Research shows that compassion training increases prosocial behavior, emotional regulation, and activation in neural circuits associated with empathy and understanding (Leiberg et al., 2011).

The Sage's compassion arises from:

- having experienced suffering
- having integrated trauma
- understanding the mechanisms of fear and confusion
- seeing the shared humanity in others
- recognizing that all internal states are temporary
- perceiving the interconnectedness of all things

Hermeticism complements this perspective through the Principle of Correspondence: inner integration leads naturally to outer compassion. As internal divisions dissolve, so does the impulse to judge, dominate, or control others.

Compassion becomes not an obligation but a spontaneous expression of inner coherence.

Intuition and Shen: The Hermetic Principle of Mentalism Refined

Where the Scholar refines rational clarity, the Sage refines **intuition**, the direct perception of patterns, meanings, and truths that arise from unconscious integration rather than conscious calculation. Intuition emerges when cognitive, emotional, and somatic pathways align, allowing insight to rise without distortion.

Research in cognitive neuroscience shows that intuitive processing is not irrational; it is the rapid synthesis of complex information drawn from embodied experience, memory, and emotional encoding (Gigerenzer, 2007). Shen corresponds to the state in which this synthesis becomes reliable and refined.

Hermeticism teaches that "All is Mind," but the Sage understands this to mean that **mind is not limited to conscious thought**. Mind includes the total field of perception, emotion, sensation, and reflective awareness.

Shen is the maturation of mind into wisdom.

Ethical Alignment: The Sage and the Hermetic Principle of Cause and Effect

True spiritual development cannot occur without ethical maturity. The Sage recognizes that every action, thought, and intention produces effects, psychological, relational, and energetic. In modern terms, this resembles moral development models that emphasize responsibility, empathy, and foresight (Kohlberg, 1984).

Ethical alignment arises from:
- clarity of perception
- empathy
- understanding of consequences
- heightened sensitivity to one's impact
- self-regulation
- honesty and humility
- the desire to reduce suffering

The Sage understands Cause and Effect not as superstition but as a psychological and behavioral law. Dishonesty fragments the psyche. Compassion integrates it. Negative actions create internal dissonance; ethical actions create internal coherence.

Ethics are therefore not imposed rules but emergent properties of integration.

The Sage and the Transformation of Polarity

The Sage recognizes that all emotions, thoughts, and experiences exist on spectrums. They do not cling to pleasure nor resist pain. They do not identify with rigid self-concepts or polarized thinking. They allow experiences to arise, change, and resolve.

This capacity aligns with:

- emotional flexibility
- mindfulness
- tolerance of ambiguity
- nuanced thinking
- psychological resilience

Modern research on psychological flexibility, a core component of well-being, mirrors this principle: individuals who can shift perspective, regulate emotional responses, and integrate opposites demonstrate higher mental health and life satisfaction (Kashdan & Rottenberg, 2010).

Shen integrates opposites in light and shadow, certainty and uncertainty, agency and surrender, producing a self that is not polarized but whole.

Presence: The Sage's Embodied Spirituality

Presence is the hallmark of Shen, a state of being fully attuned to the moment without dissociation, distraction, or reactivity. Presence emerges when Jing and Qi stabilize, giving rise to a mind that is quiet, attentive, and open.

Presence involves:

- deep interoceptive awareness
- non-reactive attention
- grounded breath
- emotional clarity
- relational attunement

- ease within uncertainty
- non-judgmental observation

Modern contemplative science associates presence with increased activity in regions of the brain linked to self-regulation, empathy, and stress reduction (Lutz, Dunne, & Davidson, 2007).

The Sage does not escape the world but engages it wholeheartedly, from a place of inner stability.

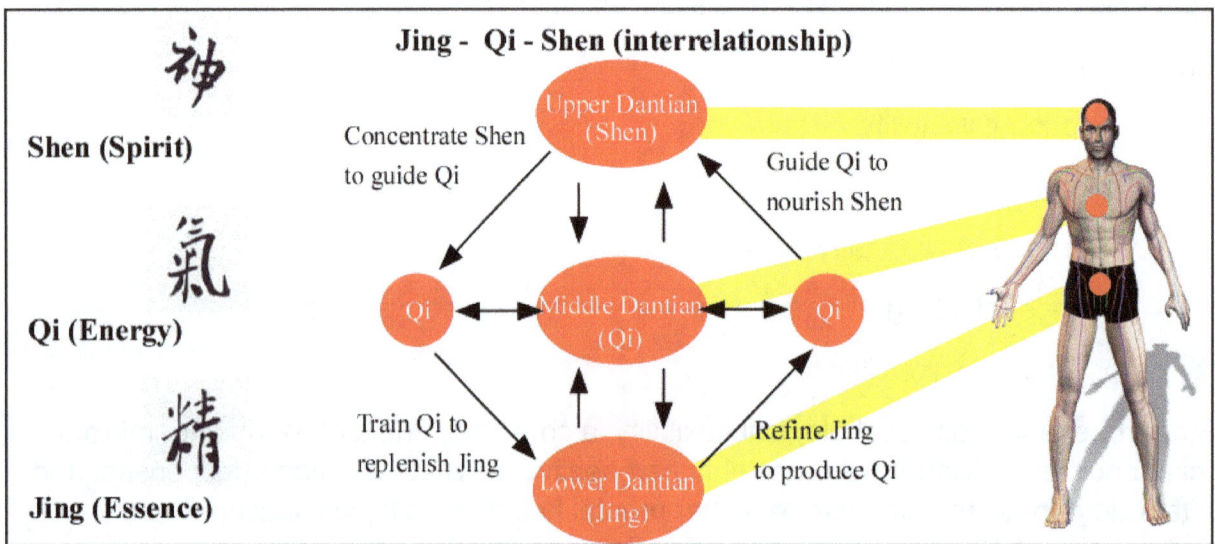

Integration: The Completion of the Lower Stages

Shen cannot be cultivated without Jing and Qi. The Warrior builds the vessel; the Scholar refines the contents; the Sage illuminates the whole. This integration reflects the Hermetic principle that the microcosm and macrocosm correspond, the inner alignment allows outer clarity.

Integration is marked by:
- coherence between thought, emotion, and action
- the ability to reflect without shame
- the ability to act without compulsion
- the ability to relate without fear
- the ability to perceive without distortion
- the ability to live with purpose and humility

This represents what modern psychology calls *self-actualization* (Maslow, 1962), *secure identity*, and *post-traumatic growth*, the ability to find meaning, strength, and clarity after adversity (Tedeschi & Calhoun, 2004).

Integration is the goal not because it is lofty, but because it is human.

Shen as the Embodied Expression of Wisdom

The Sage represents the culmination of the Hermetic Great Work, a life lived with clarity, compassion, and coherent presence. Shen emerges naturally when the Warrior and Scholar have done their part, refining body and mind into aligned, functional instruments.

The Sage is not an escape from the world but a mature engagement with it. Not detachment, but depth. Not transcendence, but integration. Not perfection, but wholeness.

With Shen established, the individual becomes a stable force in an unstable world, a presence capable of insight, empathy, ethical clarity, and lasting meaning.

The next stage of the book explores how these three developmental modes (Warrior, Scholar, Sage) interact with the Hermetic Principles to form a complete model of human growth.

Part III — The Somatic & Psychological Great Work

8. Breath, Posture and Nervous System Mastery

Hermetic development is often misunderstood as purely mental or spiritual. In reality, every stage of the Great Work is anchored in the physical body. Breath, posture, and nervous system regulation form the physiological foundation upon which mental clarity, emotional intelligence, and spiritual insight are built. Without this foundation, the Seven Hermetic Principles cannot operate coherently within an individual.

The body is not separate from consciousness; it *is* consciousness in its densest expression. Breath is the movement of life; posture is the architecture of being; the nervous system is the vibratory engine that translates internal and external information into experience.

Thus, the Great Work begins and continually returns to the mastery of breath, posture, and physiological regulation.

Modern neuroscience, psychology, and somatic therapy all confirm what Hermeticism, Taoist internal alchemy, and classical martial traditions have long taught: **the state of the body shapes the state of the mind** (Porges, 2011; Peper et al., 2016; Zaccaro et al., 2018). The Warrior–Scholar–Sage model reflects this truth. The Warrior regulates Jing and stabilizes the body. The Scholar refines Qi and clarifies the mind. The Sage illuminates Shen and expands consciousness. This integration is made possible through practices that directly influence the nervous system.

Breath as the Bridge Between Worlds

Breath is the most accessible and powerful tool for regulating the nervous system. It influences physiological arousal, emotional state, cognitive capacity, attention, intuition, and spiritual perception (Zaccaro et al., 2018). In Hermetic terms, breath is the primary means of regulating **Vibration** and restoring **Rhythm**.

Breath is unique among physiological functions in that it is both autonomic and voluntary. This makes it a perfect alchemical tool and a way to consciously influence unconscious processes.

The Functions of Breath in the Great Work

Breath affects:

- **Autonomic balance** (sympathetic vs. parasympathetic activation)
- **Heart-rate variability** (a measure of resilience)
- **Cognitive clarity**

- **Emotional stability**
- **Somatic awareness**
- **Qi circulation** (in Taoist terms)
- **Embodied presence**
- **Stress recovery**

Each of these influences supports the Seven Hermetic Principles.

Slowing the Breath, Quieting the Mind

Research shows that breathing at a rate of 4–6 breaths per minute increases vagal tone, reduces amygdala reactivity, and enhances executive functioning (Porges, 2011). In practical terms:

- anxiety decreases
- focus improves
- emotional reactions soften
- intuition becomes clearer
- the mind becomes steadier

This is the physiological expression of Hermetic **Mentalism**, the mind shaping experience by altering internal rhythm and vibration.

Breath as the Scholar's Tool

In the Scholar stage (Qi refinement), breath heightens cognitive precision and emotional intelligence. It allows individuals to self-regulate before making decisions, reflecting the **Principle of Cause and Effect**: breathing consciously produces clarity, which produces wiser actions.

Breath as the Sage's Anchor

For the Sage, breath deepens presence, compassion, and intuitive perception. Slow, smooth breathing supports Shen by stabilizing the "inner atmosphere," allowing insights to arise naturally. Breath is therefore the unifying element of all three developmental stages.

Posture: The Architecture of Consciousness

Posture is more than physical arrangement. It is the structure through which consciousness expresses itself. The body's orientation influences:

- emotional tone
- cognitive processing
- confidence
- memory access
- social communication
- moral reasoning
- nervous system activation

Peper et al. (2016) demonstrated that posture significantly affects memory recall, emotional processing, and resilience. Upright posture enhances positive affect and clarity; collapsed posture increases fear, rumination, and pessimism.

Posture expresses the Hermetic Principle of Correspondence:

As the body shifts, so do the emotions and thoughts.

Posture and Trauma

Trauma survivors often adopt protective postures:

- rounded shoulders
- collapsed chest
- tense abdomen
- restricted breath
- lowered gaze

These somatic patterns reflect the Principle of Polarity; contractive physical states mirror contractive emotional states. Changing posture begins the process of moving toward the opposite pole.

Posture and Jing

In the Warrior stage, posture stabilizes Jing. Proper alignment supports core muscles, enhances breathing, reduces stress, and provides a physical container for emotional regulation.

Posture and Qi

In the Scholar stage, posture facilitates clear thinking. Upright alignment improves blood flow, oxygenation, and neural integration.

Posture and Shen

In the Sage stage, posture becomes the embodied expression of presence. The body becomes relaxed yet awake, grounded yet open.

The Nervous System: The Engine of Inner Transformation

The nervous system determines how individuals process information, respond to challenges, and regulate emotions. Hermeticism anticipated this through the **Principles of Vibration, Polarity, Rhythm, and Cause and Effect,** all of which describe cyclical or dynamic processes reflected in neural functioning.

The Polyvagal Perspective

Porges's Polyvagal Theory explains how physiological states influence emotion, behavior, and perception (Porges, 2011):

- **Ventral vagal** → calm, connection, clarity
- **Sympathetic** → mobilization, fight-or-flight
- **Dorsal vagal** → shutdown, collapse

The Great Work aims to cultivate ventral vagal dominance of stable presence, grounded openness, and responsive engagement.

The Nervous System and the Hermetic Path

Warrior Stage (Jing)
Develops autonomic stability, reducing reactivity and increasing resilience.

Scholar Stage (Qi)
Strengthens the prefrontal cortex and emotional pathways, supporting meta-cognition and discernment.

Sage Stage (Shen)

Integrates higher-order neural networks, supporting empathy, intuition, and ethical awareness (Siegel, 2012).

Trauma and Nervous System Fragmentation

Trauma disrupts the natural oscillations of the nervous system, impairing the **Principle of Rhythm.** Recovery requires restoring this oscillation through breath, posture, grounding, and safe relational contact (van der Kolk, 2014).

Daily Practices for Nervous System Mastery

This section (and later appendix) outlines simple, powerful daily practices that integrate breath, posture, and neural regulation.

1. Coherent Breathing (4–6 breaths per minute)

Improves vagal tone; stabilizes emotions; enhances clarity.

2. Standing Meditation (Zhan Zhuang)

Strengthens Jing; improves posture; calms the mind.

3. Somatic Scanning

Increases interoception; supports integration.

4. Slow Walking with Breath Synchronization

Balances Qi; improves focus.

5. Grounding Practices

Rooting through the feet; shifting weight consciously.

6. Physiological Sigh (double inhale + long exhale)

Rapidly reduces sympathetic activation.

These practices are not mere techniques, but they are **Hermetic tools** that refine vibration, regulate rhythm, and align internal forces.

Embodied Hermeticism: Applying the Principles Through the Body

Breath, posture, and nervous system mastery directly reflect the Seven Hermetic Principles:

- **Mentalism** → breath stabilizes thought
- **Correspondence** → posture shapes emotion
- **Vibration** → nervous system states shift internal frequencies
- **Polarity** → breath transforms states
- **Rhythm** → daily practices regulate cycles
- **Cause and Effect** → habits shape outcomes
- **Gender** → balancing tension (yang) and relaxation (yin)

The **Eighth Principle of Virtue and Ethical Alignment** emerges naturally when physiological patterns become stable. Ethical behavior becomes easier because emotional reactivity decreases, clarity increases, and internal coherence improve.

Embodiment as the Heart of the Great Work

Breath, posture, and nervous system regulation are not secondary practices, they are the core mechanisms of transformation. Hermeticism is not merely a philosophy of the mind; it is a philosophy of the whole human being.

The body stabilizes the mind. The mind refines the emotions. The emotions illuminate the spirit.

Without embodied practice, spiritual insight becomes detached, cognitive clarity becomes brittle, and ethical intention collapses under stress.

Embodiment is the foundation upon which the Warrior stands, the Scholar learns, and the Sage shines. It is the living expression of the Great Work, moment by moment, breath by breath.

Rewiring the Human Nervous System: Adapting to a High-Voltage World

The human nervous system can be likened to an electrical system designed for specific voltage and amperage. Traditionally, it is assumed that most individuals are wired for 110 volts and 10 amps. However, contemporary society necessitates functioning at 220 volts and 30 amps, far exceeding the capacity originally intended by our biology. This increased "voltage" manifests as chronic stress, anxiety, burnout, and various physical ailments.

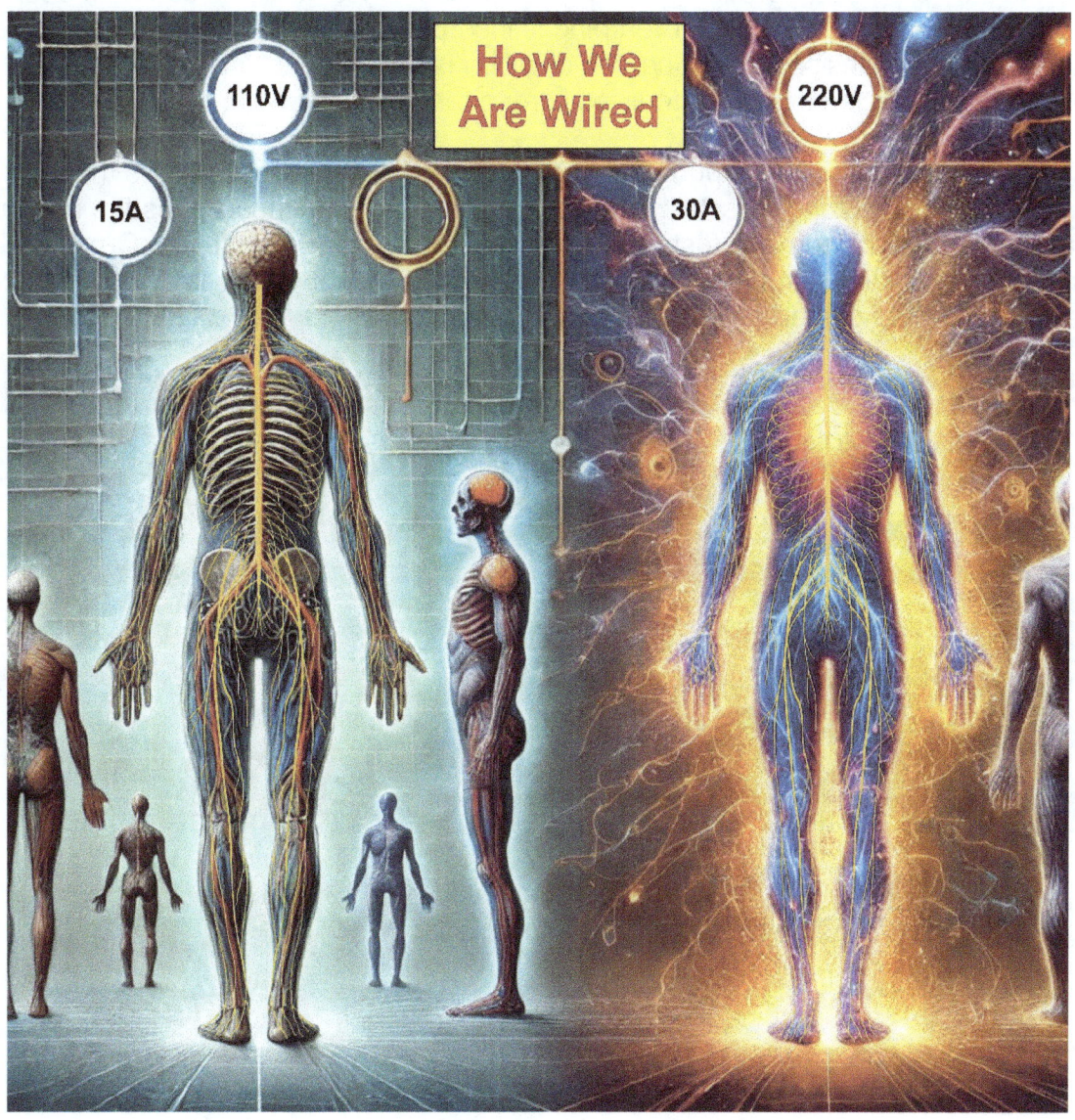

Nevertheless, just as an electrical system can be rewired to handle greater loads, the human nervous system can also be trained to adapt. Ancient practices such as martial arts, qigong, Dao Yin (Taoist yoga), yoga, and breathwork serve as effective interventions. These time-tested methods bridge the gap between the body's inherent capabilities and the demands of modern life, enabling the nervous system to withstand higher levels of stress without succumbing to being overwhelmed.

The Role of Stance Training and Controlled Stress

With over 45 years of experience in martial arts, qigong, Dao Yin, and yoga, it has been observed that certain methods can effectively enhance the nervous system. One such method is stance training, which involves holding postures for specific durations while integrating breath control.

For beginners, basic stances are introduced in succession, initially without prolonged holds. As they progress, duration gradually increases. Once students can hold each stance for 30 seconds, controlled breathing is incorporated, typically three breaths per 30 seconds. With consistent practice, the duration is extended to one-minute holds, adjusting breath cycles to around four to six respirations per minute.

This approach serves multiple purposes. On a physical level, it strengthens the legs, core, and other stabilizing muscles. On a neurological level, it encourages the nervous system to adapt to discomfort, fostering resilience, endurance, and focus. On an energetic level, it stimulates the body's internal pathways, potentially leading to enhanced vitality and internal balance.

The Science Behind the Training: The Anterior Midcingulate Cortex (aMCC)

While these practices have been in use for centuries, contemporary neuroscience provides insight into their effectiveness. A critical region of the brain implicated in resilience is the anterior midcingulate cortex (aMCC).

The aMCC is responsible for effortful control, emotional regulation, and persistence in the face of challenges. Research indicates that engaging in controlled stress—such as maintaining difficult stances, regulating breath, or training under discomfort—strengthens and enlarging the aMCC. Consequently, individuals who practice these methods may enhance their ability to manage stress more effectively, increase mental toughness, and maintain composure under pressure.

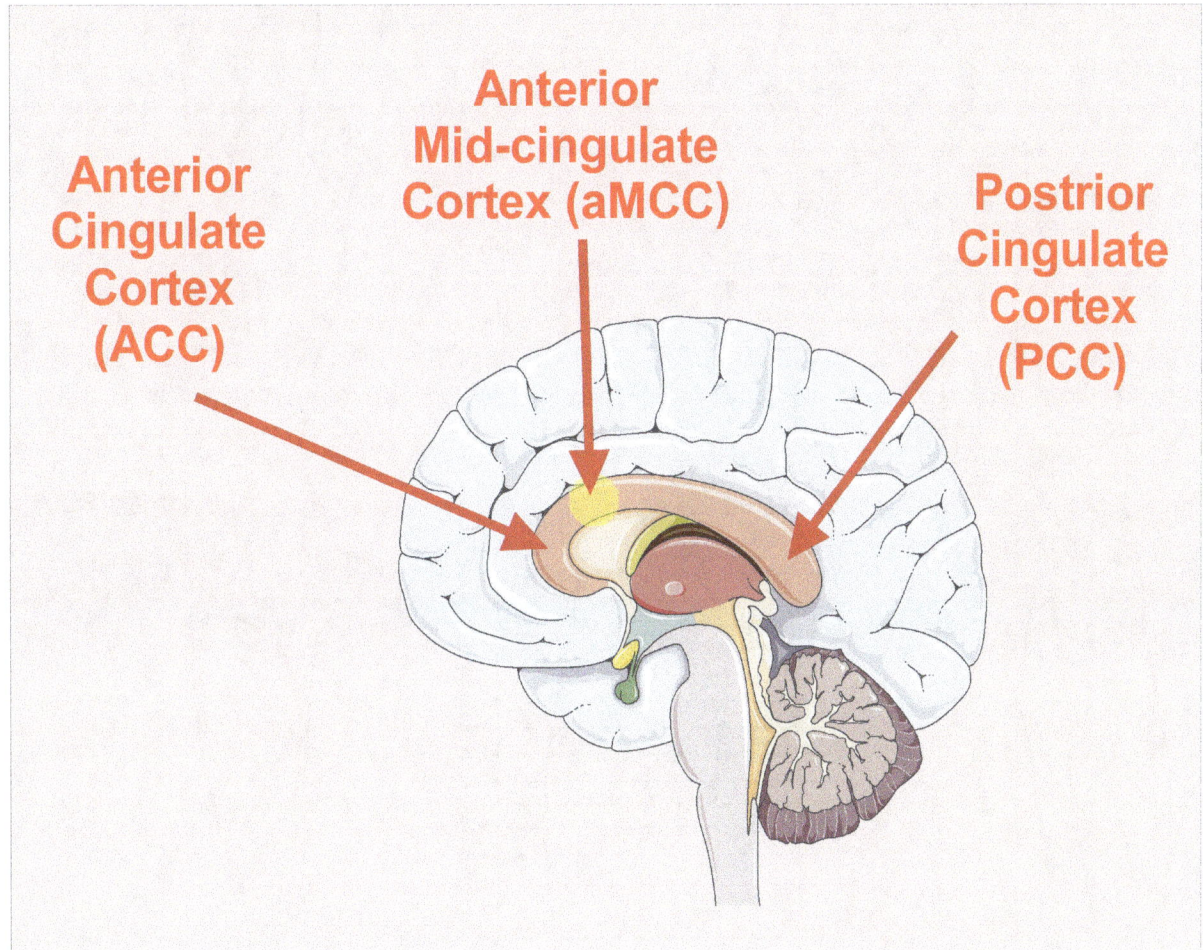

In essence, deliberate training can augment our capacity to handle life's challenges, analogous to how lifting heavier weights strengthens muscles. This concept is consistent with the principle of progressive overload, which is well-established in strength training and equally applicable to the nervous system and mental resilience.

"Burning the *Chong Mai*" – The Energetic Dimension

Beyond the physical and neurological aspects, these practices have deep roots in Taoist and Traditional Chinese Medicine (TCM). An important concept in energetic cultivation is "burning the Chong Mai."

The Chong Mai (Thrusting Vessel) is one of the eight extraordinary meridians in TCM. It serves as a primary channel for deep energy reserves, influencing the body's overall energy flow. When stance work and controlled breathing are practiced regularly, this meridian can be activated, which may allow for greater energy circulation through the other seven extraordinary vessels and the twelve main meridians.

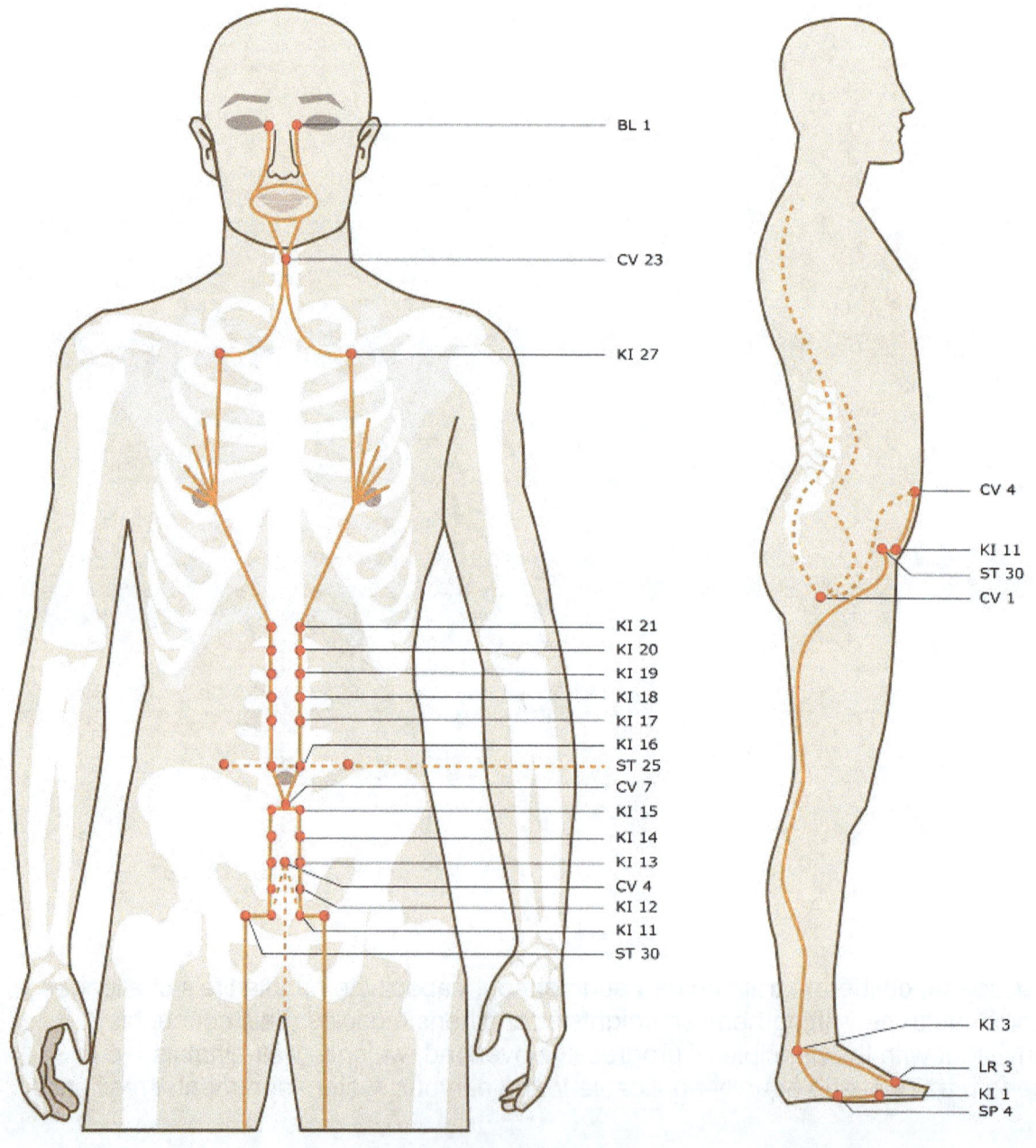

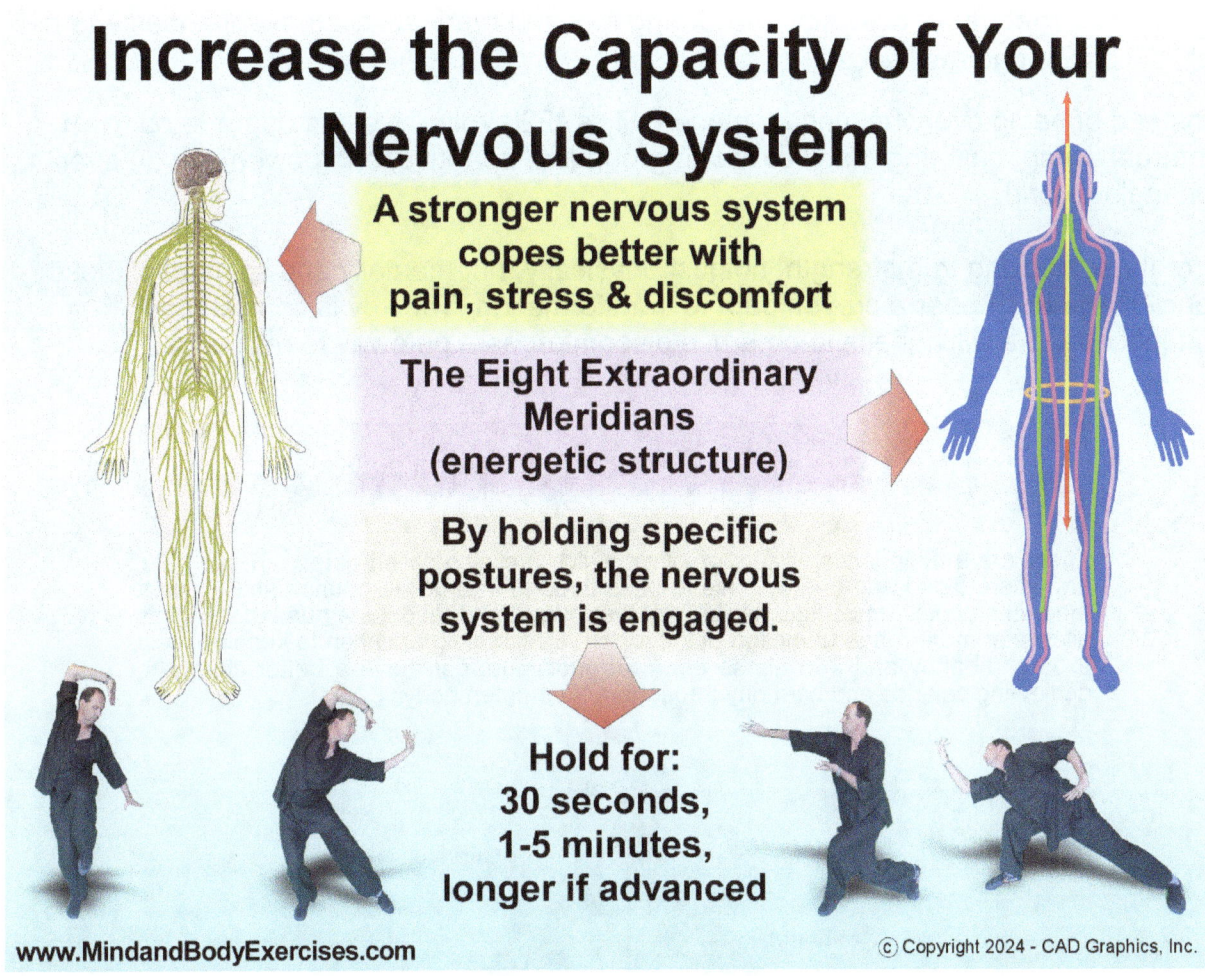

This process can be compared to upgrading a power grid. By increasing the capacity of the Chong Mai, the entire energetic system can become more efficient, stable, and resilient. This observation might explain why long-term practitioners of qigong, Dao Yin, and martial arts often report higher energy levels, improved focus, and a significant sense of internal strength.

Resilience Through Discomfort: The Path to Transformation

The old adage *"That which does not kill us makes us stronger"* perfectly encapsulates the philosophy behind these training methods. Rather than avoiding stress, we use it as a tool for growth.

- **Physically**, stance training builds strength, endurance, and structural integrity.
- **Mentally**, breath control and effortful posture-holding train the nervous system to remain calm under pressure.
- **Neurologically**, the aMCC adapts and strengthens, improving stress management and persistence.

- **Energetically**, activating the Chong Mai and meridian system enhances internal power and resilience.

Instead of being overwhelmed by modern life's "220 volts," we can upgrade our own internal wiring, ensuring that we remain grounded, adaptive, and powerful in an ever-changing world.

For those seeking true strength, not just physically, but mentally and spiritually, these ancient methods offer a proven path to transformation. The key is consistency, patience, and a willingness to embrace discomfort as a gateway to resilience.

Opening the 9 Gates   www.MindAndBodyExercises.com

9 Gates

There are 9 main joints or sets of joints, which are also called gates. These gates are where blood and energy have to pass through in order to nourish and energize the human body. Increased flexibility of the muscle and tendons around these joints, allows for more range of motion of the joints. By focusing attention to keeping these 9 gates healthy and in a sense *open*, an individual can have a better chance of achiev-ing balance and harmony throughout the human body.

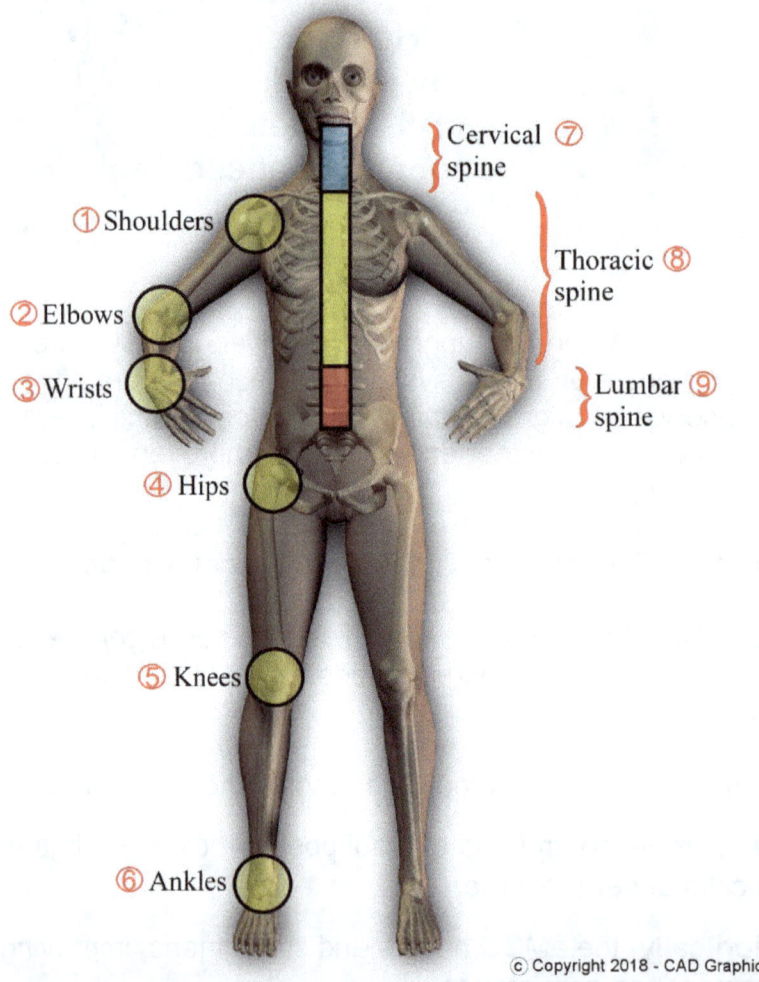

© Copyright 2018 - CAD Graphics, Inc.

Filling the 8 Vessels
www.MindAndBodyExercises.com

8 Vessels

The 8 Extraordinary Vessels are part of the body's meridian energy system. These vessels serve as reservoirs for the 12 Regular meridians. Above all else, they regulate the excess and lack of energy within the other meridians, These vessels are located in close proximity to the other meridians, often-times intersecting or running parallel with them.

12 Meridians
Lung
Heart
Pericardium
Large Intestine
Small Intestine
Triple Burner
Spleen
Kidney
Liver
Heart
Stomach
Bladder
Gall Bladder

8 Vessels
Conception
Governing
Thrusting
Belt
Yin Linking
Yang Linking
Yin Heel
Yang Heel

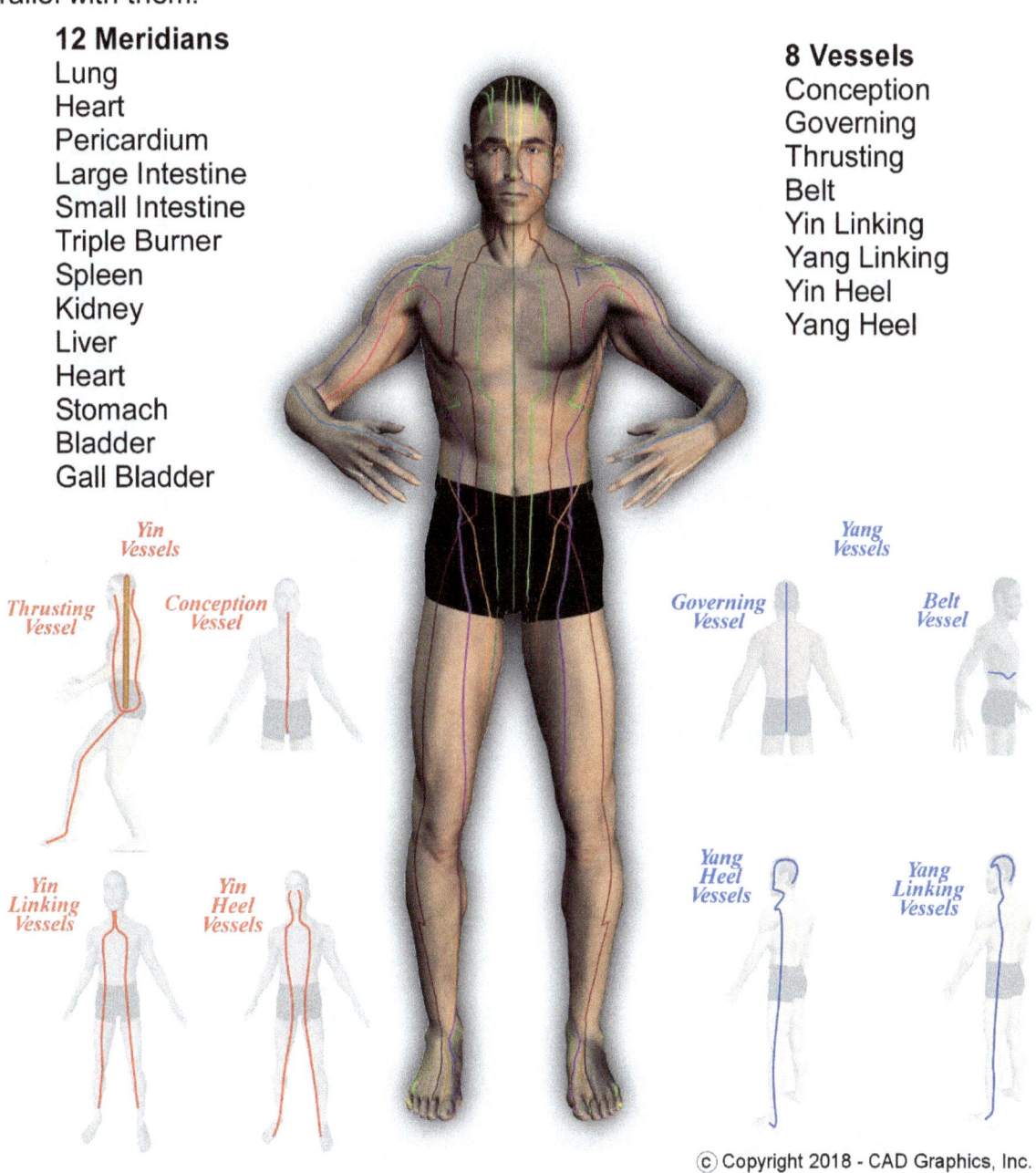

© Copyright 2018 - CAD Graphics, Inc.

The Eight Extraordinary Meridians

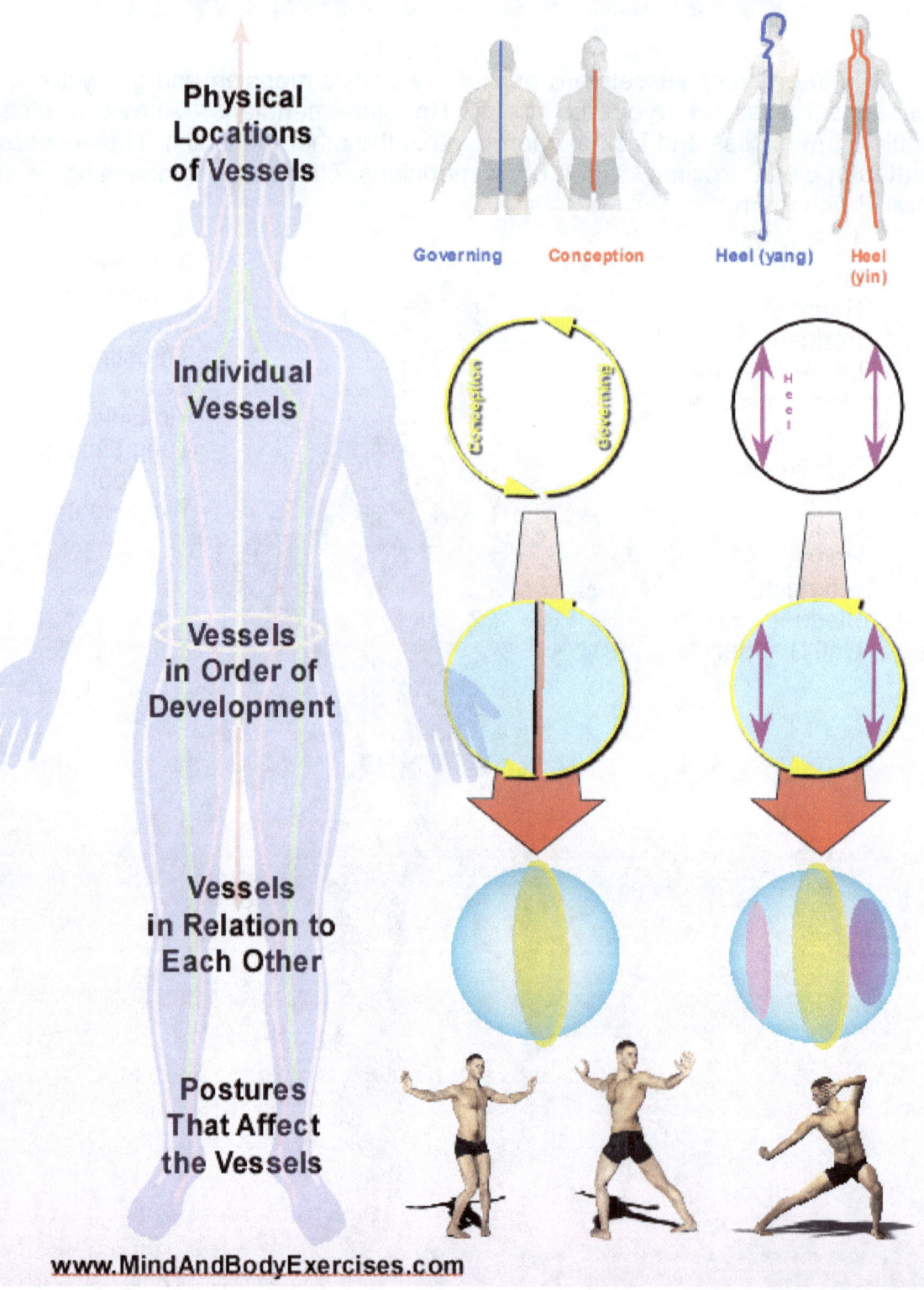

(energetic structure)

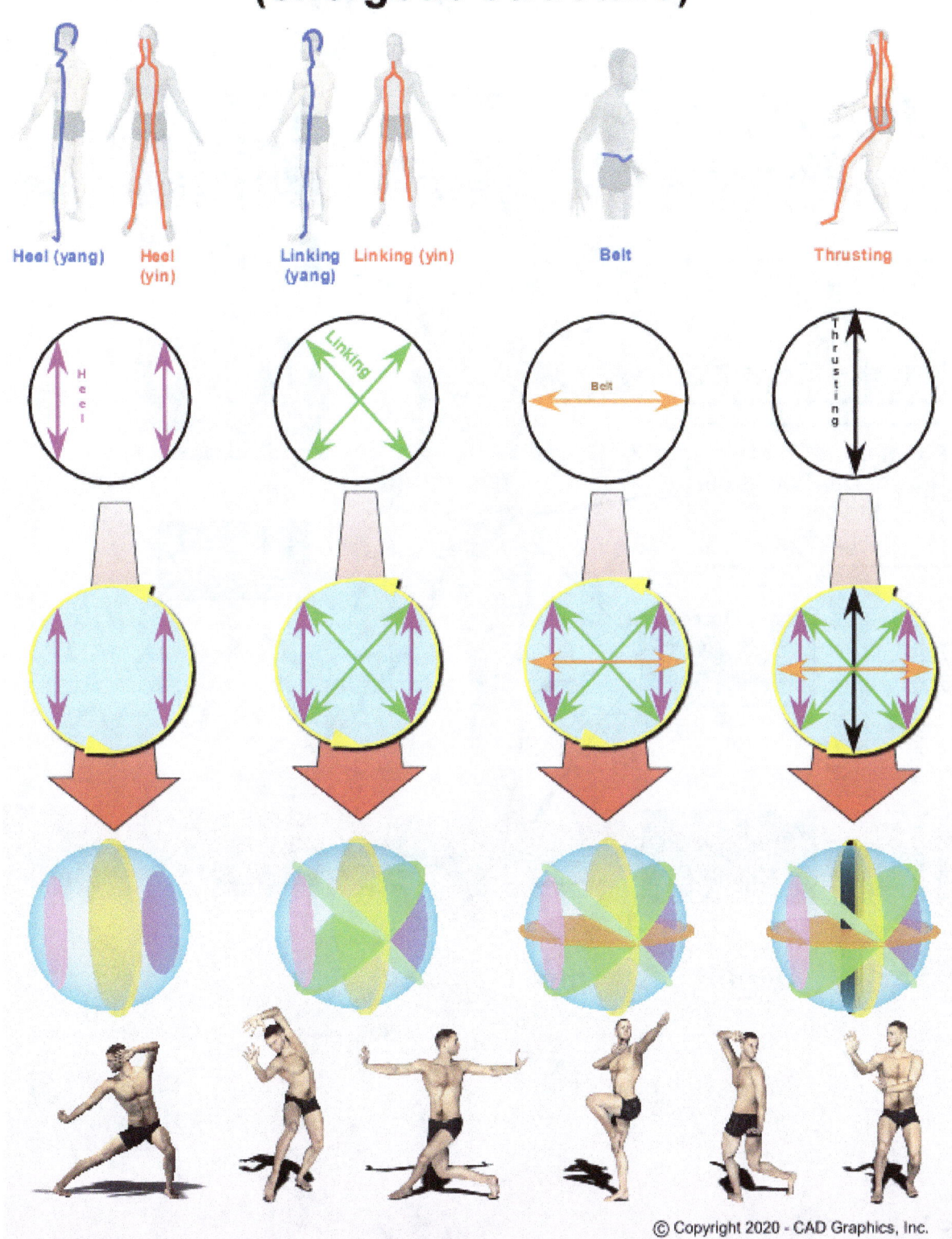

9. Practical Methods of Self-Regulation

Introductory Set

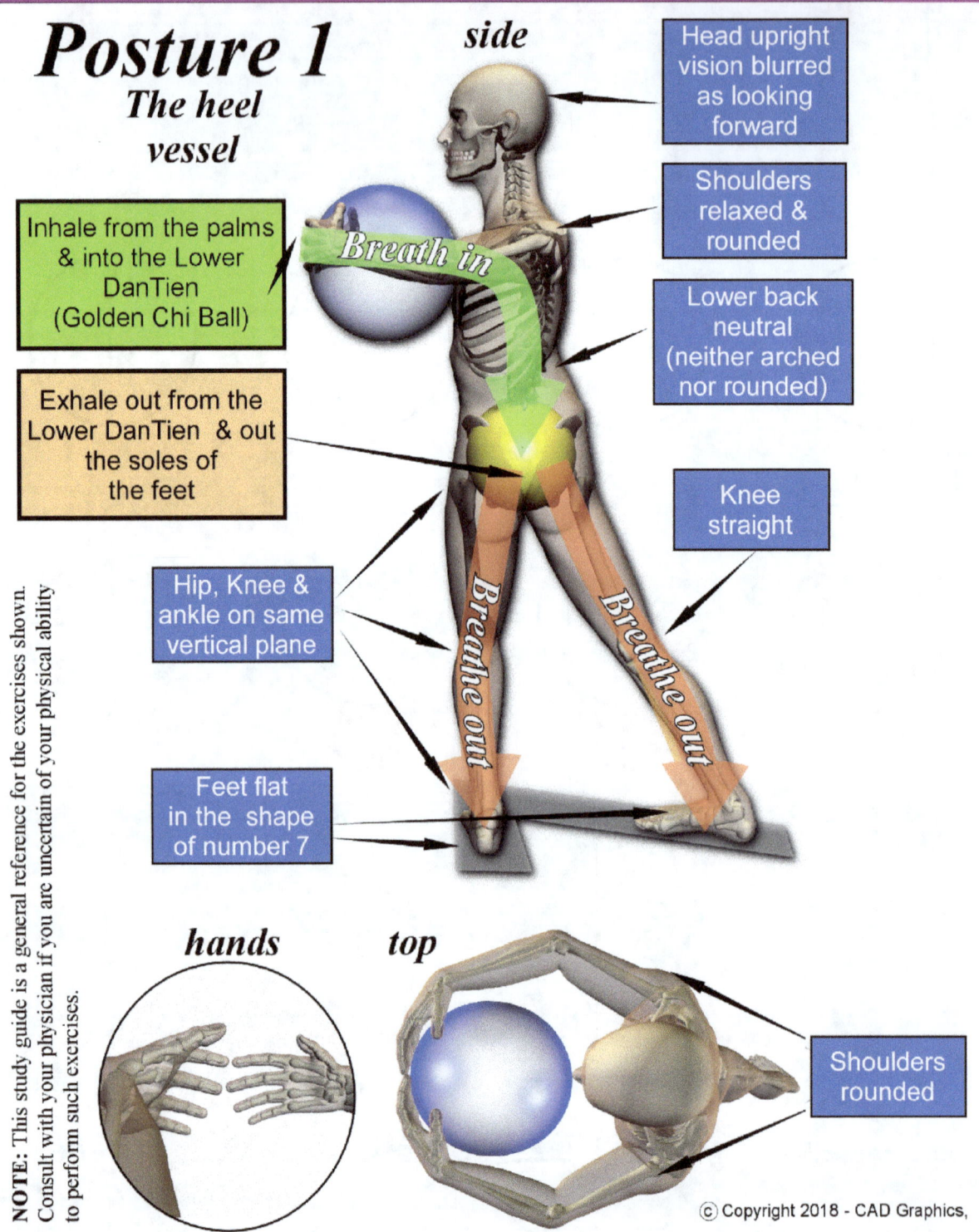

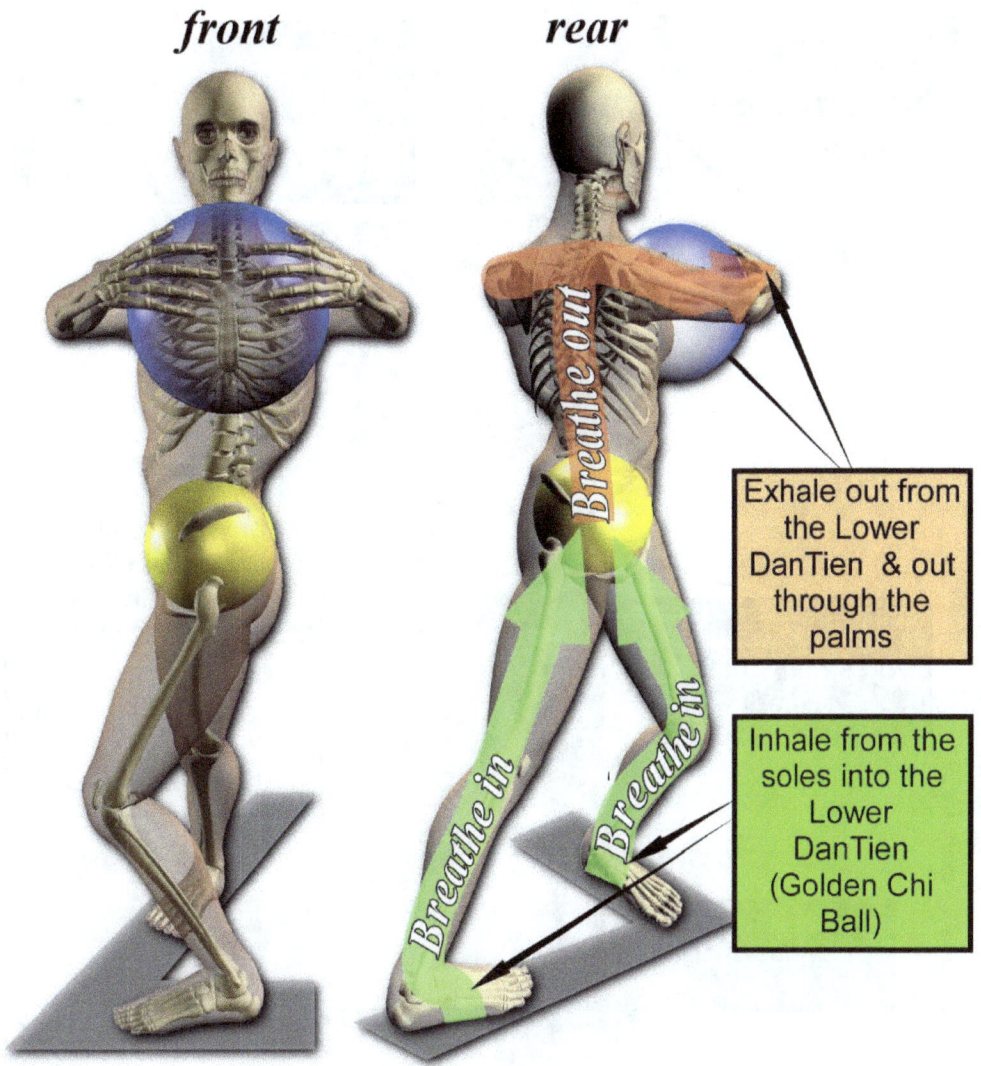

Set 1 activates all 9 gates as well as preparing the muscles, joints and bones for the next progressive stances. Start with the feet, working your way up the body as applying the proper positions and posture. Imagine holding a weightless ball between your palms and chest for this 1st exercise. Inhale from palms down into the Lower DanTien. Exhale from this point and out through the soles of the feet. Inhale from the soles into the DanTien. Exhale out from the DanTien and through to the palms to complete 1 full repetition. Execute on both sides for 1 set.

Introductory Set

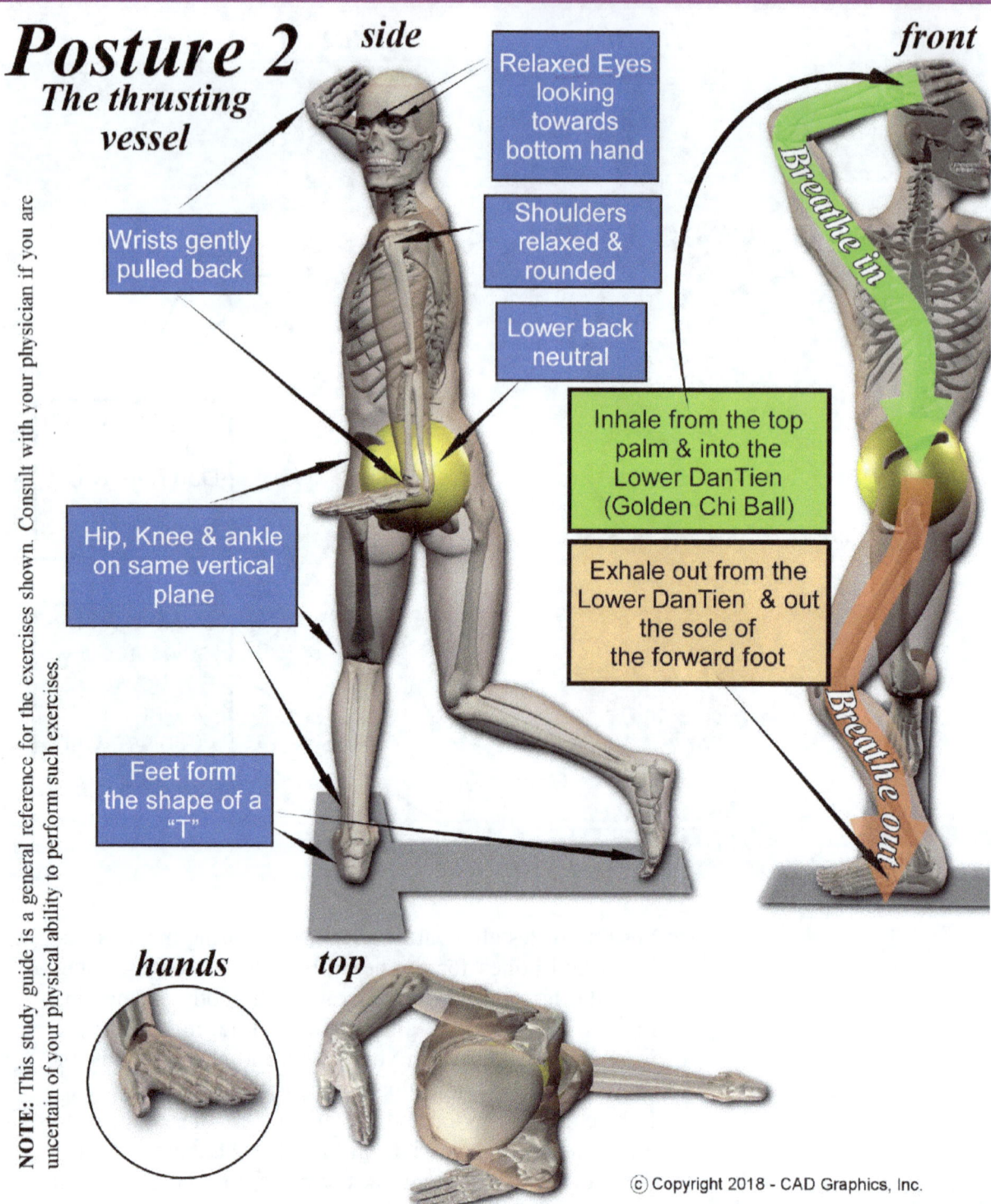

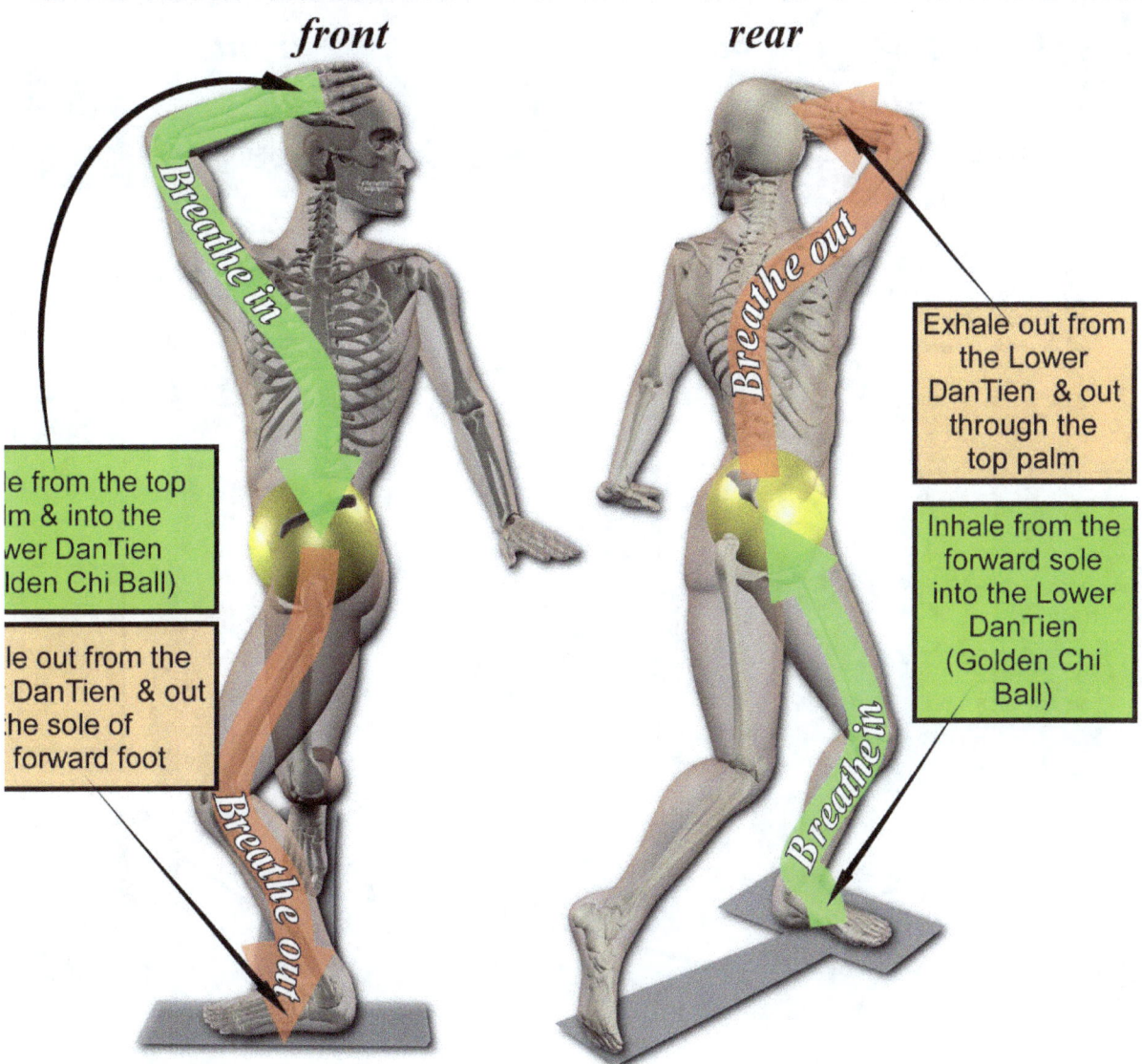

Set 2 also activates all 9 gates while putting extra resistance on the hips, thighs and ankles. Start with the feet, working your way up the body as applying the proper positions and posture. Inhale from upward palm down into the Lower DanTien. Exhale from this point and out through the sole of the forward foot. Inhale from the sole into the DanTien. Exhale out from the DanTien and through the palm to complete 1 full repetition. Execute on both sides for 1 set.

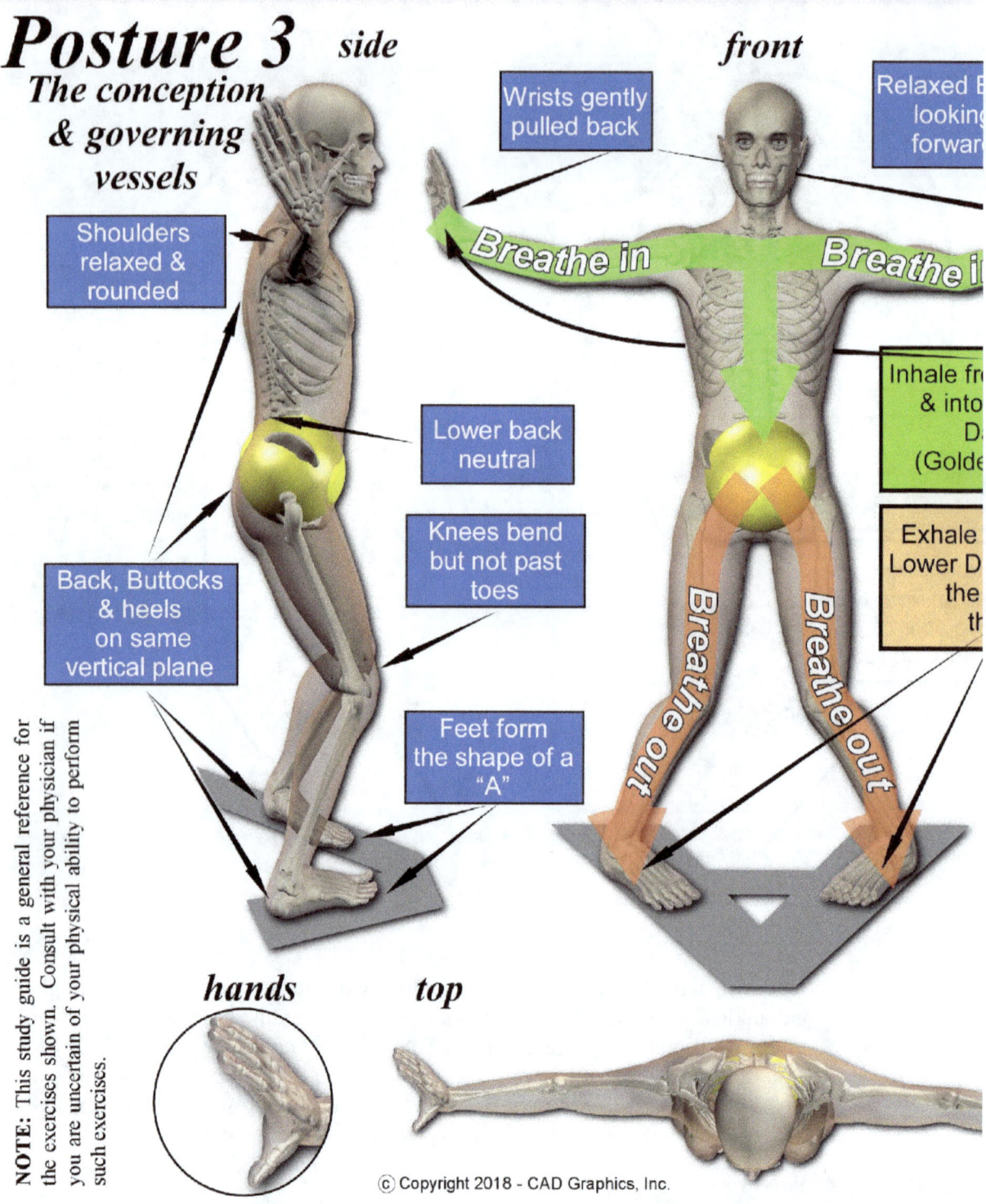

www.MindAndBodyExercises.com

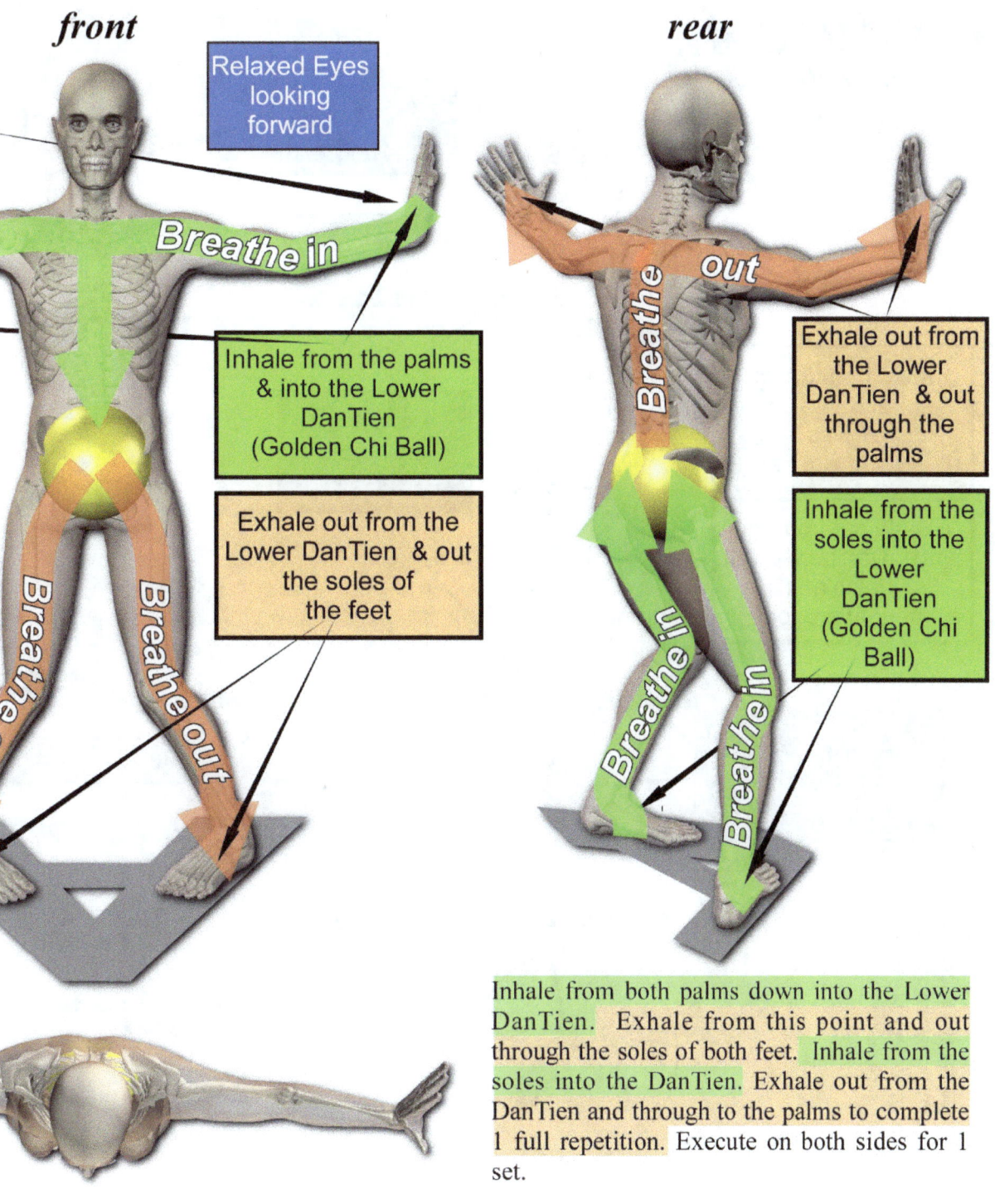

Inhale from both palms down into the Lower DanTien. Exhale from this point and out through the soles of both feet. Inhale from the soles into the DanTien. Exhale out from the DanTien and through to the palms to complete 1 full repetition. Execute on both sides for 1 set.

Introductory Set

Posture 4
The belt vessel

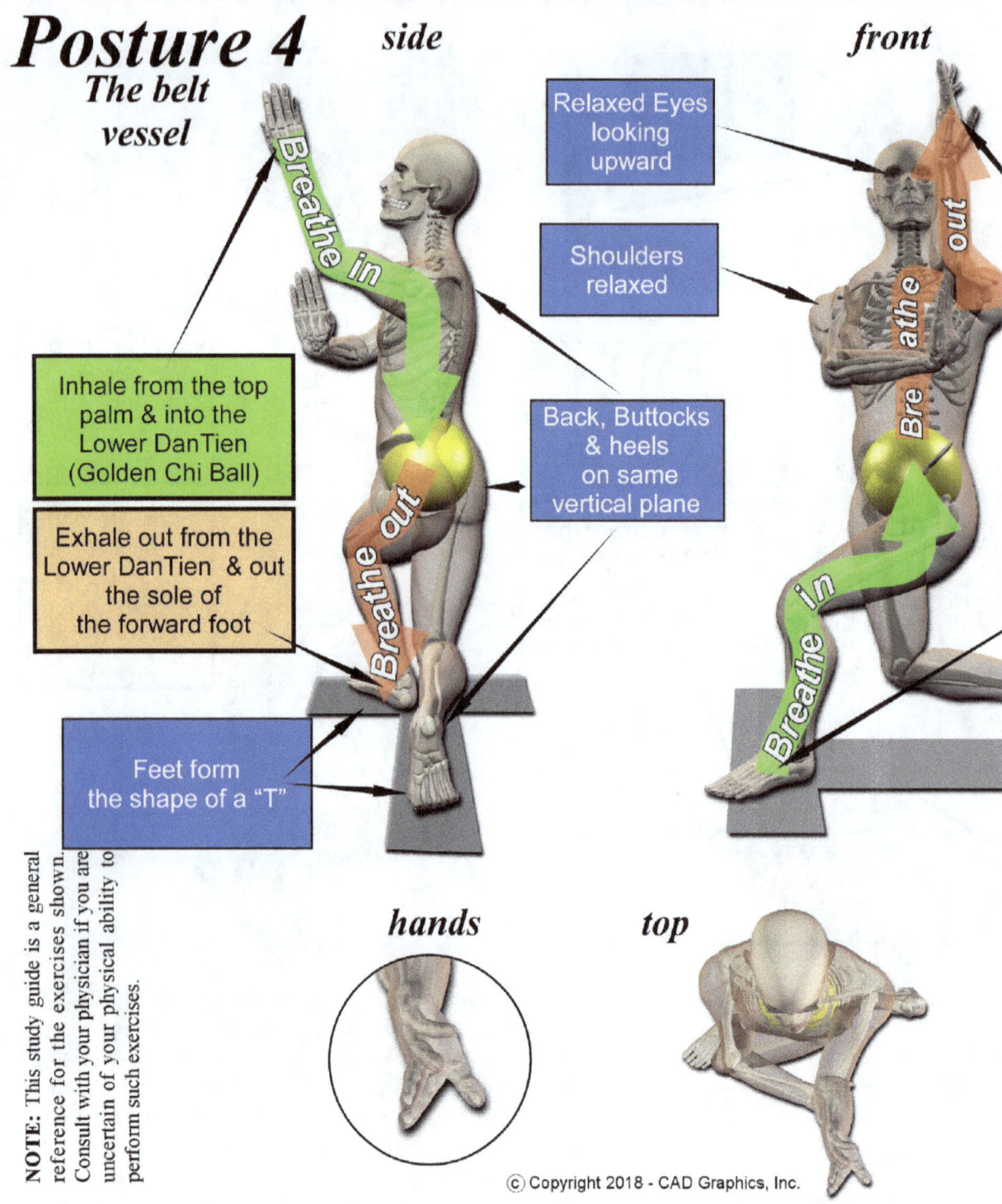

front

- Exhale out from the Lower DanTien & out through the top palm
- Inhale from the forward sole into the Lower DanTien (Golden Chi Ball)

rear

- Wrist gently twisting
- Wrist gently pulled back
- Lower back neutral

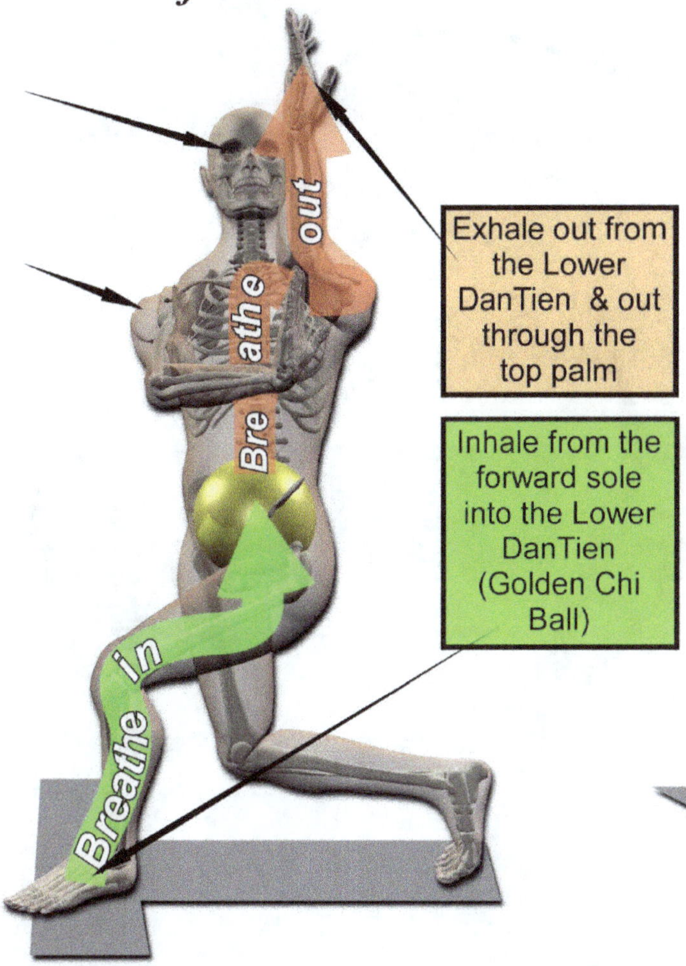

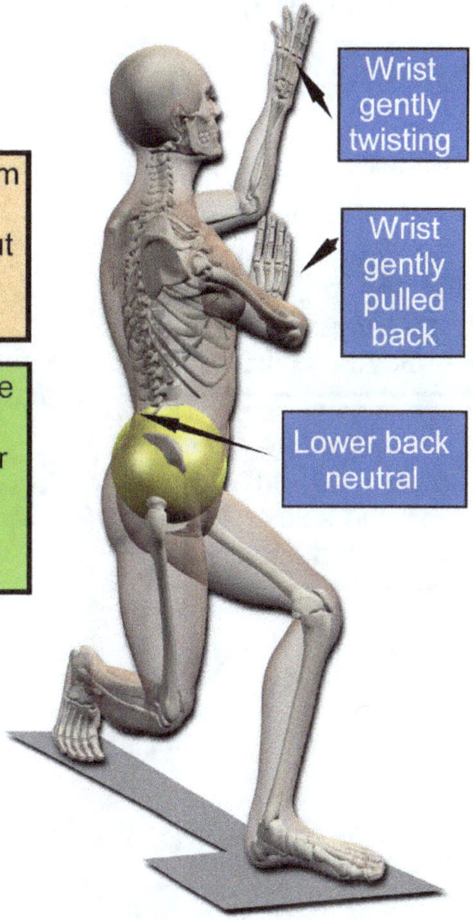

top

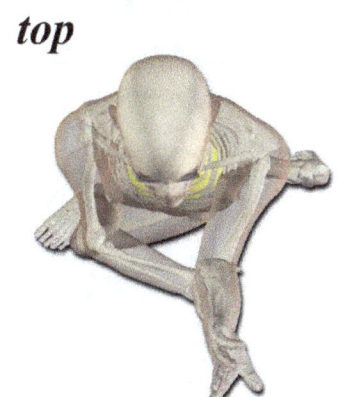

Set 4 stimulates the belt vessel by twisting the torso like a wet dish towel. This stance also strengthens the thighs, knees and ankles. Start with the feet, working your way up the body as applying the proper positions and posture. Inhale from upward palm down into the Lower DanTien. Exhale from this point and out through the sole of the forward foot. Inhale from the sole into the DanTien. Exhale out from the DanTien and through the palm to complete 1 full repetition. Execute on both sides for 1 set.

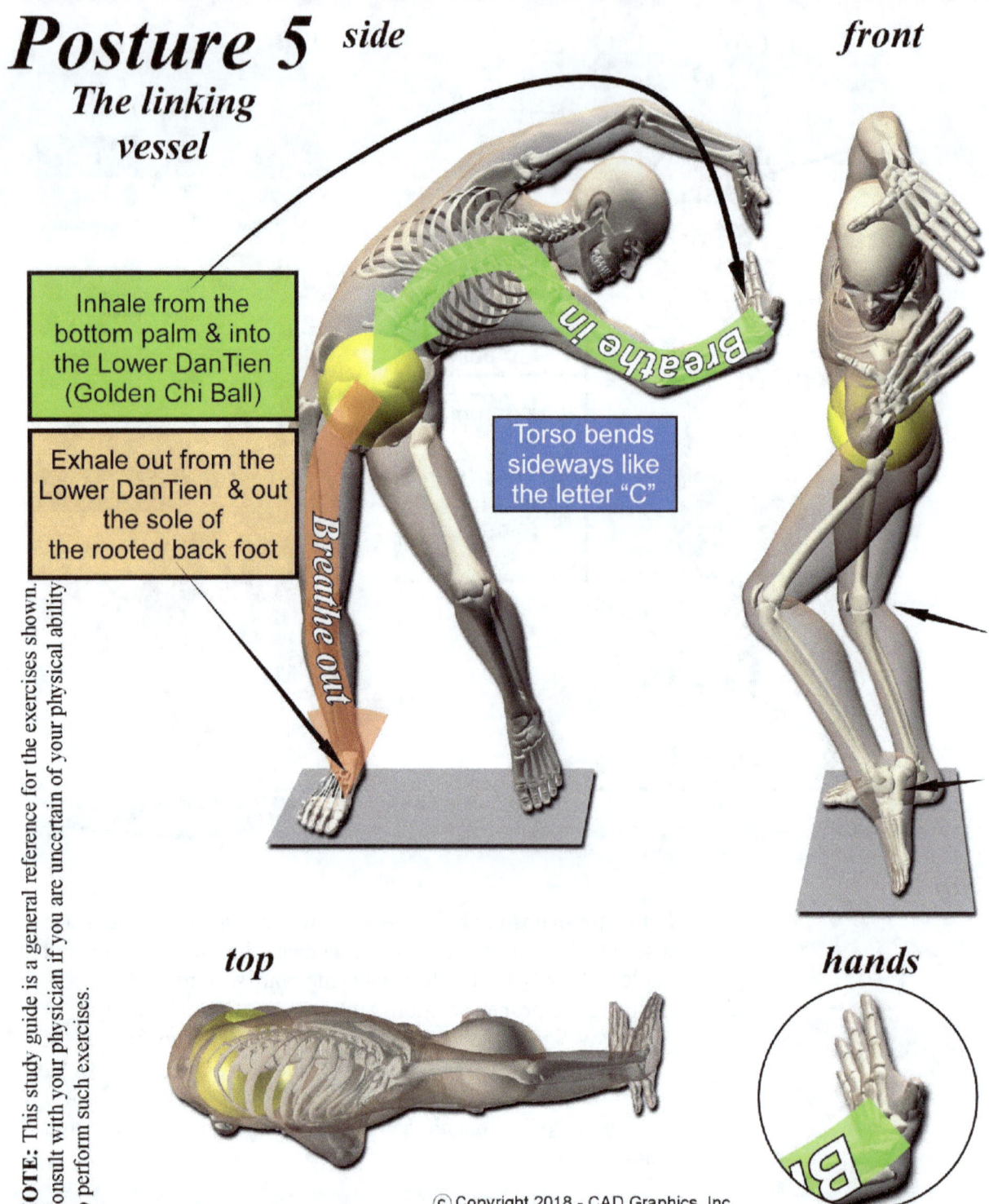

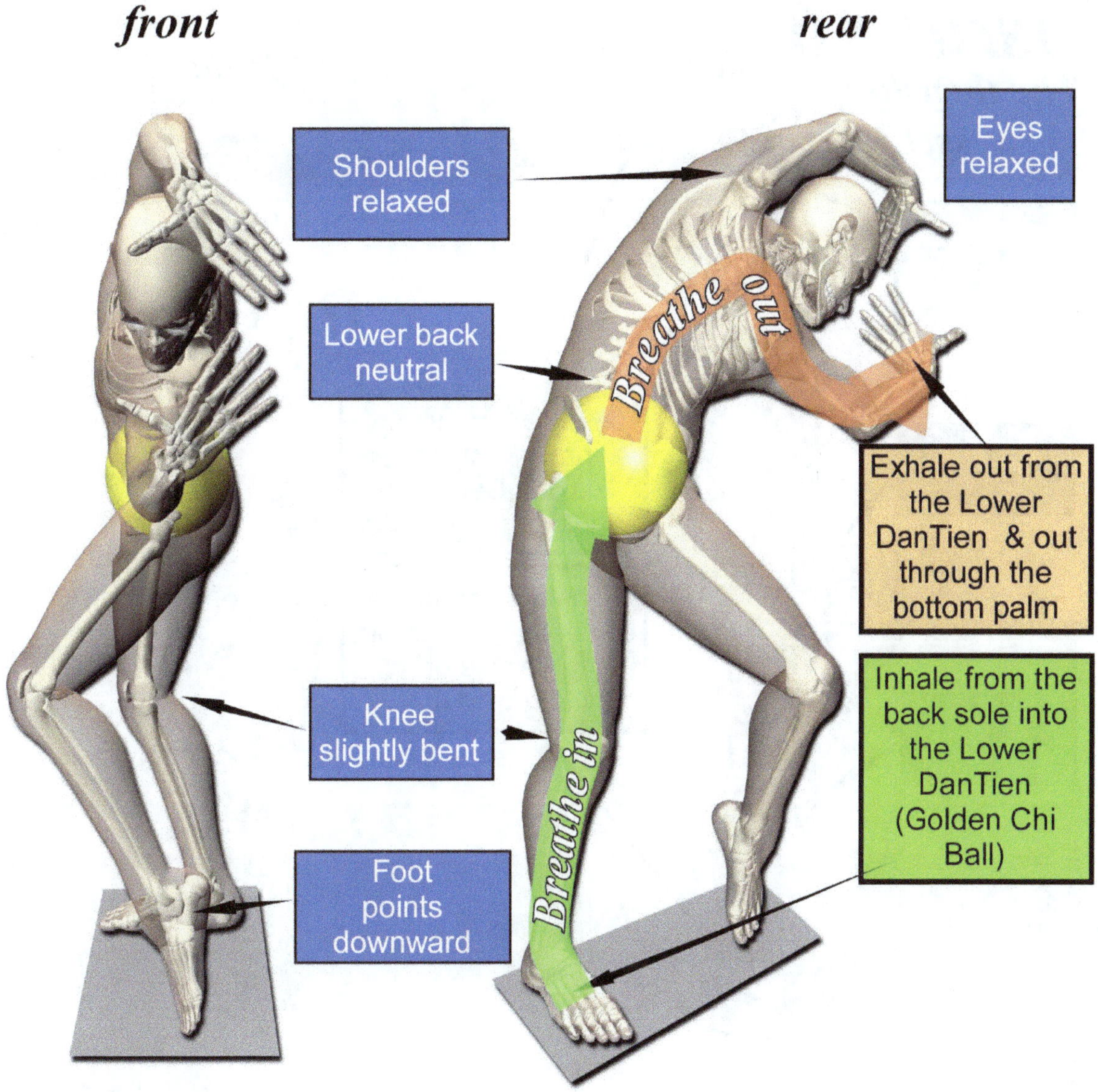

front / rear

- Shoulders relaxed
- Eyes relaxed
- Lower back neutral
- Breathe out
- Exhale out from the Lower DanTien & out through the bottom palm
- Inhale from the back sole into the Lower DanTien (Golden Chi Ball)
- Knee slightly bent
- Breathe in
- Foot points downward

hands

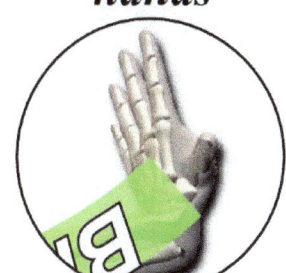

Set 5 increases the range of motion in the spine and torso. Start with the feet, working your way up the body as applying the proper positions and posture. Inhale from bottom palm down into the Lower DanTien. Exhale from this point and out through the sole of the rooted back foot. Inhale from the sole into the DanTien. Exhale out from the DanTien and through the palm to complete 1 full repetition. Execute on both sides for 1 set.

Introductory Set

Posture 6
The thrusting vessel

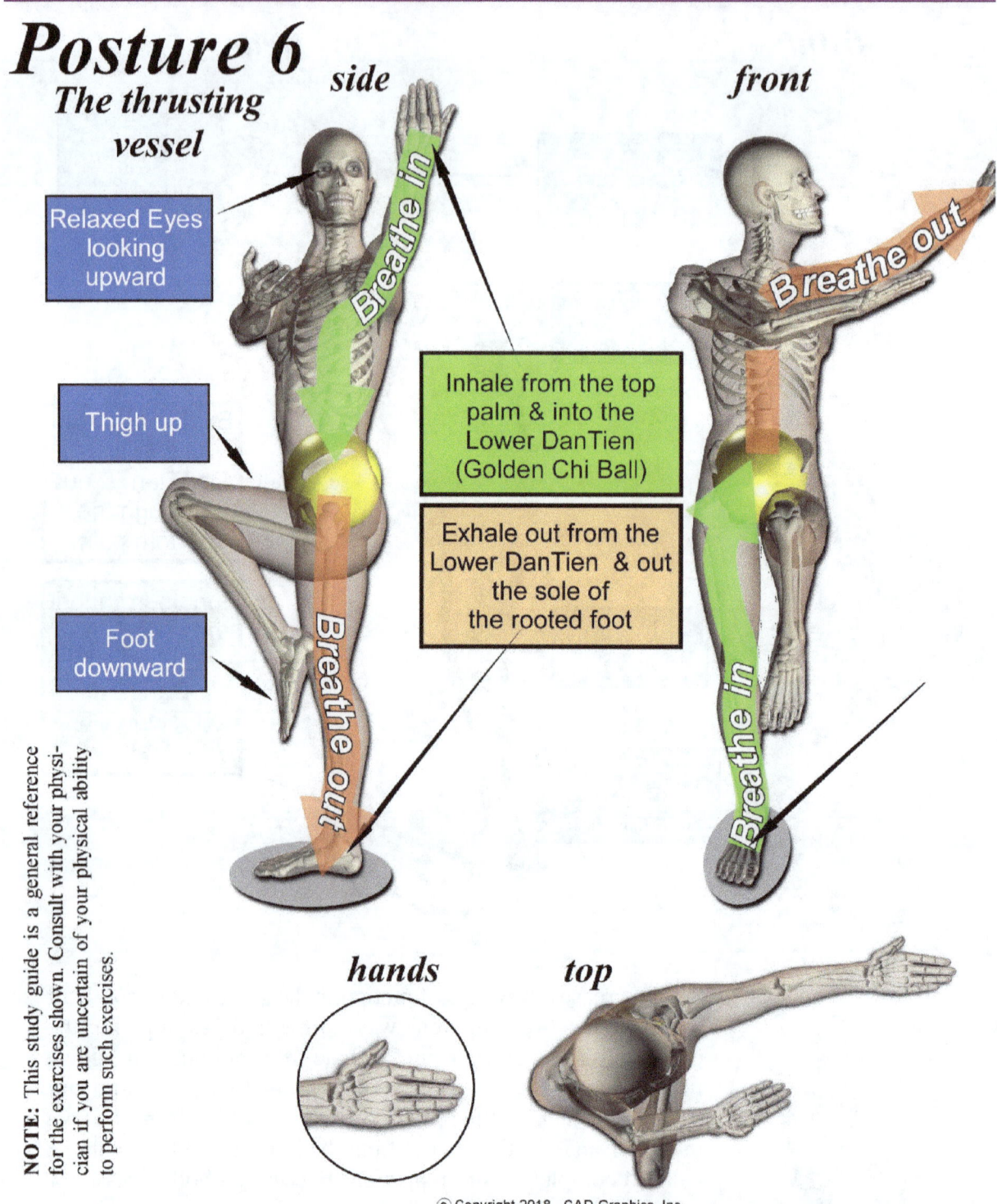

NOTE: This study guide is a general reference for the exercises shown. Consult with your physician if you are uncertain of your physical ability to perform such exercises.

© Copyright 2018 - CAD Graphics, Inc.

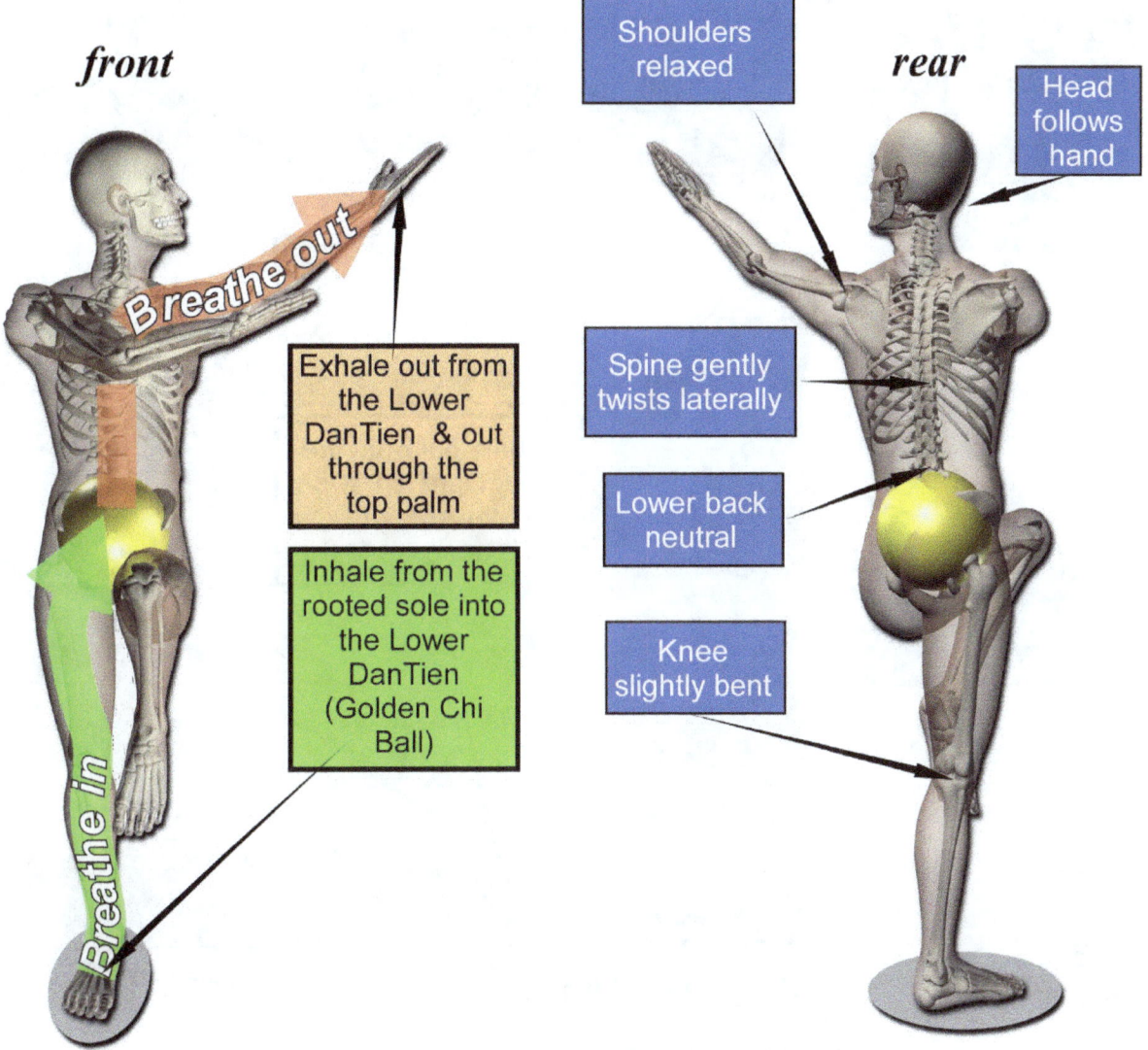

Set 6 increases balance and focus. Start with the feet, working your way up the body as applying the proper positions and posture. Inhale from upward palm down into the Lower DanTien. Exhale from this point and out through the sole of the rooted foot. Inhale from the sole into the DanTien. Exhale out from the DanTien and through the palm to complete 1 full repetition. Execute on both sides for 1 set.

Introductory Set

Posture 7
The heel vessel

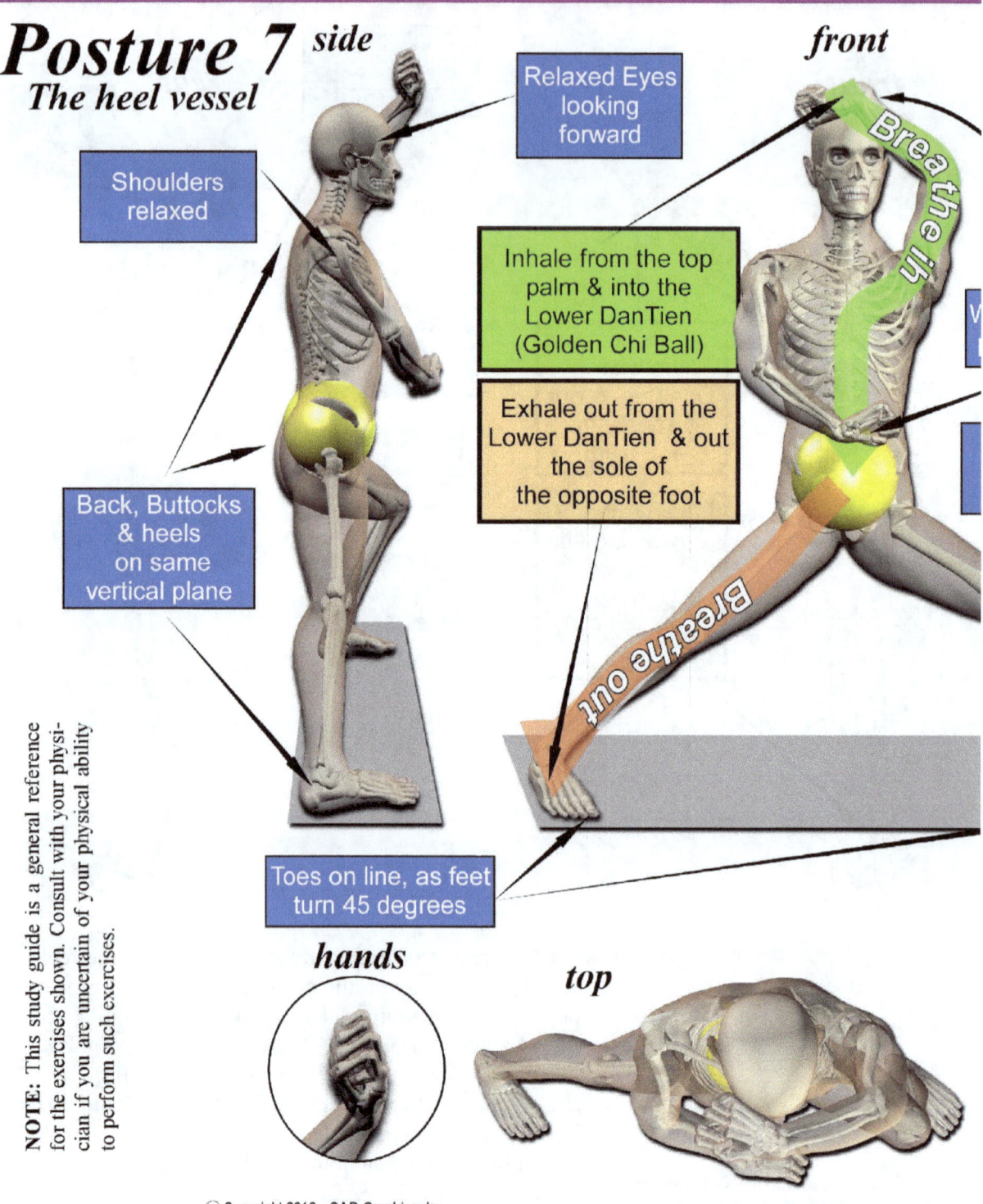

side *front*

- Relaxed Eyes looking forward
- Shoulders relaxed
- Inhale from the top palm & into the Lower DanTien (Golden Chi Ball)
- Exhale out from the Lower DanTien & out the sole of the opposite foot
- Back, Buttocks & heels on same vertical plane
- Toes on line, as feet turn 45 degrees

Breathe in / Breathe out

hands *top*

NOTE: This study guide is a general reference for the exercises shown. Consult with your physician if you are uncertain of your physical ability to perform such exercises.

© Copyright 2018 - CAD Graphics, Inc.

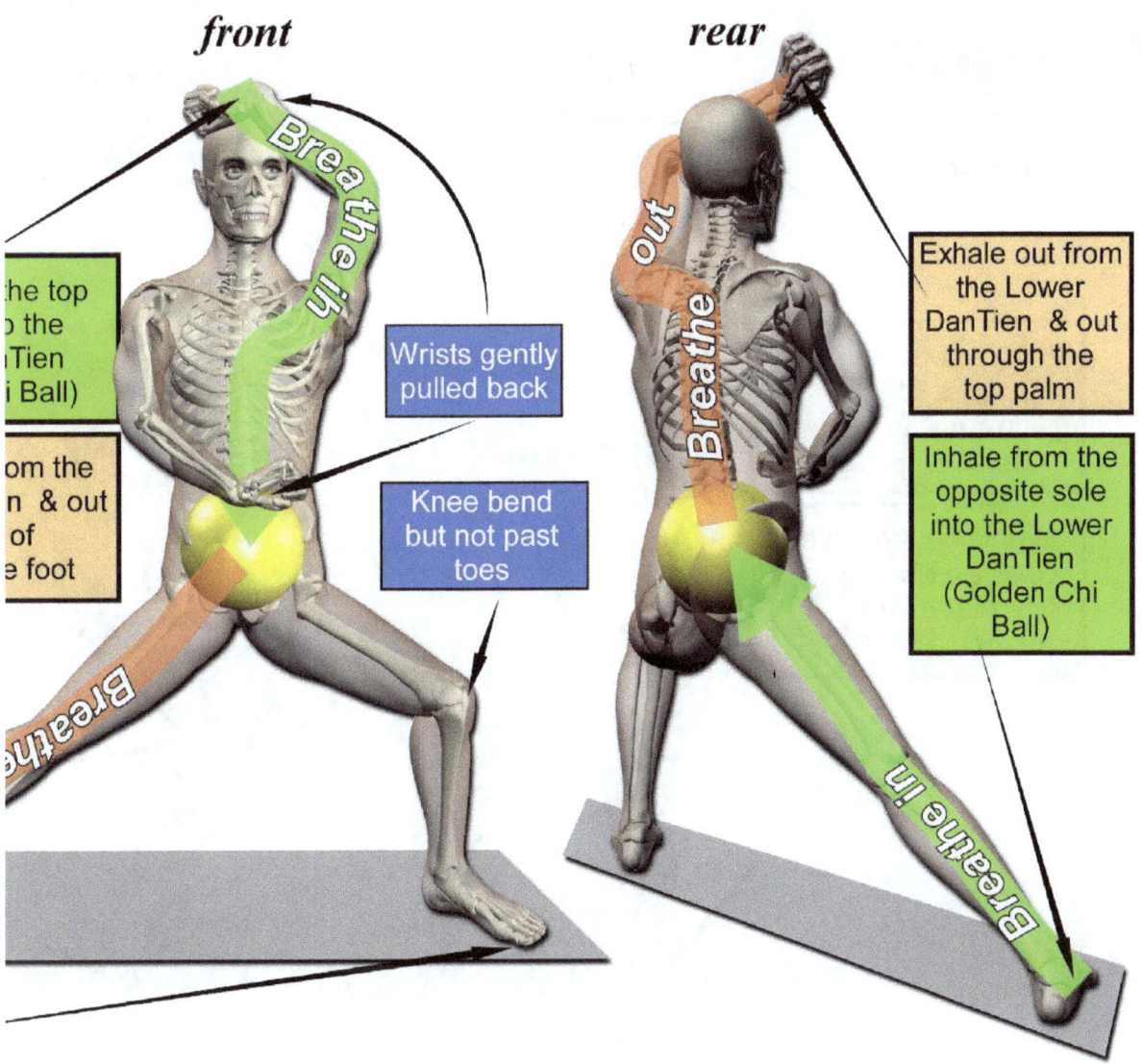

Set 7 strengthens and stretches muscles within the hips, thighs and lower back. Start with the feet, working your way up the body as applying the proper positions and posture. Inhale from upward palm down into the Lower DanTien. Exhale from this point and out through the sole of the opposite foot. Inhale from the sole into the DanTien. Exhale out from the DanTien and through the palm to complete 1 full repetition. Execute on both sides for 1 set.

Introductory Set

Posture 8
The thrusting vessel

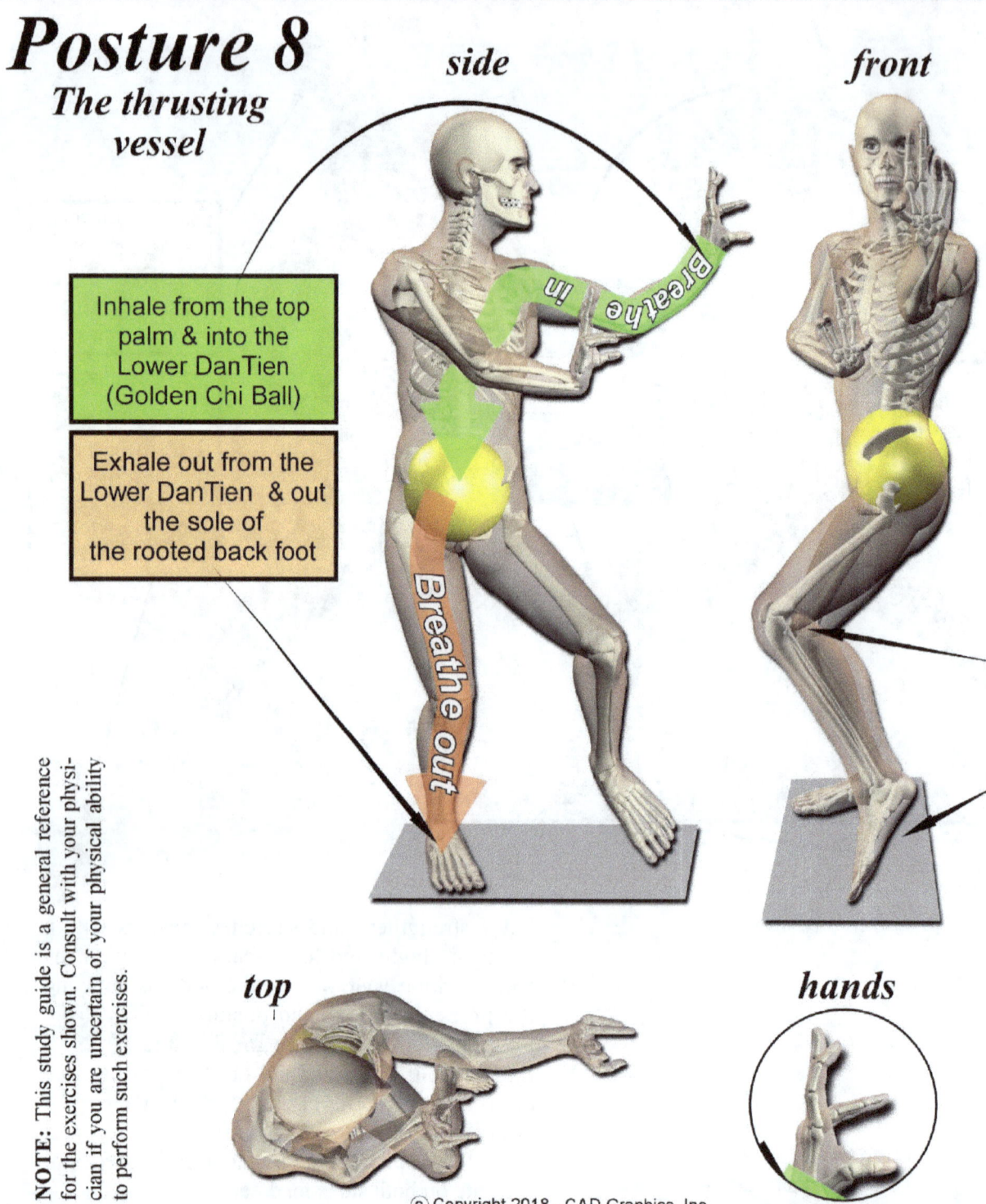

Inhale from the top palm & into the Lower DanTien (Golden Chi Ball)

Exhale out from the Lower DanTien & out the sole of the rooted back foot

NOTE: This study guide is a general reference for the exercises shown. Consult with your physician if you are uncertain of your physical ability to perform such exercises.

© Copyright 2018 - CAD Graphics, Inc.

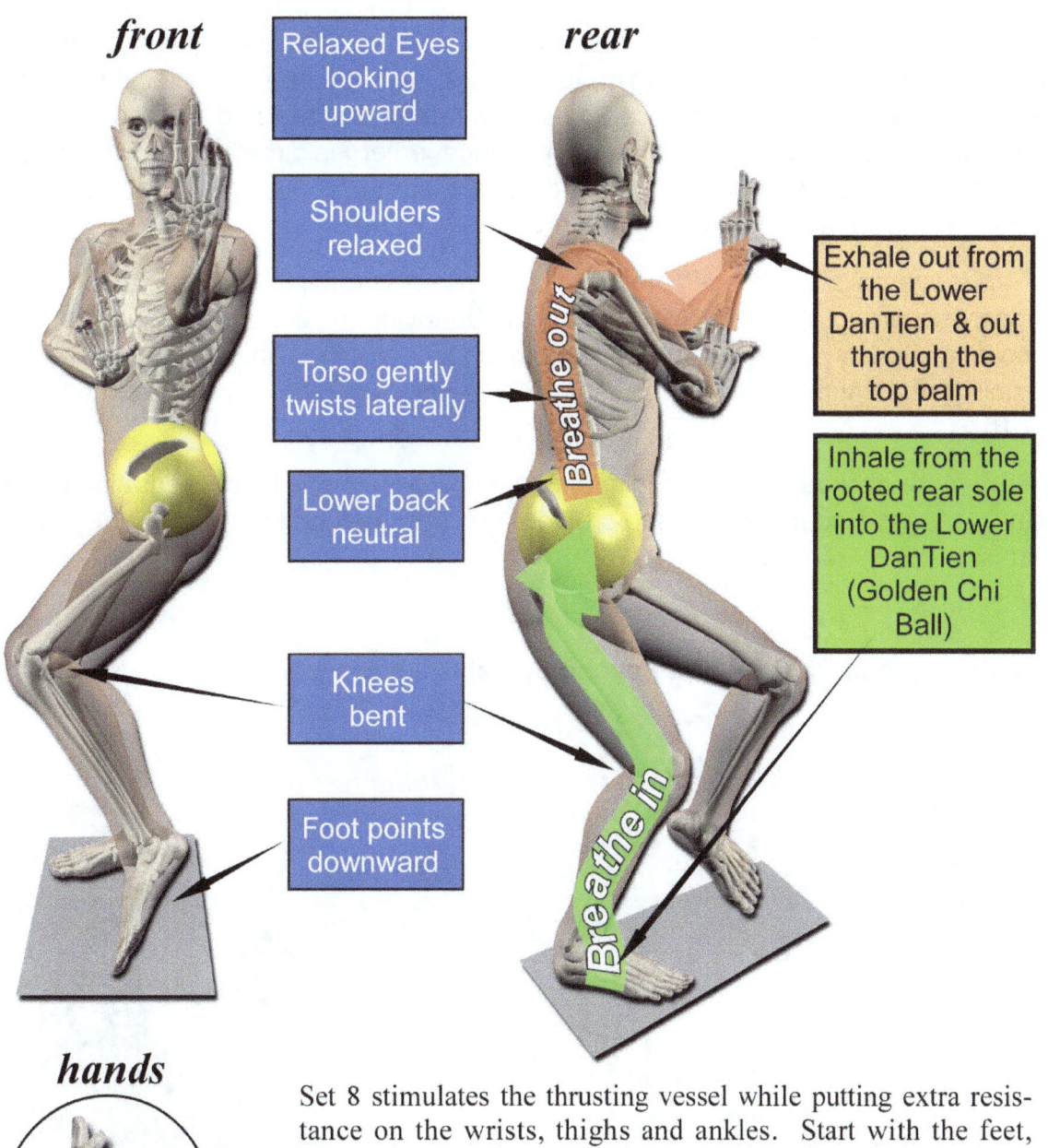

Set 8 stimulates the thrusting vessel while putting extra resistance on the wrists, thighs and ankles. Start with the feet, working your way up the body as applying the proper positions and posture. Inhale from upward palm down into the Lower DanTien. Exhale from this point and out through the sole of the rooted rear foot. Inhale from the sole into the DanTien. Exhale out from the DanTien and through the palm to complete 1 full repetition. Execute on both sides for 1 set.

10 Emotional Alchemy

Transforming Polarity and Transmuting Inner States

Hermeticism is best known for its metaphysical teachings, but its greatest contribution to modern psychology may be the **Principle of Polarity.** The insight that all emotional states exist on a continuum and can be shifted rather than resisted. Emotional alchemy, the conscious transformation of inner experience, emerges directly from this principle. It is the heart of the Great Work, where individuals learn to convert fear into courage, anger into clarity, and shame into integrity.

In Taoist internal alchemy, this process is described as refining Qi, the emotional and cognitive energies that shape perception and behavior. In contemporary psychology, emotional alchemy parallels emotion regulation, cognitive reframing, psychological flexibility, and trauma integration (Siegel, 2012; Herman, 1992; Kashdan & Rottenberg, 2010).

This chapter explores emotional alchemy through a Hermetic lens, integrating ancient principles with modern research to create a practical method for transforming inner states.

The Principle of Polarity as a Psychological Framework

The **Principle of Polarity** states:

"Everything is dual; everything has poles."

This means:

- fear ↔ courage
- sadness ↔ joy
- tension ↔ relaxation
- contraction ↔ expansion
- confusion ↔ clarity
- shame ↔ dignity
- dissociation ↔ presence

These are not separate states but different degrees of the same emotional continuum. This insight is revolutionary because it suggests that transformation is not an act of annihilation but of movement.

Modern emotion theory supports this view. Emotions are not fixed entities, but dynamic processes shaped by physiology, cognition, and context (Barrett, 2017). What changes are:

- intensity
- interpretation
- bodily activation
- thought patterns
- meaning
- behavioral response

The Principle of Polarity reveals that emotional transformation is a skill that can be practiced.

The Physiology of Emotional Alchemy

Emotions arise from the body. They are constructed from:

- autonomic nervous system states
- interoceptive signals
- muscular tension
- breath patterns
- posture
- neurotransmitters
- past conditioning

This aligns with the Hermetic Principles of Vibration and Rhythm, emotions are oscillations, not permanent conditions.

How emotions transform physiologically

1. **Breath** regulates arousal through vagal pathways (Porges, 2011).
2. **Posture** influences emotional interpretation (Peper et al., 2016).

3. **Movement** alters neural firing patterns associated with mood (Ratey, 2008).
4. **Attention** shifts meaning and cognitive appraisal (Beck, 1976).
5. **Social connection** reduces emotional intensity and increases regulation (Siegel, 2012).

These mechanisms show that emotional alchemy is not mystical; it is physiological, cognitive, and relational.

Cognitive Alchemy: Reframing and Reinterpretation

Cognitive reframing transforms the emotional meaning of a situation by shifting perspective. Tversky and Kahneman (1974) demonstrated that perception is influenced by cognitive biases and framing effects. The Scholar's clarity allows individuals to reinterpret events in ways that reduce suffering and increase agency.

Examples:

- "I was rejected" → "I was redirected."
- "I failed" → "I learned."
- "I am overwhelmed" → "I am reorganizing."
- "I am broken" → "I am healing."

Hermeticism reinforces this through **Mentalism**:

> The mind shapes experience. Reframing alters the mental vibration, which shifts emotional tone.

Somatic Alchemy: Changing Emotional Energy Through the Body

Taoist and martial practices have long recognized that emotions are stored in the muscles, breath, and organs. Somatic alchemy works directly with these elements.

Somatic methods include:

- deep diaphragmatic breathing
- shaking or tremor release
- slow intentional movement
- grounding through the feet
- tension-and-release cycles
- stretching to release emotional tension

- tapping or acupressure

These methods calm the amygdala and release stored activation (van der Kolk, 2014), allowing emotional states to transform rather than stagnate.

Somatic alchemy expresses the **Principle of Vibration**, changing frequency through movement.

Behavioral Alchemy: Action That Transforms Emotion

Behavior changes emotion by altering physiological activation and cognitive appraisal.

Examples:
- walking reduces anxiety
- smiling increases positive affect
- speaking calmly reduces anger
- setting a boundary increases dignity
- cleaning or organizing reduces overwhelm
- journaling increases clarity

Duhigg (2012) notes that habits create cognitive-emotional patterns via **Cause and Effect.** Therefore, action is a powerful tool of transmutation.

Hermetically, behavioral alchemy is the application of **Cause and Effect** to inner states.

Relational Alchemy: How Relationships Transform Emotion

Relationships influence emotional states through *co-regulation*, and how nervous systems respond to each other (Porges, 2011). Healthy relational connections can:
- neutralize fear
- calm anger
- reduce shame
- increase presence
- support emotional processing

This is the **Principle of Correspondence** applied interpersonally: the emotional state of one influence the other. Wise relationships support emotional transmutation; unhealthy relationships amplify fragmentation.

Shadow Integration: Transforming the Hidden Poles

Shadow work is the process of integrating disowned emotions, impulses, and beliefs. Jung (1959) described the shadow as the part of the psyche individuals deny or repress, leading to internal conflict and projection onto others.

Shadow integration involves:

- acknowledging uncomfortable feelings
- exploring the roots of reactivity
- identifying old wounds
- recognizing defensive patterns
- owning difficult thoughts without acting on them
- embracing emotional range

In Hermetic terms, shadow integration is conscious movement along the poles. It turns polarity into wholeness.

The Hermetic Method of Emotional Alchemy

A practical, integrated method:

1. Awareness (Mentalism)

Name the emotion without judgment.
"What am I feeling?"

2. Location (Correspondence)

Identify where it is in the body.
"Where is this sensation?"

3. Regulation (Vibration & Rhythm)

Use breath and posture to stabilize.
"How can I soothe my system?"

4. Understanding (Cause and Effect)

Explore the root trigger.
"What caused this?"

5. Reframing (Polarity)

Shift interpretation.
"What is the more constructive view?"

6. Expression (Gender)

Balance active and receptive responses.
"What action or stillness is needed?"

7. Integration (Shen)

Allow the insight to settle.
"What have I learned?"

This seven-step method transforms raw emotion into wisdom.

Post-Traumatic Growth Through Emotional Alchemy

Emotional alchemy enables post-traumatic growth, which is the development of strength, meaning, and clarity after adversity (Tedeschi & Calhoun, 2004). Trauma fragments polarity: alchemy restores it. Trauma freezes emotional rhythms; alchemy reanimates them.

Through emotional alchemy, individuals:

- reclaim agency
- reduce reactivity
- develop compassion
- organize their inner world
- internalize safety
- restore coherence
- find purpose

This is the alchemical transmutation of lead into gold, the lead of suffering into the gold of wisdom.

The Heart of the Great Work

Emotional alchemy is the central turning point of the Hermetic path. It is where the Warrior's strength meets the Scholar's clarity and gives rise to the Sage's compassion. By shifting polarity, individuals transform not only emotions but identity, relationships, and destiny.

The ability to transmute inner states determines the course of one's life. What cannot be transformed becomes suffering. What is transformed becomes wisdom.

With this psychological and emotional foundation established, the next chapter explores how discernment and boundaries function in the modern world, a continuation of the Scholar's work applied to real-life contexts.

11. Discernment and Boundaries in a Manipulative Age

Modern society has become an environment where manipulation is not an exception but a structural feature. Digital platforms are engineered to capture attention, emotional triggers are exploited to influence behavior, and misinformation spreads faster than truth. Social pressures, ideological echo chambers, and performance-driven culture distort perception and weaken critical thinking. In such a landscape, discernment and boundaries are not merely optional virtues, they are essential survival skills.

Hermeticism provides a sophisticated framework for navigating manipulation by empowering individuals to understand how perception is shaped, how emotional states are influenced, and how inner sovereignty can be maintained. The Warrior–Scholar–Sage developmental arc reinforces this by grounding discernment in the body (Jing), clarifying it through the mind (Qi), and integrating it through ethical presence (Shen).

This chapter examines the mechanisms of modern manipulation, the psychological vulnerabilities that enable it, and the Hermetic tools necessary to preserve autonomy in an increasingly coercive world.

Manipulation as a Violation of Correspondence

At the core of all manipulation is a disruption of the Hermetic **Principle of Correspondence**. When external messages, pressures, or influences overpower internal perception, individuals lose the ability to interpret reality through their own lens. Manipulation replaces internal correspondence with external programming.

Examples include:

- persuasive advertising designed to bypass rational thinking
- political messaging that activates fear-based responses
- online echo chambers that distort perception
- charismatic authorities who override internal judgment
- social dynamics that reward conformity over authenticity
- abusive relationships that erode self-trust

Modern psychology confirms that human cognition is highly susceptible to external framing, authority cues, and emotional priming (Tversky & Kahneman, 1974). This susceptibility is amplified in environments of chronic stress, trauma, and digital overstimulation (Haidt, 2024).

The antidote is restoring correspondence: aligning inner perception with truth, grounded in embodied awareness and cognitive sovereignty.

The Scholar's Shield: Discernment as Cognitive Sovereignty

Discernment is the Scholar's greatest tool. It is the ability to:

- analyze without reacting
- question without collapsing into doubt
- interpret without projecting
- evaluate motives and patterns
- sense incongruence
- identify manipulation
- choose responses intentionally

Discernment is not cynicism; it is clarity. It requires emotional regulation (Warrior), cognitive sharpness (Scholar), and intuitive insight (Sage).

Modern threats to discernment

1. **Information overload** overwhelms cognitive filters.
2. **Chronic stress** degrades executive functioning.
3. **Trauma** distorts evaluation and creates hypervigilance or naïveté.
4. **Echo chambers** limit perspective.
5. **Social comparison** distorts self-perception.
6. **Algorithmic curation** narrows awareness.
7. **Authority bias** reduces critical thinking (Milgram findings).
8. **Groupthink** suppresses independent thought.

Hermeticism counteracts these through **Mentalism, Polarity, and Cause and Effect**, returning interpretive power to the individual.

Boundaries as the Warrior's Ethical Armor

Boundaries are not defensive walls, but rather they are structures of clarity that define what is acceptable, healthy, and aligned. In modern life, boundaries must extend to:

- time
- energy

- emotional availability
- digital exposure
- relationships
- environments
- commitments
- attention

Healthy boundaries prevent manipulation by reducing cognitive overload, emotional depletion, and susceptibility to coercion (Herman, 1992).

Types of boundaries

- **Physical boundaries**: posture, space, embodied presence.
- **Emotional boundaries**: refusing responsibility for others' feelings.
- **Cognitive boundaries**: thinking independently.
- **Digital boundaries**: limiting exposure to manipulative platforms.
- **Relational boundaries**: selecting healthy connections.
- **Ethical boundaries**: refusing actions that violate values.

Boundaries reflect the Principle of Polarity, differentiating self from other, internal truth from external influence.

Trauma and the Erosion of Discernment

Trauma weakens discernment by altering:

- self-trust
- fear responses
- emotional processing
- attachment patterns
- moral intuition
- cognitive framing

Survivors of high-control environments, abusive relationships, or manipulative mentors often internalize distorted messages that override intuition. This makes them more vulnerable to coercion and more likely to mistrust their own perceptions (Herman, 1992).

Healing requires:

- grounding (Warrior)
- reframing (Scholar)
- compassion (Sage)
- restoration of boundaries
- development of emotional intelligence

Discernment is not only a skill, but also a trauma-informed corrective process.

Manipulation Through Emotional Vibration

Manipulation works through *emotional activation*, which corresponds to the Hermetic **Principle of Vibration**. Emotions like fear, shame, excitement, and anger create internal resonance that can override rational thought.

This is exploited by:

- advertising
- political rhetoric
- social media outrage cycles
- toxic relationships
- charismatic leaders
- fear-based messaging

Regulating vibration through breath, grounding, and somatic awareness, is the first line of defense against manipulation.

When vibration stabilizes:

- fear subsides
- clarity returns
- autonomy increases
- insight becomes accessible

This reflects the Scholar's and Sage's integration of Qi and Shen.

The Hermetic Triad of Protection: Warrior–Scholar–Sage

Each developmental mode protects autonomy in its own way.

The Warrior protects through the body

- strong posture
- stable breath
- grounded presence
- clear physical boundaries
- reduced reactivity

The Warrior counters manipulation by strengthening Jing, reducing somatic vulnerability.

The Scholar protects through the mind

- questioning assumptions
- evaluating claims
- recognizing emotional triggers
- separating fact from narrative
- noticing cognitive distortions

The Scholar strengthens Qi, making perception clearer.

The Sage protects through insight

- sensing incongruence
- perceiving hidden motives
- recognizing subtle dynamics
- maintaining compassion without naivete
- acting from wisdom, not impulse

The Sage strengthens Shen, adding ethical clarity and intuitive discernment.

Together, they produce sovereignty.

Discernment as a Daily Practice

Discernment must be cultivated through consistent effort. Practical exercises include:

1. The Pause

Before reacting, take a conscious breath. This interrupts emotional hijacking.

2. The Inquiry

Ask:

- "What am I feeling?"
- "What is influencing me?"
- "Whose voice is this?"
- "What is the evidence?"

3. The Boundary

If something feels off, create distance in the physical, emotional, or cognitive.

4. The Observation

Notice patterns in others' behavior, tone, and consistency.

5. The Reality Check

Verify information from multiple sources; avoid echo chambers.

6. The Alignment Check

Ask:

- "Does this align with my values?"
- "Does this feel manipulative?"
- "Does this serve my highest development?"

Discernment is not a talent; it is a muscle.

Hermetic Boundaries: A Framework for Autonomy

Boundaries reflect the integration of all Hermetic Principles:

- **Mentalism** → clear thinking requires protected mental space.
- **Correspondence** → inner boundaries create outer boundaries.
- **Vibration** → emotional regulation prevents manipulation.
- **Polarity** → distinguishing self from others.
- **Rhythm** → establishing daily routines that preserve stability.
- **Cause and Effect** → actions reflect values.
- **Gender** → balancing assertiveness and receptivity.
- **Virtue** → ensuring boundaries align with ethical principles.

Healthy boundaries are not barriers, they are the structure that allows freedom, creativity, and growth.

Discernment and Boundaries as Modern Hermetic Necessities

The modern world requires a level of discernment that previous eras did not. Information is abundant; wisdom is scarce. Influence is constant; autonomy is fragile. Manipulation is subtle; sovereignty must be intentional.

Discernment protects the mind. Boundaries protect the nervous system. Virtue protects the soul. Together, they ensure that the individual remains aligned with the Great Work; capable of navigating a chaotic world without losing clarity, integrity, or purpose.

As the manuscript moves forward, the next chapter explores **meaning-making, purpose, and the search for direction,** integrating Hermetic principles with the deep human need for significance and coherence.

12. Meaning-making, Purpose and Personal Integration

The search for meaning is universal. Every individual, regardless of culture or upbringing, grapples with the fundamental questions:

- *Why am I here?*
- *What is the purpose of my life?*
- *What am I meant to do?*
- *How do I make sense of suffering?*

Hermeticism provides a powerful framework for meaning-making by linking the inner world with the outer world, the mundane with the spiritual, and the personal with the universal. The Seven Hermetic Principles, combined with the **Eighth Principle of Virtue and Ethical Alignment**, form a map for understanding one's place within the cosmos.

Modern psychology affirms that meaning-making is central to mental health, resilience, and post-traumatic growth. Viktor Frankl (2006) argued that humans are meaning-seeking beings and that the capacity to assign meaning to suffering determines whether one collapses or transcends adversity. Trauma research similarly shows that meaning-making is a primary factor in recovery, identity reconstruction, and psychological integration (Park, 2010; Tedeschi & Calhoun, 2004).

This chapter explores how Hermetic principles guide meaning-making and how purpose emerges organically through personal development.

Meaning-Making as a Hermetic Function

Hermeticism teaches that everything is connected through Correspondence: *"As above, so below; as within, so without."* Meaning emerges when individuals understand how their personal experiences relate to universal patterns.

This creates coherence between:

- events and lessons
- suffering and transformation
- identity and destiny
- chaos and order
- inner changes and outer outcomes

Meaning-making is the process of discovering these correspondences.

The Principle of Mentalism teaches that meaning is not found, it is constructed through interpretation, attention, and reflection. **The Principle of Cause and Effect** shows that meaning grows when individuals understand the consequences of thoughts, behaviors, and choices.

Meaning-making is, therefore, a form of conscious alchemy.

Purpose as an Emergent Quality of Integration

Purpose is not a goal one chooses; it is an orientation that emerges when Jing, Qi, and Shen become aligned.

- When the Warrior stabilizes the body, purpose becomes grounded.
- When the Scholar clarifies perception, purpose becomes coherent.
- When the Sage integrates compassion, purpose becomes meaningful.

Purpose is not external. It is an internal compass that guides direction and action. Research shows that people who feel purposeful demonstrate greater resilience, better health outcomes, and higher psychological well-being (McKnight & Kashdan, 2009). Purpose protects against anxiety, despair, and moral confusion.

Hermeticism teaches a similar view: purpose arises through the alignment of personal will with universal principles.

Suffering and the Hermetic Path to Meaning

Suffering is inevitable. But it is also one of the primary catalysts for meaning-making. In Hermetic philosophy, suffering activates the **Principle of Polarity**, exposing the extremes of human experience and creating opportunities for transformation.

Suffering becomes meaningful when it reveals:

- hidden patterns
- personal strengths
- moral clarity
- resilience
- empathy
- insight
- spiritual depth

In trauma research, this is known as **post-traumatic growth (PTG),** the emergence of new strengths, deeper relationships, and greater appreciation of life after hardship (Tedeschi & Calhoun, 2004).

Meaning is not found in suffering itself but in the interpretation and integration of experience.

Identity, Coherence, and the Construction of Meaning

Identity is not static, but rather it is a narrative that is continually updated to reflect experiences, beliefs, and relationships. Meaning-making requires coherence: the ability to weave events into a unified story.

Psychologists call this *narrative identity,* or the internal story individuals live by, shaping how they understand themselves and their lives (McAdams, 2013).

Hermeticism supports this through the Principle of Correspondence: personal narratives are expressions of universal patterns.

When narrative identity is fragmented, individuals experience confusion, lack of direction, and inner conflict. Trauma deepens fragmentation by disrupting continuity, distorting meaning, and weakening self-trust (Herman, 1992).

Rebuilding meaning involves restoring narrative coherence:

- integrating past experiences
- reorganizing memory
- redefining identity
- reconnecting with purpose
- forming a new vision for the future

The Sage represents the completion of this integration in identity aligned with truth, virtue, and presence.

The Warrior, Scholar, and Sage as Meaning-Makers

Each developmental mode contributes to meaning-making in distinct ways.

The Warrior: Meaning Through Embodiment

The Warrior finds meaning through action, discipline, and responsibility. The body becomes an instrument of purpose. Physical practice, boundaries, posture, and breath anchor meaning in the lived, embodied world.

The Scholar: Meaning Through Understanding

The Scholar finds meaning by interpreting patterns, analyzing experience, and clarifying thought. Purpose becomes articulate, structured, and coherent.

The Sage: Meaning Through Insight

The Sage finds meaning through intuition, compassion, and ethical alignment. Purpose becomes expansive, relational, and spiritually grounded.

Together, they produce a fully integrated meaning-making system that is physical, cognitive, emotional, relational, and spiritual.

Meaning-Making and the Hermetic Principles

Each Hermetic Principle contributes to the development of meaning:

- **Mentalism** → meaning is shaped by interpretation.
- **Correspondence** → meaning emerges from pattern recognition.
- **Vibration** → emotional tone influences meaning.
- **Polarity** → transformation requires embracing opposites.
- **Rhythm** → meaning evolves through cycles.
- **Cause and effect** → choices shape destiny.
- **Gender** → creation of meaning involves active intention + receptive insight.
- **Virtue (the Eighth Principle)** → meaning becomes ethical and coherent when aligned with inner truth.

Meaning-making is thus the synthesis of the Great Work at a personal level.

Purpose as a Path Rather Than a Destination

Purpose is not a static endpoint. Purpose is a living, evolving process. Individuals often experience different expressions of purpose at different developmental stages:

- The Warrior finds purpose in strength, discipline, and personal sovereignty.
- The Scholar finds purpose in knowledge, clarity, and understanding.
- The Sage finds purpose in service, wisdom, and connection.

Purpose deepens as consciousness evolves. It becomes less about achievement and more about alignment.

Frankl (2006) emphasized that purpose is discovered through:

- creativity
- love
- responsibility
- suffering
- commitment
- presence

Hermeticism agrees that purpose arises when the individual aligns with higher principles of truth and virtue.

Pitfalls in Purpose-Seeking

Individuals often misinterpret purpose due to:

- external pressure
- comparison
- cultural expectations
- trauma-driven beliefs
- fear of failure
- perfectionism
- lack of embodiment
- spiritual bypassing

These distortions reflect the **Principle of Polarity**, where purpose confusion is simply the opposite pole of clear purpose. Movement, reflection, and integration can shift individuals toward clarity.

Hermetic Meaning-Making Practices

Practical methods include:

1. Pattern Reflection (Correspondence)

Identify recurring themes, lessons, or struggles and interpret their deeper meaning.

2. Emotional Inquiry (Polarity)

Explore how difficult emotions contain hidden wisdom.

3. Breath-Centered Presence (Vibration)

Use respiration to shift perception toward clarity.

4. Narrative Reconstruction (Mentalism)

Rewrite personal stories to emphasize agency and growth.

5. Ethical Alignment Check (Virtue)

Ensure that decisions support integrity and compassion.

6. Shadow Dialogue

Engage disowned parts of the psyche to reveal hidden insights.

7. Purpose Journaling

Reflect on values, strengths, and meaningful experiences.

Through these practices, meaning becomes not an abstract concept but a lived experience.

Meaning as the Soul's Direction

Meaning-making is the spiritual heart of the Great Work. It transforms random events into purposeful lessons, suffering into growth, and identity into destiny. Purpose emerges not from external validation but from internal coherence when Jing stabilizes, Qi clarifies, and Shen illuminates.

The next chapter expands upon this foundation by exploring **the cultivation of higher states of consciousness**, building on meaning-making to enter deeper realms of intuitive wisdom.

PART IV — Expanded Consciousness & Creative Self

13. Expanded Consciousness

The Sage's Higher Perception and the Hermetic Mind

Expanded consciousness is not a mystical abstraction; it is the natural evolution of human awareness when the body is stable (Jing), the mind is clear (Qi), and the spirit is integrated (Shen). Hermeticism has always taught that the mind is the fundamental substratum of reality, stating in the Principle of Mentalism that *"the All is Mind."* But this principle is not merely metaphysical, it is psychological, physiological, and developmental.

As individuals progress through the Warrior–Scholar–Sage arc, their perceptual field widens. They become capable of perceiving subtle patterns, emotional undercurrents, relational dynamics, moral implications, and existential truths that remain invisible to the untrained mind. Expanded consciousness is therefore the culmination of the Great Work, an integrated mode of perception where intuition, reason, embodiment, and ethics operate as a unified system.

Modern neuroscience, contemplative science, Taoist internal alchemy, and trauma integration models all support the idea that consciousness can evolve through developmental milestones (Siegel, 2012; Lutz, Dunne, & Davidson, 2007). Hermeticism anticipated these findings by describing progressive refinements of mind, culminating in illumination.

This chapter examines expanded consciousness as a mature, grounded, ethically aligned state of awareness, free of mystical exaggeration yet retaining the profound depth of ancient esoteric tradition.

Expanded Consciousness as Integrated Awareness

Expanded consciousness does not refer to supernatural vision or psychic ability, though such concepts were historically associated with sages and adepts. Instead, expanded consciousness describes the integration of:

- somatic awareness
- emotional intelligence
- cognitive clarity
- intuitive perception
- moral insight
- existential understanding
- relational attunement

In modern psychological terms, this is an expression of *neural integration*, a process in which separate brain regions communicate harmoniously, producing coherence and insight (Siegel, 2012).

This integrated mode of awareness corresponds directly to Shen, as the radiant mind of Taoist philosophy. Shen emerges naturally when the nervous system is regulated, emotional processes are integrated, and meaning-making is mature.

Expanded consciousness is therefore not a mystical gift but a developmental achievement.

The Hermetic Principles as Perceptual Lenses

The Seven Hermetic Principles can be understood as perceptual filters that expand consciousness by revealing hidden aspects of reality.

1. Mentalism → Recognizing inner narratives

Perception expands when individuals understand the role of thought in shaping experience.

2. Correspondence → Seeing patterns

Expanded awareness perceives similarities between internal and external processes.

3. Vibration → Detecting emotional and energetic states

Individuals become attuned to shifts in mood, tone, and underlying intention.

4. Polarity → Holding opposites without fragmentation

High consciousness tolerates paradox and complexity.

5. Rhythm → Understanding cycles

Insight grows from recognizing developmental and emotional cycles.

6. Cause and Effect → Tracking consequences

Expanded awareness sees how choices ripple through time.

7. Gender → Integrating active and receptive qualities

Consciousness becomes balanced, fluid, and creative.

8. Virtue → Distinguishing truth from distortion

Ethics refine perception.

These perceptual capacities emerge not from doctrine but from lived integration.

The Biology of Expanded Awareness

Expanded consciousness has clear biological correlates in:

1. Prefrontal Cortex Activation

Supports executive function, empathy, and moral reasoning (Miller & Cohen, 2001).

2. Default Mode Network (DMN) Modulation

Regulates self-referential thinking and facilitates insight (Brewer et al., 2011).

3. Increased Heart Rate Variability (HRV)

Indicates emotional regulation and physiological flexibility (Porges, 2011).

4. Enhanced Interoception

Supports somatic awareness and intuition (Craig, 2008).

5. Integration of Limbic and Cortical Systems

Allows emotions and cognition to work synergistically (Siegel, 2012).

Thus, "higher consciousness" is an embodied neural phenomenon and not merely a philosophical ideal.

Intuition as the Sage's Second Sight

Intuition is one of the hallmark features of expanded consciousness. It is not guesswork or speculation but rapid, unconscious pattern recognition arising from integrated neural networks (Gigerenzer, 2007).

Intuition allows the Sage to:

- sense incongruence
- understand emotional subtext
- anticipate consequences
- detect manipulation
- perceive relational dynamics
- integrate complex information instantly

Intuition is the **Principle of Mentalism** operating at high resolution.

Intuition vs. Trauma Reactions

Intuition must be distinguished from trauma-driven hypervigilance. Trauma creates *false positives*: fear-based interpretations mistaken for insight (Herman, 1992).

Genuine intuition is calm, grounded, and clear.
Trauma reactions are urgent, emotional, and narrowed.

Expanded consciousness develops intuition by integrating trauma and refining emotional intelligence.

Moral Insight as a Feature of Shen

As consciousness expands, moral clarity emerges naturally. This reflects the **Principle of Virtue**, the Eighth Principle where perception becomes ethically attuned.

Moral insight involves:

- recognizing the ethical implications of actions
- sensing harm before it occurs
- understanding relational dynamics
- choosing responsibility over self-interest
- feeling the interconnectedness of all beings

Research shows that higher moral reasoning correlates with cognitive integration and emotional regulation (Kohlberg, 1984; Haidt, 2024).

Thus, the Sage's morality is not imposed but developed.

Systems Perception: Seeing the Larger Patterns

Expanded consciousness perceives systems rather than isolated events. This includes:

- relational systems
- family dynamics
- cultural structures
- trauma cycles
- collective behavior patterns
- historical influences
- psychological archetypes

This perspective aligns with the Principle of Correspondence, micro and macro patterns reflecting each other.

Systems perception prevents the Sage from being lost in personal emotion or superficial interpretations. It reveals the deeper architecture of experience.

Presence: The Gateway to Expanded Consciousness

Presence is the quality of being fully attuned to the current moment, somatically, emotionally, mentally, and ethically. Presence emerges through:

- regulated breathing
- upright posture
- grounded attention
- emotional stability
- cognitive clarity
- reduced internal noise

Presence corresponds to *ventral vagal activation*, a state of calm engagement (Porges, 2011). This state enhances perception, empathy, and relational attunement.

Presence is the Sage's home base.

Shadow Integration and the Expansion of Awareness

Expanded consciousness requires integrating the shadow. Jung (1959) noted that individuals who do not explore their shadow remain controlled by unconscious drives. Hermeticism sees unintegrated polarity creates distortion.

Shadow integration expands awareness by:

- revealing unconscious motives
- transforming shame
- acknowledging projections
- integrating repressed emotions
- dissolving inner fragmentation

When the shadow is integrated, perception becomes clearer and less reactive.

Higher States Without Bypassing

Hermeticism insists that expanded consciousness is not an escape from reality but deeper engagement with it. *Spiritual bypassing* is where one uses spiritual concepts to avoid emotional or psychological work and contradicting the Great Work.

Expanded consciousness integrates:

- embodiment
- emotional maturity
- cognitive clarity
- ethical responsibility
- relational attunement

Higher states are grounded states.

Practical Methods for Expanding Consciousness:

1. Slow, Coherent Breathing

Deepens interoception and stabilizes attention.

2. Mindful Observation

Watching thoughts without identification.

3. Pattern Recognition Journaling

Tracking recurring themes or synchronicities.

4. Shadow Dialogue

Confronting uncomfortable emotions without judgment.

5. Ethical Reflection

Aligning daily choices with core values.

6. Meditation and Qigong

Integrating Shen through stillness and movement.

7. Discernment Practice

Examining motives, influences, and reactions.

8. Silence and Solitude

Creating space for insight.

These practices do not create expanded consciousness, but rather they reveal it.

The Hermetic Mind as a Mature Consciousness

Expanded consciousness is the culmination of the Sage's development. It is not supernatural but deeply human, as a natural flowering of the integrated body, mind, and spirit. The Hermetic Mind sees patterns, perceives truth, feels compassion, and acts responsibly.

This mature awareness becomes the foundation for the next stage of Hermetic development: **co-creating one's reality through aligned intention, emotional regulation, and virtuous action**, which is explored in the following chapter.

14. Co-creation and Hermetic Art of Shaping Reality

Hermeticism teaches that the mind is not a passive observer of reality but an active participant in its formation. **The Principle of Mentalism** — *"All is Mind"* — suggests that consciousness plays a central role in how individuals experience and influence the world around them. While popular interpretations have distorted this teaching into magical thinking or simplistic manifestations, the authentic Hermetic view is both profound and practical: *human beings are co-creators of their reality through perception, interpretation, emotion, action, and virtue.*

This concept aligns closely with modern psychology, neuroscience, and trauma studies. Research shows that perception shapes experience; interpretation filters meaning; emotion influences memory, behavior, and physiology; intention directs attention; and consistent action creates habits, circumstances, and outcomes (Barrett, 2017; Duhigg, 2012; Siegel, 2012). The Hermetic art of co-creation therefore reflects real psychological and physiological mechanisms and not superstition.

Co-creation is the active, ethical participation in shaping the internal and external conditions of life. It is an advanced expression of Jing, Qi, and Shen working together through the Warrior's embodiment, the Scholar's clarity, and the Sage's insight. This chapter explains how reality is co-created in alignment with the Hermetic Principles and how individuals can cultivate this capacity with responsibility and purpose.

Co-Creation as Psychological and Spiritual Agency

The Hermetic idea that *"the All is Mind"* does not imply that thoughts alone reshape external events. Instead, it points to the fundamental truth that *the way individuals think, perceive, and interpret reality governs their responses, behaviors, relationships, and emotional states.* These responses in turn shape outcomes.

Modern cognitive science calls this *constructivism,* the idea that the mind creates internal meaning structures that determine how we experience reality (Beck, 1976; Barrett, 2017). Trauma psychology further reveals how past experiences shape perception and behavior, often unconsciously (Herman, 1992).

Thus, co-creation involves:

- awareness of internal patterns
- interpretation of meaning
- emotional regulation
- behavioral consistency
- virtuous action

- alignment with values

The Hermetic Principles offer a complete system for understanding this process.

The Hermetic Laws of Co-Creation

Each principle plays a role in shaping personal reality:

1. Mentalism — The Mind Shapes Experience

Thoughts, internal narratives, and interpretations determine emotional responses, choices, and behavior patterns.

2. Correspondence — Patterns Repeat Across Levels

Internal chaos leads to external chaos; internal coherence produces external stability.

3. Vibration — Emotion Determines Perception

Fear narrows perception; calm expands it. Emotional vibration influences cognition and behavior (Porges, 2011).

4. Polarity — Shifting from One Emotional Pole to Another

Changing inner polarity transforms outer action.

5. Rhythm — Life Operates Through Cycles

Co-creation requires recognizing and working with cycles, not against them.

6. Cause and Effect — Behavior Produces Outcomes

Intention without action is powerless; action without intention is blind.

7. Gender — Creation Requires Both Active and Receptive Modes

Intention (masculine/yang) and openness (feminine/yin) must be balanced.

8. Virtue — Ethical Alignment Ensures Co-Creation Is Beneficial

Without virtue, co-creation becomes manipulation or self-deception.

Co-creation emerges from the synthesis of all eight principles.

The Neuroscience of Shaping Reality

Hermetic co-creation mirrors several modern mechanisms:

1. Neuroplasticity

Repeated thoughts and actions rewire neural pathways (Doidge, 2007).
This reflects Mentalism and Rhythm.

2. Predictive Processing

The brain predicts reality using internal models, shaping perception through expectation (Clark, 2016). This mirrors Correspondence and Vibration.

3. Emotion–Cognition Integration

Emotion regulates decision-making, attention, and behavior (Damasio, 1999).
This supports Polarity and Vibration.

4. Behavioral Activation

Consistent action changes environment, habits, and identity (Duhigg, 2012). These expresses Cause and Effect.

Science confirms what Hermeticism intuited centuries ago: the mind, emotions, and actions shape reality at every level.

Co-Creation Through the Warrior–Scholar–Sage

Each developmental mode contributes to the ability to shape reality.

The Warrior (Jing): Co-Creation Through Embodiment

- posture
- breath

- strength
- self-regulation
- boundaries
- courageous action

The Warrior shapes reality through **physical presence**, stability, and consistent action.

The Scholar (Qi): Co-Creation Through Cognition

- discernment
- emotional intelligence
- reframing
- problem-solving
- learning

The Scholar shapes reality by interpreting events wisely and making informed decisions.

The Sage (Shen): Co-Creation Through Insight

- intuition
- compassion
- ethical clarity
- systems perception
- meaning-making

The Sage shapes reality by aligning intention with virtue and perceiving the larger pattern. Co-creation becomes most powerful when the three work together.

The Misuse of Co-Creation: Avoiding Magical Thinking

Hermeticism warns against the illusion that the mind can bypass action or override reality. Co-creation fails when:

- individuals avoid responsibility
- emotions are unregulated

- trauma distorts perception
- narratives replace truth
- ethics are ignored
- intuition is mistaken for impulse
- spirituality becomes bypassing

True Hermetic co-creation is grounded, embodied, ethical, and disciplined.

Aligned Intention: The Sage's Creative Force

Intention is not wishful thinking; it is a coherent alignment of:

- thought
- emotion
- physiology
- action
- attention
- values

This alignment is the Hermetic expression of *Shen in motion*. When intention is aligned, individuals experience a sense of purpose, clarity, and direction.

Aligned intention has three qualities:

1. **Clarity** — knowing exactly what one seeks.
2. **Coherence** — the body, mind, and emotions support the goal.
3. **Virtue** — the intention aligns with ethical principles.

Unaligned intention produces confusion and frustration.

Co-Creation Through Emotional Vibration

Emotion determines the "energetic state" from which individuals act. Research shows that emotional states:

- shape decision-making
- influence interpersonal behavior
- affect memory and attention

- determine risk-taking
- influence how others perceive us (Keltner, 2009)

Thus, emotional regulation is essential in co-creation. In Hermetic terms:

Vibration precedes manifestation.

A calm regulated nervous system creates stability, clarity, and wise choices. A dysregulated system creates chaos, impulsivity, and confusion.

Behavioral Co-Creation: Manifestation Through Action

Behavior is the primary vehicle of co-creation. Small, consistent actions alter:

- health
- habits
- relationships
- career
- environment
- identity
- opportunities

As James Clear (2018) notes, identity is shaped through repeated action. Hermeticism expresses this as Cause and Effect. Action grounds intention into lived reality.

Ethical Co-Creation: The Role of Virtue

The Eighth Principle ensures that co-creation is beneficial rather than self-serving. Virtue acts as a governor on intention and action.

Ethically aligned co-creation:

- strengthens integrity
- builds meaningful relationships
- creates long-term stability
- supports well-being
- contributes to collective good
- prevents harm

Ethically misaligned co-creation collapses under its own weight. Virtue is therefore the *true foundation* of shaping reality.

A Practical Framework for Hermetic Co-Creation:

1. Clarify (Mentalism)

Define the intention clearly.

2. Align (Vibration + Rhythm)

Regulate emotions and physiology to match the intention.

3. Discern (Correspondence)

Ensure the intention matches values and universal principles.

4. Transform (Polarity)

Shift fear, shame, or resistance into courage and clarity.

5. Act (Cause and Effect)

Take consistent, meaningful action.

6. Balance (Gender)

Mix effort with receptivity.

7. Evaluate (Virtue)

Ensure the process remains ethical and constructive.

This method embodies the Hermetic Great Work.

Co-Creation as a Mature Spiritual Discipline

Co-creation is not manipulation of reality nor magical thinking, but rather it is the disciplined, embodied, emotionally regulated, ethically aligned participation in one's destiny. It unites the Warrior's strength, the Scholar's clarity, and the Sage's wisdom into a unified process.

Co-creation is the natural flowering of the Great Work:

> *to think clearly, feel openly, act courageously, and live ethically.*

The next chapter explores how co-creation expresses itself socially and relationally and how the Hermetic adept interacts with family, community, and the larger world.

15. The Hermetic Adept in Society

Relationships, Leadership and the Field of Influence

Hermeticism has often been portrayed as an inward-looking discipline focused on meditation, alchemy, and inner transformation. Yet the true Hermetic adept is not isolated from society. Rather, the adept becomes a stabilizing force within it. Once Jing is strengthened, Qi refined, and Shen illuminated, the individual naturally radiates coherence into their relationships, communities, and environments. This outward expression of the Great Work is not merely social behavior, it is an energetic, psychological, and ethical phenomenon.

Modern neuroscience confirms that human beings constantly influence one another through emotional contagion, interpersonal regulation, and shared neural states (Siegel, 2012; Cozolino, 2014). Trauma research adds that relationships can either fragment or integrate the psyche (Herman, 1992). Hermeticism anticipated these findings through the **Principles of Correspondence, Vibration, Gender, and Cause and Effect.**

This chapter explores how the Hermetic adept participates in society, shapes social fields, leads ethically, and maintains sovereignty within complex relational environments.

The Adept as a Stabilizing Presence

A central feature of the Sage is **presence,** as a grounded, calm, attentive awareness that influences others without force or coercion. Presence is the outward expression of Shen through the nervous system.

In interpersonal neurobiology, this is known as *co-regulation,* the phenomenon where an individual's regulated nervous system calms others (Porges, 2011).

A Hermetic adept stabilizes social environments through:
- calm tone
- empathetic listening
- steady posture
- grounded breath
- clear boundaries
- emotional intelligence
- ethical consistency

The **Principle of Vibration** explains this influence:

the vibratory state of one person entrains to others.

Therefore, the adept becomes a source of coherence in a chaotic world.

Relationships as Hermetic Laboratories

Relationships reveal the degree of inner integration. They activate:

- old wounds
- unconscious patterns
- attachment tendencies
- shadow aspects
- moral dilemmas
- emotional challenges

Thus, relationships serve as laboratories for emotional alchemy (Chapter 9).

The **Principle of Correspondence** teaches:

what arises in relationships mirrors what arises within.

Healthy relationships reflect integration; dysfunctional relationships reflect fragmentation.

A Hermetic adept engages relationships consciously by:

- observing emotional triggers
- communicating clearly
- holding compassionate boundaries
- evaluating relational patterns
- practicing patience
- offering presence rather than control

Relationships are not distractions from the Great Work, they *are* the Great Work applied.

Discernment in Social Environments

Modern society is saturated with conflicting narratives, social pressure, ideological polarization, and manipulation. Discernment becomes essential for navigating these environments without losing autonomy.

Discernment (Chapter 10) operates socially through:

- reading verbal and nonverbal cues
- sensing incongruence
- detecting manipulation
- identifying emotional undertones
- evaluating motives
- understanding group dynamics

Hermetically, this is the **Principle of Mentalism** applied to social fields:

recognizing how thoughts, assumptions, and emotional resonance shape interpretation.

The adept interacts with society from a position of clarity rather than reactivity.

Boundaries: The Social Application of Jing

Boundaries are the structure through which the adept maintains stability in social contexts. Without boundaries, personal energy becomes entangled with others' chaos, trauma, or emotional projections.

Boundaries are Hermetic because they express:

- **Polarity** — differentiation of self from other
- **Correspondence** — inward order shaping outward limits
- **Vibration** — regulating emotional influence
- **Cause and effect** — actions with predictable relational outcomes
- **Virtue** — ethical self-respect

Healthy boundaries enable the adept to remain compassionate without becoming overwhelmed, and to remain open without becoming naïve.

Leadership Through Virtue and Shen

Hermetic adepts may or may not hold formal leadership roles, but they inevitably possess *influence*. Influence emerges naturally when:

- emotional regulation is stable
- intuition is clear
- integrity is consistent
- communication is grounded
- presence is compassionate
- decisions are ethically aligned

This form of leadership mirrors what modern leadership theory calls *transformational leadership,* by guiding not through authority but through example, inspiration, and moral clarity (Bass & Riggio, 2006).

Leadership qualities of the adept:

1. **Ethical Wisdom (Shen)**
   Seeing long-term consequences and acting with virtue.

2. **Discernment (Qi)**
   Making clear, informed decisions.

3. **Courage (Jing)**
   Facing conflict without aggression or avoidance.

4. **Compassion**
   Understanding the emotional reality of others.

5. **Non-reactivity**
   Maintaining presence in chaos.

6. **Integrity**
   Aligning action with principle.

Leadership becomes an extension of the Great Work.

The Adept's Influence on Family and Community

Families and communities are emotional ecosystems. The adept influences these systems not by controlling others but by embodying stability, virtue, and coherence.

Within families, the adept may:
- deescalate conflicts
- model healthy communication
- provide emotional safety
- clarify boundaries
- serve as a grounding presence

Within communities, the adept may:
- promote cooperation
- mediate tension
- offer insight
- encourage growth
- inspire moral clarity

Cozolino (2014) notes that human beings thrive in networks of emotionally attuned relationships. Hermetic adepts contribute to this by stabilizing interpersonal environments.

Navigating Social Shadows and Collective Trauma

Societies contain collective shadows, such as unconscious fears, biases, traumas, and destructive behaviors. These shadows manifest through:
- polarization
- violence
- addiction
- neglect
- exploitation
- misinformation
- apathy

The adept must navigate these forces without being swallowed by them.

This requires:
- emotional boundaries (Warrior)

- cognitive clarity (Scholar)
- ethical presence (Sage)
- discernment (Hermetic Principle of Virtue)
- compassion without enabling
- courage without aggression

By holding inner coherence, the adept resists collective fragmentation.

Interpersonal Alchemy: Transforming Social Dynamics

Just as emotional alchemy transforms inner states, interpersonal alchemy transforms relational dynamics.

Key practices include:

1. **Non-reactive listening**
   Calming emotional resonance.

2. **Naming underlying patterns**
   Bringing unconscious dynamics into awareness.

3. **Softening one's own nervous system**
   Allowing others to co-regulate.

4. **Setting boundaries without hostility**
   Combining softness and strength.

5. **Asking clarifying questions**
   Revealing hidden motives.

6. **Empathic reflection**
   Reducing defensiveness.

This is the living expression of the Principle of Vibration in social life.

The Adept as a Beacon: The Field of Influence

As Shen matures, individuals begin radiating a subtle field of influence. This is not metaphysical in a supernatural sense but neurological and psychological.

Research demonstrates that:

- emotional states spread through mirror neurons
- nervous systems attune to each other within seconds

- social groups synchronize physiologically and emotionally
- calm individuals can lower group stress
- anxious individuals can raise it (Cozolino, 2014; Porges, 2011)

Thus, the adept's presence becomes:
- a calming force
- a moral compass
- a source of coherence
- a catalyst for deeper thinking
- a reminder of virtue

Influence does not require speech; it is transmitted through being.

Hermeticism as a Social Art

The Hermetic adept does not withdraw from the world; they deepen their participation in it. Their influence arises not from authority, force, or charisma but from coherence, virtue, and clarity.

They embody the Great Work through:
- stabilizing relationships (Warrior)
- clarifying perception (Scholar)
- illuminating wisdom (Sage)

In doing so, they shape families, communities, and cultures, not through dominance but through quiet transformation.

The next chapter moves deeper into this theme by exploring **conflict, relational turbulence, and the Hermetic methods of resolving interpersonal challenges.**

16. Conflict, Shadow Dynamics and the Hermetic Approach to Resolution

Conflict is inevitable in human relationships. It arises from differences in values, needs, perceptions, trauma histories, and developmental stages. But to the Hermetic adept, conflict is not something to fear, as it is a mirror, a catalyst, and a laboratory for the Great Work.

Conflict reveals hidden patterns, unconscious wounds, and shadow material that may remain invisible during periods of calm. It exposes inconsistencies between beliefs and behavior. It tests boundaries, discernment, emotional regulation, and ethical alignment. When navigated consciously, conflict becomes a powerful instrument of transformation.

Hermeticism, Taoist internal alchemy, and modern psychological frameworks all recognize that inner conflict and interpersonal conflict are mirrors of one another. The Principle of Correspondence, *"as within, so without"* applies directly: external conflict often reflects internal fragmentation, while internal coherence reduces the intensity and frequency of external discord.

This chapter explores conflict through the Hermetic lens, examining how the adept perceives, navigates, and resolves conflict without abandoning virtue, clarity, or compassion.

Conflict as an Expression of Polarity

The Principle of Polarity states that opposites are identical in nature but vary in degree. Conflict represents poles struggling to reconcile. Opposites appear in relationships as:

- autonomy vs. connection
- stability vs. change
- logic vs. emotion
- restraint vs. expression
- boundaries vs. openness
- duty vs. desire

Conflict becomes destructive only when individuals become rigidly attached to one pole. The adept learns to shift, balance, and integrate polarity rather than identify with a single position.

Modern psychology agrees that emotional flexibility, not avoidance, is what predicts healthier relationships and greater psychological well-being (Kashdan & Rottenberg, 2010). Conflict is not the problem; fragmentation is.

Shadow Dynamics in Conflict

Jung (1959) argued that people often project their unacknowledged shadow onto others. Conflict intensifies this projection dynamic, causing individuals to see in others what they refuse to see in themselves.

Examples include:

- accusing others of selfishness while ignoring one's own unmet needs
- labeling others as controlling while engaging in covert control
- condemning dishonesty while hiding personal truths
- reacting strongly to traits that mirror buried emotions

The **Principle of Correspondence** explains this phenomenon:

> *the shadow projected onto others corresponds to the shadow unintegrated within.*

Conflict is therefore a portal into deeper self-understanding.

Trauma Reactivity and the Nervous System

Trauma amplifies conflict through:

- hypervigilance
- emotional flooding
- black-and-white thinking
- survival-based reactions
- collapse or shutdown
- difficulty trusting intent
- over-identification with pain

These reactions reflect dysregulated **Vibration**, as emotional frequency overwhelms cognitive clarity (Herman, 1992).

The adept approaches conflict by stabilizing Jing and Qi before responding. This requires:

- conscious breathing
- grounding

- regulating posture
- slowing speech
- separating past from present
- calming the limbic system

Only then can conflict be addressed from a place of wisdom rather than fear.

The Warrior, Scholar, and Sage in Conflict

Each developmental mode offers different strengths for navigating conflict:

The Warrior (Jing): Stabilizing the Body

- maintains grounded posture
- resists impulsive reactions
- keeps breathing steady
- holds physical boundaries
- avoids escalation

The Warrior prevents physiological collapse or aggression.

The Scholar (Qi): Clarifying the Mind

- questions assumptions
- identifies distortions
- separates emotion from fact
- recognizes triggers
- evaluates motives
- reframes patterns

The Scholar prevents cognitive distortion and confusion.

The Sage (Shen): Illuminating the Heart

- sees the deeper dynamic

- recognizes the shadow in self and other
- holds compassion without enabling
- communicates ethically
- seeks understanding
- prioritizes virtue

The Sage prevents moral or emotional regression.

Together, they enable conflict to become an alchemical process rather than an explosion.

The Hermetic Approach to Conflict Resolution

The Hermetic method integrates all eight principles into a cohesive process:

1. Mentalism → Recognize the story you are telling

Interpretation shapes emotional response and behavior.

2. Correspondence → Look at the inner mirror

What part of you is being activated?

3. Vibration → Regulate emotion first

No resolution is possible in dysregulation.

4. Polarity → Explore the opposing pole

Both sides contain truth; integration reveals the larger pattern.

5. Rhythm → Allow emotional waves to settle

Conflict cannot be resolved in peak intensity.

6. Cause and Effect → Evaluate consequences of each action

Ethical foresight guides wise choices.

7. Gender → Balance assertiveness and receptivity

Speak truth with compassion; listen without collapse.

8. Virtue → Align with values and integrity

Act in a way that sustains dignity, respect, and moral clarity.

Conflict becomes a spiritual discipline rather than a battlefield.

Communication as Alchemical Dialogue

Effective conflict resolution requires communication that builds safety, clarity, and understanding.

Key practices include:

- speaking slowly and clearly
- using "I" statements instead of accusations
- acknowledging emotions without shame
- identifying needs directly
- asking clarifying questions
- validating the other person's experience
- setting boundaries calmly

These practices reduce defensiveness and promote trust. Interpersonal neurobiology shows that attuned communication mirrors secure attachment, calming both individuals (Siegel, 2012). Hermetically, communication expresses **Gender,** a balance of active expression and receptive listening.

Energetic Coherence in Conflict

The adept monitors internal vibration during conflict:

- rapid heart rate
- shallow breath
- contracted muscles
- rigid posture

- racing thoughts

These signals indicate the need for somatic regulation. The adept resets vibration through:

- exhalation emphasis
- loosening shoulders
- grounding feet
- slowing speech
- pausing before responding

This physiological coherence allows conflict to remain safe and constructive.

Ethical Boundaries and Non-Negotiables

Not all conflicts can be resolved through dialogue. The adept recognizes when conflict shifts into:

- manipulation
- dishonesty
- coercion
- boundary violation
- emotional abuse
- psychological destabilization

In such cases, ethical boundaries must be asserted clearly. Virtue requires:

- refusing to participate in harmful dynamics
- maintaining integrity
- protecting one's mental and emotional well-being
- disengaging when necessary

Hermeticism is not passive; it calls for disciplined sovereignty.

Forgiveness, Repair, and Closure

Forgiveness is not the erasure of pain but the release of inner entanglement. Repair requires:

- acknowledgment
- responsibility
- empathy
- changed behavior
- shared commitment to growth

Closure, when repair is impossible, requires:

- acceptance
- boundary reinforcement
- narrative integration
- renewed purpose

This is the completion of emotional alchemy applied relationally.

Conflict as the Crucible of the Great Work

Conflict tests the depth of the Hermetic path. It exposes shadow, reveals wounds, challenges perception, and demands courage, clarity, and compassion.

The adept transforms conflict by:

- regulating vibration (Warrior)
- clarifying interpretation (Scholar)
- acting with virtue (Sage)

Through this alchemical process, conflict becomes a teacher, a mirror, and ultimately, a doorway to greater integration.

The next chapter extends these relational themes into **service, contribution, and the Hermetic role within collective evolution**, exploring how the individual's transformation contributes to the transformation of society.

PART V — Destiny, Virtue & Cosmic Principle at Work

17. Service, Contribution and the Hermetic Role in Collective Evolution

When the Great Work matures within an individual, Jing is stabilized, Qi refined, and Shen illuminated. The natural next step is outward movement. Inner growth becomes outer contribution. Personal coherence becomes social coherence. The adept's presence, virtue, and clarity ripple outward, influencing families, communities, and culture.

In Hermeticism, this outward expression is not accidental; it is the culmination of the path. The *Corpus Hermeticum* repeatedly emphasizes that one who has attained gnosis is compelled to uplift others, not through coercion, but through example, compassion, and ethical clarity (Copenhaver, 1992).

Modern psychology and sociology agree that individuals who experience high levels of integration, purpose, and expanded consciousness naturally express their development

through prosocial behavior, mentorship, community service, and moral action (Richards, 2018; Siegel, 2012). Service is therefore not altruism alone; it is a developmental outcome.

This chapter explores how the Hermetic adept contributes to collective evolution through presence, leadership, compassion, and the transmission of wisdom.

The Principle of Correspondence and Collective Evolution

"As above, so below; as within, so without."

This principle forms the foundation of collective transformation. Societal change begins with individual change. Trauma, fear, aggression, and fragmentation within individuals contribute to collective dysfunction. Conversely, inner coherence, emotional regulation, and ethical alignment within individuals strengthen communities and cultures.

Collective evolution is not achieved through ideology or force; it begins with the microcosm:

- individual nervous systems
- individual relationships
- individual ethical decisions
- individual self-awareness

By transforming the self, the adept participates in transforming the whole.

The Eighth Principle: Virtue as Social Contribution

The **Eighth Principle of Virtue and Ethical Alignment** ensures that service arises from integrity rather than ego, savior complexes, or manipulation. Ethical service requires:

- humility
- responsibility
- wisdom
- boundaries
- compassion
- discernment
- courage

Service grounded in virtue becomes sustainable and transformative rather than codependent or self-serving. Virtue is therefore the moral foundation of Hermetic contribution.

Service as the Expression of Shen

Shen or the luminous spirit naturally expresses itself through care, compassion, presence, and wisdom. In Taoist and Confucian philosophy, the Sage does not withdraw from society; he or she becomes a stabilizing force within it.

Service is not sacrifice; it is overflow. It arises when inner abundance meets outer need.

Shen expresses itself socially through:

- emotional regulation that calms others
- insight that clarifies confusion

- ethical behavior that inspires trust
- compassionate listening that heals
- wisdom that guides without dominating
- presence that steadies the nervous system
- humility that prevents ego distortion

Service is the Sage's signature.

The Warrior and Scholar in Service

The Warrior and Scholar contribute to collective evolution in complementary ways.

The Warrior's Service: Stability and Protection

The Warrior offers:

- grounded presence
- courage in adversity
- protection without aggression
- clear boundaries
- accountability
- embodied integrity

Warriors serve by stabilizing the emotional field around them.

The Scholar's Service: Clarity and Insight

The Scholar offers:

- critical thinking
- discernment
- education
- mentorship
- communication
- problem-solving

Scholars serve by illuminating confusion and fostering understanding. Together with the Sage, they complete the triad of service.

The Adept as Mentor, Teacher, and Guide

Hermetic adepts often serve through informal or formal mentorship. This role involves:

- modeling integration
- encouraging personal responsibility
- offering guidance without control
- teaching principles and practices
- helping others navigate shadow material
- supporting autonomy rather than dependence

Modern psychology refers to this as *transformational mentorship*, where the mentor catalyzes growth through presence and modeling rather than authority (Bass & Riggio, 2006).

Hermetically, mentorship expresses the **Principle of Cause and Effect:**

actions shape future generations.

Collective Trauma and the Adept's Role in Healing

Modern society carries layers of collective trauma, such as war, oppression, addiction, disconnection, fragmentation, and chronic stress. These wounds manifest as:

- fear-based politics
- polarized communities
- interpersonal mistrust
- rising violence
- emotional numbness
- spiritual confusion

The adept contributes to collective healing by:

- creating emotionally safe spaces
- modeling regulation
- understanding trauma responses

- interrupting cycles of reactivity
- offering compassion without rescuing
- promoting truth and discernment
- encouraging meaning-making

Just as an individual integrates their shadow, societies must integrate their collective shadow. The adept serves as a catalyst for this integration.

Leadership Reimagined Through Hermetic Virtue

Leadership, in the Hermetic sense, is not about hierarchy or authority. It is about:

- ethical presence
- stable nervous system regulation
- inner clarity
- relational wisdom
- integrity in action
- vision guided by virtue

Leadership becomes a natural extension of the adept's coherence. Research on leadership supports this: people gravitate toward those who exude calm, confidence, empathy, and consistency (Goleman, 2006).

Hermetic leadership offers:

- clarity in confusion
- groundedness in chaos
- wisdom in conflict
- compassion in suffering
- courage in uncertainty

Such leaders elevate groups without coercion.

The Field of Influence: How Presence Shapes Communities

A growing body of research in social neuroscience shows that individual emotional states influence groups through:

- emotional contagion
- mirror neuron activation
- collective nervous system attunement
- shared psychological fields (Cozolino, 2014; Porges, 2011)

This field of influence is what Hermeticism refers to metaphorically as "aura" or "vibration."

When the adept enters a room:
- chaos becomes more orderly
- tension eases
- communication improves
- behavior becomes more ethical
- conflict softens
- people feel safer

This is not magic. It is neurobiology. Shen radiates through physiology, expression, and presence.

Service Without Self-Sacrifice

Service becomes distorted when:
- boundaries collapse
- guilt drives behavior
- ego seeks validation
- trauma reenacts old patterns
- compassion becomes enabling
- exhaustion replaces presence

Hermetic service is sustainable because it is rooted in:
- Jing (physical stability)

- Qi (emotional clarity)
- Shen (spiritual insight)
- Virtue (ethical alignment)
- Discernment (cognitive sovereignty)

Service that destroys the self cannot uplift others.

Co-Creating a More Coherent Collective Reality

When Hermetic adepts operate within society, they become catalysts for increased coherence. This manifests through:

- more ethical interpersonal dynamics
- calmer relational fields
- clearer decision-making
- reduced reactivity
- greater empathy
- increased meaning-making
- strengthened community bonds

Collective evolution accelerates when individuals embody the Great Work.

The Adept as Contributor to Collective Awakening

Service is the outward expression of the inward transformation. It is the Sage extending Shen into the world through action, compassion, and ethical influence.

Hermetic adepts uplift society not through preaching or force, but through:

- coherence
- presence
- virtue
- wisdom
- compassion
- courage
- clarity

Through service, the personal Great Work becomes a *collective Great Work*, guiding humanity toward greater integration, meaning, and ethical maturity.

The next chapter moves deeper into this theme by exploring **the Hermetic view of destiny, free will, and the unfolding of one's path.**

18. Destiny, Freewill and the Unfolding of the Hermetic Path

Questions of destiny and freewill lie at the heart of every spiritual, philosophical, and psychological tradition. Hermeticism is no exception. The *Corpus Hermeticum* frequently references Fate (*Heimarmene*) and Necessity (*Ananke*), describing them as forces that shape the structure of the cosmos. Yet these same texts emphasize the power of human consciousness to transcend mechanical patterns through knowledge, virtue, and alignment with the Divine Mind (Copenhaver, 1992).

Modern psychology echoes this duality. Human behavior is shaped by genetics, environment, trauma, conditioning, and unconscious drives (Bargh & Chartrand, 1999). Yet research also shows that individuals possess the capacity to consciously intervene in these patterns by rewiring neural pathways through attention, behavior, and meaning-making (Doidge, 2007; Siegel, 2012).

Taoist internal alchemy contains the same dual truth: while the flow of the Tao carries all things, individuals can refine their Jing, Qi, and Shen to harmonize with it—choosing a path of virtue, clarity, and integration rather than confusion and fragmentation.

In Hermeticism, destiny and free will are not opposites but two poles of the same continuum. Destiny provides the structure; free will provides the movement. Together, they shape the unfolding of the Hermetic path.

The Principle of Correspondence and the Architecture of Destiny

"As above, so below; as within, so without."

Destiny unfolds through patterns such as biological, psychological, relational, and spiritual. These patterns reflect Correspondence:

- personal patterns mirror ancestral patterns
- relational patterns mirror internal patterns
- cultural patterns mirror collective consciousness
- developmental patterns mirror universal cycles

Destiny is not a predetermined script, but a pattern-based trajectory influenced by:

- genetics
- early childhood experience
- trauma or stability

- cultural environment
- personal choices
- relational dynamics
- unconscious beliefs
- moral development

In other words, destiny is the structure of one's developmental field. But structure is not finality; it is the starting point.

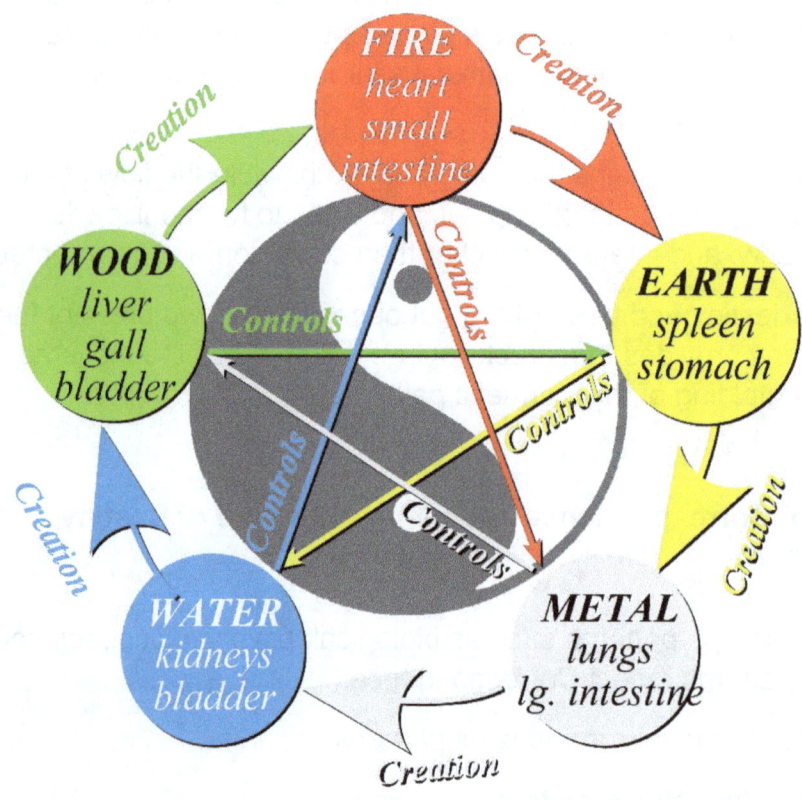

The Principle of Cause and Effect and the Mechanics of Free Will

Hermeticism teaches that every action has a consequence. This principle aligns closely with behavioral psychology and neuroscience, where repeated actions mobilize habit loops, decision pathways, and identity formation (Duhigg, 2012; Miller & Cohen, 2001).

Free will expresses itself through:

- intentional action
- conscious reflection

- emotional regulation
- cognitive reframing
- choosing virtue over impulse
- modifying behavior
- aligning with values

Free will does not negate destiny; it interacts with it. Destiny provides the conditions; free will directs the response.

This is the essence of the Hermetic Great Work:

to consciously influence the trajectory of one's life within the architecture of fate.

Fate, Trauma, and Conditioning: The Lower Poles of Polarity

Trauma, conditioning, and early relational experiences create powerful unconscious patterns. These patterns manifest as:

- emotional triggers
- attachment styles
- limiting beliefs
- repeated relational failures
- maladaptive habits
- distorted interpretations

From the Hermetic standpoint, these forces represent the lower pole of the **Principle of Polarity.** Individuals who remain unconscious are governed by these lower poles, just as the unenlightened in the *Corpus Hermeticum* remain bound by Fate. Modern trauma psychology confirms this: without intervention, trauma responses will dominate thought, behavior, and relationships (Herman, 1992). Thus, those who lack self-awareness live out "destiny" as an unconscious repetition of the past.

Transcending Mechanical Fate: The Scholar and Sage as Liberators

Hermeticism teaches that inner awakening allows individuals to step beyond mechanical patterns. In the ancient texts, this is referred to as *rising above the cosmic spheres*, a metaphor for transcending unconscious conditioning (Copenhaver, 1992).

In psychological terms, this involves:

- increased insight
- emotional regulation
- cognitive flexibility
- moral development
- shadow integration
- meaning-making
- higher-order consciousness

This is the work of **Qi (Scholar)** and **Shen (Sage)**, which liberate individuals from reactive behavior. Transcending mechanical fate does not eliminate destiny, it refines it, allowing the individual to choose a higher trajectory.

Destiny as Potential, Not Predetermination

Destiny is best understood as potential, the set of possibilities encoded within ones:

- temperament
- body
- nervous system
- environment
- talents
- challenges
- emotional landscape
- relational patterns
- existential themes

These potentials unfold through life experiences, but they are not fixed. They can be expanded, redirected, or transformed through the Great Work. Hermeticism teaches that destiny is a *natural inclination*, not an unalterable fate. Psychology confirms that personality trajectories can change through:

- emotional integration
- secure relationships
- conscious decision-making

- new experiences
- spiritual development
- trauma healing

Destiny is a river; free will is the boat.

The Taoist Perspective: Aligning with the Flow

Taoism offers a complementary view through the concept of *Wu Wei,* or effortless action. Alignment with the Tao does not mean passivity; it means acting in harmony with one's nature and the flow of circumstances.

In Hermetic terms:

- Jing aligns the body with nature.
- Qi aligns the mind with truth.
- Shen aligns the spirit with virtue.

This produces a destiny that feels coherent, meaningful, and fluid. The Taoist adept does not force destiny; they unfold with it.

Wu Wei "Doing Nothing"

Rather than literal non-action, wu wei means "effortless action."

It refers to a state of being at peace even in difficult situations, so that one can act with maximum skill and efficiency.

In English, we often describe this state as being "in the zone."

Three Layers of Destiny According to the Hermetic–Psychological Model

Destiny can be understood through three layers:

1. Biological Destiny (Jing)

- genetic predispositions
- temperament
- physiological tendencies
- health potentials

2. Psychological Destiny (Qi)

- early conditioning
- trauma imprints
- cognitive patterns

- emotional tendencies
- attachment styles

3. Spiritual or Existential Destiny (Shen)

- meaning-making themes
- moral orientation
- archetypal patterns
- life purpose
- inner calling

Free will operates at all three levels, but strongest at the psychological and spiritual layers.

Synchronicity and the Hermetic Path

Jung's concept of **synchronicity** (meaningful coincidence) aligns with the Hermetic **Principle of Correspondence.** Synchronicities often emerge when:

- inner work deepens
- consciousness expands
- intuition sharpens
- emotional patterns integrate
- ethical alignment strengthens

These experiences do not prove predetermination; they reflect increasing coherence between inner state and outer events. Synchronicity is destiny responding to consciousness.

When Destiny "Calls": The Emergence of Purpose

As individuals progress along the Hermetic path, they often experience the emergence of a "calling," a sense of profound direction that feels both chosen and discovered.

This calling arises through:

- the integration of shadow
- the healing of trauma

- the refinement of virtue
- strengthened intuition
- alignment with values
- recognition of life themes

Purpose becomes the active expression of destiny. Where destiny provides potential, purpose provides direction, and free will provides movement.

The Hermetic Adept's Relationship to Destiny

With Shen matured, the adept understands:

- destiny is a field of possibility
- free will influences polarity
- virtue shapes long-term outcomes
- consciousness alters interpretation
- emotional regulation affects choices
- intention guides flow
- action solidifies direction

The adept participates in destiny without resisting or surrendering to it. Destiny becomes a dialogue, not a decree.

Conclusion: Destiny as Co-Created Evolution

Hermeticism resolves the ancient debate between fate and free will by reframing both:

- **Destiny** is the architecture of possibility.
- **Free will** is the capacity to navigate, reshape, and elevate that architecture.
- **Virtue** is the compass.
- **Consciousness** is the guide.
- **Integration** is the path.
- **The Great Work** is the unfolding of one's highest potential.

Destiny does not dictate the path; it provides the material from which the path is shaped. Free will does not create circumstances; it creates meaning and direction within them. Together, they form the symphony of the Hermetic journey.

The next chapter explores **how the adept maintains equilibrium amid life's fluctuations,** applying the Hermetic Principle of Rhythm to real-world challenges and psychological cycles.

19. The Principle of Rhythm

Navigating Cycles, Seasons, and Life's Periods of Expansion and Contraction

Life moves in cycles. Everything in nature, the body, emotions, relationships, societies, and consciousness itself, operates through rhythms of expansion and contraction, activity and rest, clarity and confusion, stability and change. The Hermetic Principle of Rhythm teaches that these cycles are not interruptions to life but the fundamental structure of it.

> *"For every action, there is an equal and opposite reaction; for every rise, a fall; for every forward movement, a return."*

This principle describes the oscillations governing all phenomena.

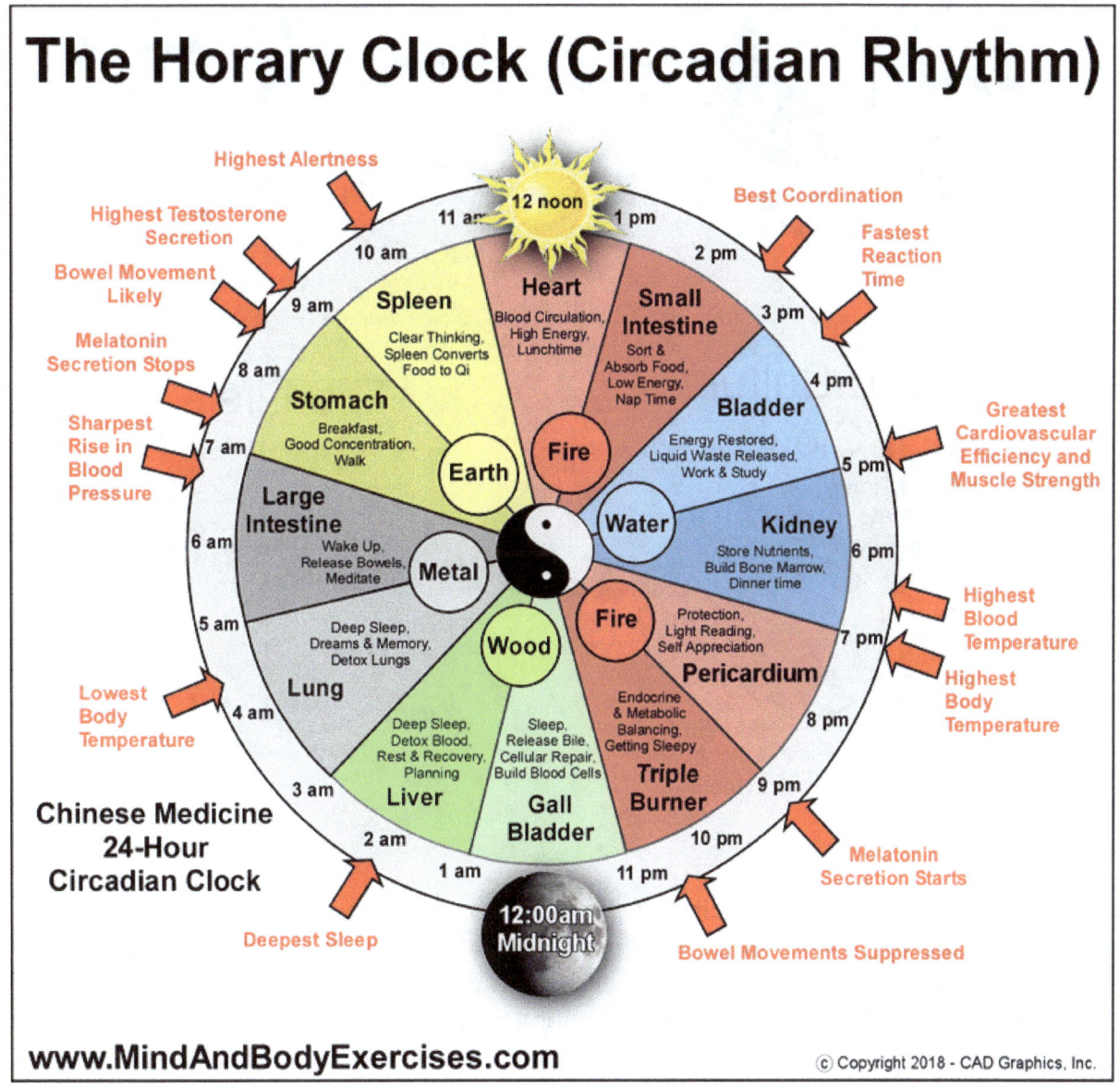

Taoist philosophy echoes this through the *yin–yang* dynamic, the alternation of seasons, and the concept of *wuji → taiji*, the interplay of stillness and movement. Modern biology and psychology confirm that human behavior, hormones, mood, and cognition all fluctuate according to circadian rhythms, ultradian cycles, developmental phases, and environmental conditions (Foster, 2021; McEwen, 2011).

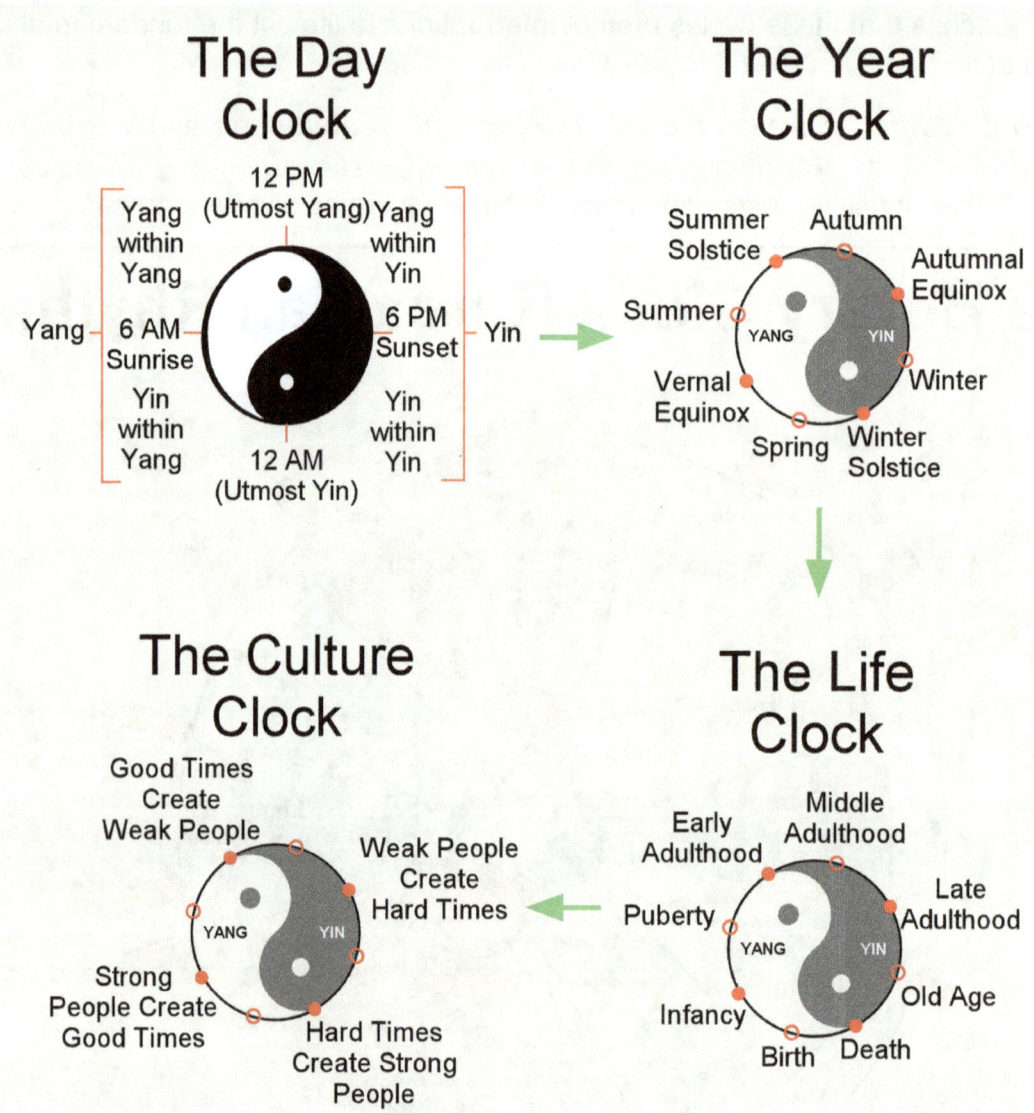

To the Hermetic adept, the Principle of Rhythm is not merely a cosmological observation, it is a guide for living. Mastery of the Great Work requires learning to move *with* cycles rather than against them. Doing so protects the nervous system, stabilizes emotions, empowers discernment, and deepens wisdom.

This chapter explores how to navigate cycles consciously and how the Warrior, Scholar, and Sage integrate Rhythm into their daily lives.

Rhythm as a Universal Law

Rhythm governs:

- natural cycles (seasons, lunar phases, tides)
- biological cycles (breath, heartbeat, hormones, neural oscillations)
- emotional cycles (arousal and recovery)
- psychological cycles (motivation, learning, creativity)
- relational cycles (approach and withdrawal)
- societal cycles (expansion and collapse)
- spiritual cycles (contraction and awakening)

Everything moves through periods of growth, plateau, decline, and renewal.
This is not failure, but rather it is natural law.

The Principle of Rhythm teaches that resisting cycles creates suffering. Accepting and aligning with cycles creates flow.

The Warrior and the Physical Cycles of Jing

The Warrior's body is governed by clear rhythms:

- energy peaks and dips
- muscular tension and relaxation
- activity and recovery
- alertness and fatigue
- hormonal fluctuations
- age-related changes

Ignoring these rhythms leads to burnout, injury, and emotional instability.
Respecting them builds strength, resilience, and longevity.

Warrior practices include:

- honoring sleep cycles

- periodizing physical training
- responding to early signs of fatigue
- using breath to regulate arousal
- grounding during overstimulation
- resting during emotional contraction

This stabilizes the physical foundation of the Great Work.

The Scholar and the Mental–Emotional Cycles of Qi

Qi fluctuates through patterns of:
- motivation and disinterest
- clarity and confusion
- emotional expansion and withdrawal
- cognitive sharpness and mental fog
- curiosity and disorientation

These cycles mirror neural rhythms and emotional regulatory patterns (Siegel, 2012). The Scholar recognizes that mental waves are not signs of weakness but indicators of developmental integration.

Scholar practices include:

- respecting cognitive limits
- structuring work in focus–rest cycles
- journaling emotional waves
- reframing difficult periods as integration phases
- using mindfulness to observe fluctuations
- adjusting expectations during low cycles

Wisdom emerges when individuals stop resisting the natural ebb and flow of Qi.

The Sage and the Existential Cycles of Shen

Shen unfolds in deeper cycles:

- periods of insight followed by consolidation
- spiritual expansion followed by grounding
- compassion followed by introspection
- heightened intuition followed by silence
- engagement followed by solitude

These cycles reflect the maturation of consciousness. Spiritual growth is nonlinear, where periods of stagnation often precede breakthroughs.

Sage practices include:
- embracing silence during inner contraction
- allowing periods of confusion without panic
- sensing when to withdraw and when to engage
- practicing patience with developmental timing
- trusting intuition to return after quiet phases
- maintaining humility during peak experiences

This allows Shen to expand without destabilizing the psyche.

Emotional Oscillation: The Hermetic View of Mood Cycles

Human emotion naturally oscillates between:
- high and low energy
- openness and guardedness
- joy and sadness
- anger and calm
- hope and doubt

These shifts reflect the Principle of Rhythm operating within the nervous system. Emotional oscillation is normal; emotional volatility reflects dysregulation.

Hermetic emotional navigation includes:
- identifying where one is in the emotional cycle

- avoiding major decisions during emotional extremes
- using breath to soften high-intensity states
- grounding during contraction
- reflecting during emotional quiet
- practicing gratitude during expansion

This turns emotional cycles into allies rather than enemies.

The Danger of "Anti-Rhythm" Living

Modern culture encourages lifestyle patterns that violate the Principle of Rhythm:

- constant productivity
- overstimulation through devices
- suppressed rest
- perfectionism
- chronic stress
- emotional numbing
- avoidance of introspection

These anti-rhythmic habits disrupt:

- circadian cycles
- nervous system balance
- hormonal function
- emotional stability
- cognitive clarity

Long-term, this leads to burnout, anxiety, and depression (McEwen, 2012). The Hermetic adept must counteract cultural anti-rhythms by returning to natural cycles.

Rhythm and Recovery: The Forgotten Half of the Great Work

In Taoist alchemy, refinement occurs not only during effort but during rest. Growth happens during:

- sleep

- stillness
- emptiness
- reflection
- recovery
- silence

The Sage recognizes that contraction is not regression, it is assimilation. Every expansion requires a corresponding return. This mirrors biological processes: muscles build during rest; memories consolidate during sleep; emotions integrate during calm periods. The **Principle of Rhythm** reveals that *recovery is not optional, it is essential for transformation.*

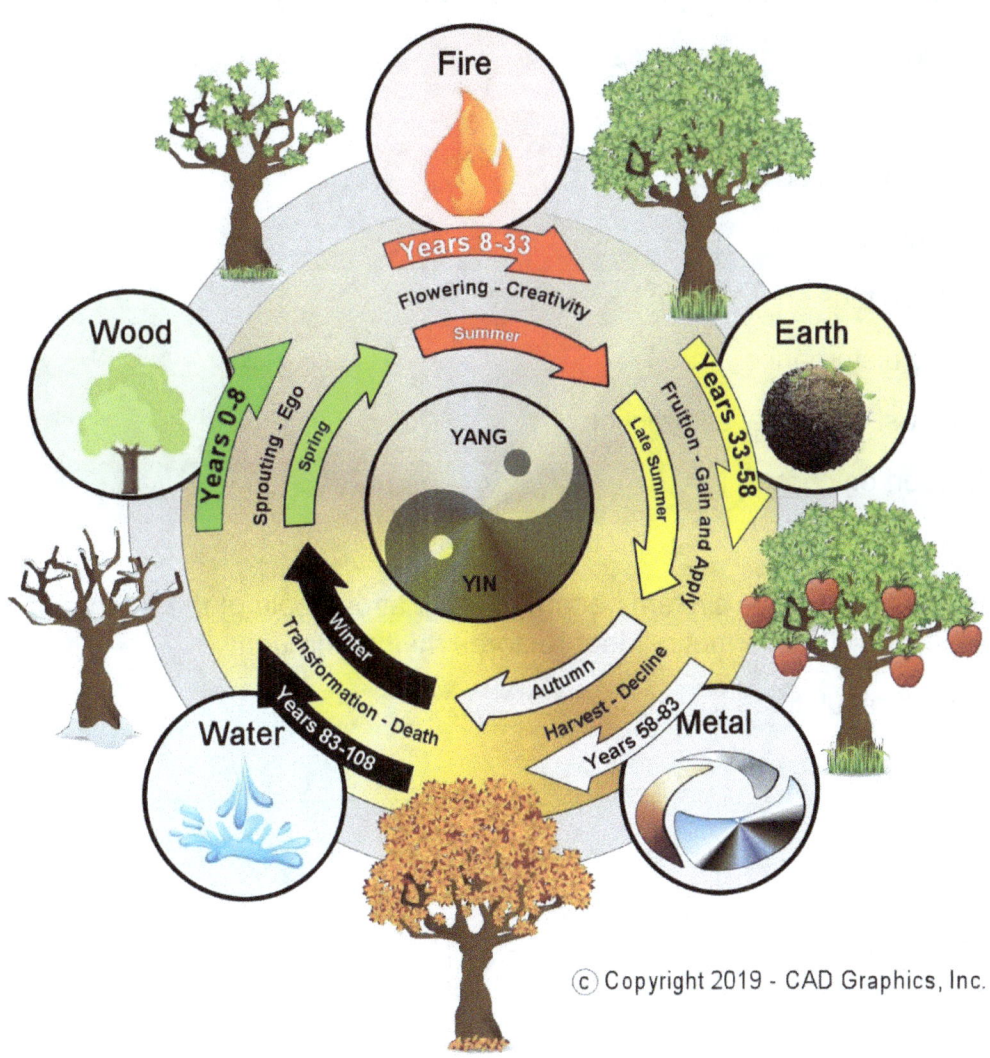

The Cycles of Life: Childhood, Adulthood, Eldership

Life itself unfolds through sacred rhythms:

- childhood (Jing development)
- adolescence (emotional/identity Qi development)
- adulthood (Shen refinement and social participation)
- elderhood (wisdom, integration, service)

Understanding these cycles reduces self-judgment and aligns individuals with their developmental tasks. Eldership, in particular, reflects the Sage's rhythm: less striving, more guiding; less accumulation, more distillation; less external focus, more internal illumination.

Rhythm, Trauma, and the Restoration of Natural Cycles

Trauma disrupts rhythm. It creates:

- hyperarousal
- emotional flooding
- shutdown
- chronic tension
- sleep disturbance
- mistrust of natural contraction
- fixation on control

The traumatized nervous system becomes stuck at one pole of the rhythm spectrum (Herman, 1992). The Hermetic adept restores rhythm through:

- breath regulation
- gentle movement
- grounding
- self-compassion
- relational safety
- pacing
- somatic awareness

This re-establishes the natural oscillation between activation and rest.

The Hermetic Practice of "Riding the Pendulum"

To navigate Rhythm consciously, the adept practices:

1. Awareness

Recognizing the current phase of the cycle.

2. Acceptance

Understanding that contraction is as sacred as expansion.

3. Adjustment

Aligning behavior with the energetic season.

4. Anticipation

Knowing that cycles will shift again.

5. Anchoring

Maintaining virtue and presence regardless of the phase.

This transforms cycles from forces that dominate one's life into rhythms one skillfully rides.

Conclusion: Rhythm as the Internal Clock of the Great Work

Rhythm teaches:

- that no state is permanent
- that expansion requires contraction
- that confusion precedes clarity
- that integration follows upheaval
- that growth is cyclical, not linear
- that rest is as important as effort

Mastering Rhythm allows the adept to remain centered in all phases of life. The pendulum may swing, but the center remains still.

The next chapter explores the **Principle of Gender** in its deepest Hermetic sense, not about biological sex, but about the dynamic interplay of creation, balance, and the fusion of opposites.

20. The Principle of Gender

Creative Polarity and the Fusion of Opposites

The Principle of Gender is among the most profound and misunderstood teachings in the Hermetic tradition. Unlike modern interpretations that reduce "gender" to biological sex or social identity, Hermeticism frames Gender as a universal law of creative polarity, governing creation, transformation, and the interplay of complementary forces throughout existence.

In the *Kybalion* and in earlier Hermetic writings, Gender refers to the dynamic between the **active** and the **receptive**, the **projective** and the **formative**, the **initiating** and the **nurturing** aspects of all processes ((Initiates, 2013). Every phenomenon, whether physical, psychological, relational, and spiritual, emerges from the interaction of these complementary forces.

Taoism echoes this principle in the *yin–yang* dynamic, where opposites are not in conflict but in continuous interplay, generating movement, balance, and transformation. Modern psychology frames these forces in terms of activation and receptivity, sympathetic and parasympathetic balance, executive function and emotional attunement, cognitive focus and intuitive openness (Porges, 2011; Siegel, 2012).

To the Hermetic adept, Gender is not a concept. It is a lived experience, visible in breath, behavior, relationships, creativity, and spiritual development. It is the key to understanding how the Warrior, Scholar, and Sage integrate into a unified whole.

Gender in the Cosmos: Creative Duality as Universal Structure

In nature, Gender appears through countless complementary pairs:

- sun and moon
- light and shadow
- expansion and contraction
- action and stillness
- seed and soil
- electricity and magnetism
- structure and flow
- order and spontaneity

These are not opposites in conflict; they are complementary halves of creative unity. Creation emerges through the interaction of these polarities.

The Five Aspects of Yin and Yang

The 5 Aspects of yin and yang complement and balance each other via these aspects, which define the relationship between each.

 1) Opposition

 2) Interdependence

 3) Mutual Consuming-Increasing

 4) Mutual Transforming

 5) Infinite Divisibility

www.MindAndBodyExercises.com © Copyright 2024 - CAD Graphics, Inc.

The Hermetic **Principle of Gender** declares that everything contains both "masculine" and "feminine" aspects, not in sexual terms, but in terms of function:

- the masculine corresponds to initiation, direction, structure
- the feminine corresponds to receptivity, cultivation, embodiment

The cosmos itself unfolds through these dynamics.

Gender Within the Human Psyche

From a psychological perspective, the **Principle of Gender** corresponds to the interplay between:

Masculine (Active) Functions

- goal pursuit
- decision-making
- assertiveness
- structure
- focus
- initiation
- boundary-setting

Feminine (Receptive) Functions

- emotional awareness
- intuition
- empathy
- relational sensitivity
- creativity
- receptivity
- nurturing

Healthy psychological functioning requires balance between these two modes. Overemphasis on one leads to imbalance:

- excessive masculine → rigidity, aggression, control
- excessive feminine → passivity, confusion, enmeshment

The Scholar helps one understand these dynamics; the Warrior embodies the active principle ethically; the Sage harmonizes the two.

Gender and the Nervous System

The nervous system reflects the **Principle of Gender** through the interplay of:

- sympathetic activation (masculine)
- parasympathetic receptivity (feminine)

Optimal functioning requires fluid movement between these states, a process called *autonomic flexibility*, which predicts emotional resilience and mental well-being (Porges, 2011).

In practical terms:

- the breath initiates (masculine) during inhalation
- the breath yields (feminine) during exhalation

Every moment of breathing expresses Gender.

Jing, Qi, Shen: The Taoist Expression of Gender

Taoist internal alchemy describes the interplay of Gender through the trinity of:

- **Jing** (essence)
- **Qi** (vital energy)
- **Shen** (spirit)

Each contains masculine and feminine aspects:

Jing

- masculine: stabilization, structure
- feminine: nourishment, restoration

Qi

- masculine: activation, circulation
- feminine: cultivation, modulation

Shen

- masculine: insight, illumination
- feminine: compassion, receptivity

The Sage unifies these aspects to produce inner alchemy.

Hermetic Gender in Relationships: The Dance of Complementary Forces

Healthy relationships function like energetic ecosystems. When the **Principle of Gender** is respected, relationships become:

- dynamic
- mutual
- adaptive
- creative
- compassionate

When Gender is distorted:

- power struggles emerge
- resentment builds
- communication collapses
- polarity disappears
- confusion replaces clarity

Healthy relationships require:

- active expression paired with receptive listening
- honesty paired with compassion
- boundaries paired with connection
- independence paired with interdependence

Hermetic Gender teaches the adept how to embody these relational dynamics consciously.

Gender and Creativity: The Process of Manifestation

All creation requires both:

1. Masculine (Active) Component
- vision
- direction
- initiation
- decision
- action

2. Feminine (Receptive) Component
- incubation
- intuition
- refinement
- integration
- embodiment

Without vision, nothing begins. Without incubation, nothing grows. This rhythm reflects the Hermetic interplay:

- thought → form
- intention → manifestation
- concept → embodiment

Every creative act is a fusion of Gender.

The Shadow of Gender: Trauma, Conditioning, and Imbalance

Trauma disrupts Gender balance by:
- collapsing receptivity (hypervigilance)
- damaging assertiveness (freeze response)
- skewing boundaries (fawn response)
- distorting relational dynamics

- amplifying control or avoidance

Early relational experiences often shape one's Gender patterns:

- authoritarian environments produce defensive masculinity
- inconsistent environments produce hypervigilant femininity
- neglect produces fragmentation of both poles

Healing requires integrating the wounded masculine and wounded feminine into healthy forms.

The Warrior, Scholar, and Sage Through the Lens of Gender

Each archetype expresses both masculine and feminine aspects.

The Warrior

- masculine: courage, protection, firmness
- feminine: patience, restraint, endurance

The Scholar

- masculine: logic, structure, analysis
- feminine: curiosity, openness, synthesis

The Sage

- masculine: insight, truth-telling, moral clarity
- feminine: compassion, presence, attunement

These archetypes unfold properly only when both poles are expressed harmoniously.

The Alchemy of Gender: Union of Opposites

In the highest Hermetic sense, Gender culminates in union, the merging of active and receptive forces into a unified field.

This union appears in:

- Taoist internal fusion

- Jung's (1968) alchemical *coniunctio*
- the integration of shadow and persona
- the awakening of Shen
- the attainment of gnosis
- the balancing of brain hemispheres
- the coherence of heart and mind

The *Corpus Hermeticum* describes this union as the "marriage of heaven and earth," the merging of the divine masculine intellect with the divine feminine soul (Copenhaver, 1992).

This union does not erase polarity; it harmonizes it.

Gender in Ethical Action: The Virtuous Fusion

The **Eighth Principle of Virtue** requires balancing:

- firmness with kindness
- honesty with empathy
- boundaries with compassion
- justice with mercy
- initiative with cooperation

Ethical action arises from the union of masculine clarity and feminine care. The Sage embodies both simultaneously.

Gender as the Engine of Conscious Evolution

The **Principle of Gender** reveals that all growth, creation, and transformation require:

- the active and the receptive
- the directive and the yielding
- the structural and the fluid
- the solar and the lunar
- the initiating and the nurturing

Mastery of Gender allows the adept to:

- create harmoniously
- relate authentically
- heal deeply
- act ethically
- manifest purposefully
- embody the Warrior, Scholar, and Sage fully

By integrating the two poles of Gender, the adept participates consciously in the creative force of the cosmos.

The next chapter brings these concepts down to the ground by examining **Hermetic ethics and moral action,** how the adept navigates ethical dilemmas, interpersonal responsibility, and the moral implications of spiritual knowledge.

21. Ethics, Moral Discernment and the Responsibilities of the Hermetic Adept

As the Hermetic path deepens, power and perception increase. With this increase comes responsibility, ethical, relational, and spiritual. The *Corpus Hermeticum* repeatedly warns that knowledge without virtue becomes corruption, and power without wisdom becomes tyranny (Copenhaver, 1992). True Hermeticism is therefore not merely a metaphysical framework; it is a moral discipline.

Modern psychology, leadership theory, and trauma-informed science affirm the same idea: individuals who develop heightened awareness, emotional insight, and cognitive clarity become influential within their relational and social ecosystems (Goleman, 2006; Cozolino, 2014). This influence can either uplift or harm. Thus, ethical maturity is not optional, it is foundational.

This chapter explores how Hermeticism frames ethics, how the Warrior–Scholar–Sage triad expresses moral responsibility, how trauma and shadow impact moral discernment, and how an adept navigates complex ethical dilemmas in a fragmented world.

The Eighth Principle: Virtue as the Foundation of the Great Work

Hermeticism recognizes **Virtue** as the balancing principle, an eighth and essential force that governs the moral use of the other seven principles. Virtue is not merely moral behavior; it is ethical *alignment* with:

- truth
- integrity
- compassion
- justice
- humility
- self-responsibility
- non-harm

In Hermetic ethics, an adept must embody virtue in:

- thought (alignment with truth)
- speech (clarity and non-deception)
- behavior (non-harm, responsibility)

- intention (purity of motive)
- emotional presence (compassion)
- boundaries (respect for self and others)

The Great Work is incomplete without Virtue. Knowledge becomes dangerous when not held in alignment with ethical principles.

Ethics as Balance: The Interplay of Polarity

The **Principle of Polarity** applies directly to ethical action. Every moral dilemma involves balancing complementary values:

- honesty and compassion
- justice and mercy
- firmness and flexibility
- transparency and prudence
- loyalty and autonomy
- personal needs and collective needs

Rigid adherence to one pole creates imbalance:

- honesty without compassion becomes cruelty
- compassion without boundaries becomes enabling
- justice without mercy becomes oppression
- mercy without accountability becomes chaos

Ethical discernment requires holding both poles of the masculine and feminine, Warrior and Sage simultaneously.

This dynamic mirrors the Taoist view that virtue arises from balancing yin and yang, not from choosing one over the other.

The Scholar and Moral Clarity

The Scholar's Qi provides the cognitive tools for ethical discernment:

- evaluating consequences
- identifying biases

- understanding psychological motives
- discerning manipulation
- recognizing cognitive distortions
- separating emotion from judgment
- analyzing social systems

Modern psychology emphasizes that ethical insight requires cognitive flexibility, self-awareness, and emotional regulation (Rest, 1986; Siegel, 2012). Without these capacities, moral judgment becomes reactive, distorted, or emotionally driven. Thus, the Scholar ensures that ethical decisions are clear, informed, and rational.

The Warrior and Moral Courage

Knowing what is right is insufficient; one must have the courage to act.

The Warrior provides:

- courage in confrontation
- integrity under pressure
- boundaries against harm
- protection of oneself and others
- courage to disappoint others for the right reasons
- resistance to manipulation or coercion
- commitment to truth despite discomfort

Moral courage is often the rarest form of courage. It requires the ability to:

- speak truth in environments of deception
- remain calm under emotional attack
- uphold boundaries under pressure
- act ethically even when costly

The Warrior enforces virtue through embodied action.

The Sage and Moral Presence

The Sage brings Shen with the capacity to sense the deeper moral structure underlying in situations. The Sage's ethical contribution is intuitive, empathic, and rooted in compassion. This includes:

- perceiving hidden pain beneath harmful behavior
- responding without ego
- discerning intent from impact
- offering wise intervention
- remaining grounded and non-reactive
- practicing forgiveness without abandoning boundaries

The Sage transforms conflict into growth and suffering into wisdom. Ethical maturity emerges when Warrior courage, Scholar clarity, and Sage compassion align.

Shadow, Trauma, and Ethical Distortion

Ethics cannot be understood without discussing the shadow. Unresolved trauma often distorts moral judgment:

- hypervigilance creates false accusations
- fear-based boundaries become avoidance or hostility
- shame inhibits moral agency
- unresolved anger fuels reactivity
- emotional enmeshment blurs boundaries
- trauma bonds distort loyalty
- projection replaces discernment

Jung (1959) emphasized that shadow material, when unacknowledged projects onto others, turning relational or ethical challenges into exaggerated moral narratives.

The Hermetic adept must integrate shadow before claiming moral authority. Trauma-informed ethics require:

- self-awareness
- humility
- regulation

- accountability
- emotional integration

Without these, ethics become a mask for unresolved wounds.

Discernment: The Hermetic Skill of Seeing Clearly

Discernment is the ability to perceive:
- truth from distortion
- intuition from fear
- compassion from enabling
- boundaries from avoidance
- integrity from manipulation
- humility from self-abandonment
- wisdom from ego

Discernment requires:

1. Emotional Regulation

One cannot discern from a dysregulated nervous system.

2. Shadow Awareness

Otherwise projections are mistaken for insight.

3. Intellectual Clarity

Otherwise biases distort judgment.

4. Intuition

Otherwise one ignores deeper realities.

5. Virtue

Otherwise power corrupts awareness.

Discernment is the Sage's highest gift.

The Ethics of Influence: The Adept's Responsibility

As the adept grows, they influence others through:

- emotional presence
- clarity of speech
- energetic regulation
- moral example
- mentorship
- leadership
- spiritual insight

This influence is not optional, it is inherent to the developmental process.
Modern social neuroscience confirms that individuals with high emotional regulation and coherence shape group dynamics without effort (Cozolino, 2014).

Thus, the Hermetic adept has responsibilities:

1. To avoid using insight manipulatively

Knowledge amplifies temptation to control.

2. To avoid exploiting others' vulnerability

Compassion must temper power.

3. To maintain boundaries and avoid overreach

Service must not become saviorism.

4. To speak truth without cruelty

Honesty must be humane.

5. To embody virtue consistently

Ethics must permeate behavior, not merely belief.

Ethical power is exercised through restraint as much as through action.

Navigating Ethical Dilemmas

Hermetic ethics are not rigid commandments. They are principles that guide decision-making in complex situations. Dilemmas arise when:

- competing values conflict
- relationships carry emotional history
- trauma complicates clarity
- social systems exert pressure
- truth risks destabilizing peace
- boundaries require firmness
- compassion risks enabling harm

The adept navigates dilemmas through:

- slowing down
- regulating emotion
- exploring both poles (Polarity)
- anticipating consequences (Cause and Effect)
- sensing timing (Rhythm)
- using intuition (Gender)
- maintaining virtue (Eighth Principle)

Ethics require wisdom, not formulas.

The Moral Function of the Adept in Community

The adept contributes to moral coherence by:

- modeling integrity
- offering calm in chaos

- speaking truth to distortion
- providing stable boundaries
- intervening against harm
- uplifting others through presence
- mentoring ethically
- embodying compassion without self-abandonment
- reducing collective reactivity

Like a tuning fork, the adept stabilizes the moral resonance of a group. This is not idealism; it is social neurobiology.

Conclusion: Ethics as the Crown of the Great Work

Ethical maturity is the culmination of Hermetic development. Without ethics:

- knowledge becomes manipulation
- power becomes oppression
- insight becomes arrogance
- intuition becomes fantasy
- boundaries become walls
- compassion becomes weakness
- courage becomes recklessness

Ethics integrate the Warrior, Scholar, and Sage into a unified whole.

Virtue transforms the Great Work from personal refinement into collective uplift.
It is through ethical discernment that the adept becomes a stabilizing presence in the world, a moral anchor in times of confusion, fragmentation, and volatility.

The next chapter expands this outward movement even further by exploring **the Hermetic relationship between suffering, meaning, adversity, and resilience,** and how the adept transforms hardship into wisdom.

PART VI — The Final Transmutation

22. Suffering, Adversity and the Alchemy of Meaning

Suffering is an unavoidable aspect of the human condition. Illness, loss, betrayal, fear, trauma, aging, and existential uncertainty affect every individual regardless of status, belief, or circumstance. But in Hermeticism, suffering is not regarded as punishment or misfortune; it is the crucible through which the Great Work is refined.

The *Corpus Hermeticum* teaches that those who seek wisdom must confront the illusions, wounds, and constraints that obscure the divine spark within (Copenhaver, 1992). This confrontation often takes the form of adversity. Modern psychology echoes this view, recognizing that suffering, when navigated consciously, can lead to growth, resilience, and profound reorganization of identity (Tedeschi & Calhoun, 2004).

For the Hermetic adept, suffering is neither to be glorified nor avoided. It is to be understood, integrated, and transmuted. This chapter explores how adversity becomes a portal to meaning, how suffering reshapes identity, and how the Warrior, Scholar, and Sage each participate in the alchemy of hardship.

The Hermetic View of Suffering: Obscurity Before Illumination

Hermetic texts describe suffering as a state of obscured consciousness. When individuals identify with illusion, shadow, or the lower poles of Polarity, they experience psychological fragmentation and spiritual disorientation. This "darkening" reflects:

- confusion
- fear
- disconnection
- egoic rigidity
- attachment to false beliefs
- emotional reactivity

Suffering, in this sense, indicates separation from inner truth.

Hermeticism teaches that the cure is not external rescue but internal awakening. The adept must:

- face shadow
- integrate wounds
- purify intention

- refine perception
- align with virtue

This process transforms suffering into clarity, just as heat refines metal in alchemical symbolism. Taoist internal alchemy describes this transformation through the conversion of Jing (raw experience) into Qi (insight) and Qi into Shen (wisdom).

The Psychology of Adversity: Trauma, Stress, and Growth

Modern psychology reveals that adversity affects every aspect of human functioning:

- attachment and trust
- emotion regulation
- cognitive patterns
- nervous system reactivity
- worldview
- sense of identity

Trauma disrupts the autonomic nervous system, resulting in hyperarousal, shutdown, or oscillation between the two (Porges, 2011). Stress without meaning becomes toxic and deteriorates mental and physical health (McEwen, 2012).

Yet research on post-traumatic growth (PTG) shows that suffering when integrated can lead to:

- increased appreciation for life
- stronger relationships
- new priorities
- personal strength
- spiritual development
- deeper meaning (Tedeschi & Calhoun, 2004)

This mirrors the Hermetic idea that adversity is an opportunity for refinement.

The Warrior: Endurance, Stability, and Grounding in Hardship

The Warrior represents the body, the realm of Jing, and is the first responder in times of adversity. Suffering activates survival responses; the Warrior provides the physical foundation for navigating stress.

Warrior capacities include:

- resilience under pressure
- grounding during chaos
- physical endurance
- breath control
- stabilization of posture and presence
- courage to face pain without collapse

The Warrior prevents suffering from overwhelming the system. Without this grounding, individuals become emotionally flooded or shut down. The Warrior's stability allows the Scholar and Sage to engage in adversity consciously.

The Scholar: Meaning-Making, Insight, and Cognitive Reframing

The Scholar interprets suffering, transforming raw experience (Jing) into intelligible patterns (Qi). This process aligns with cognitive and narrative psychology, which shows that meaning-making is essential for resilience (Pennebaker & Chung, 2011).

Scholar functions include:

- understanding the roots of suffering
- distinguishing between past and present
- reframing limiting beliefs
- identifying lessons and themes
- analyzing patterns in adversity
- transforming chaos into coherence

Meaning does not erase suffering, but it prevents suffering from becoming meaningless. The Scholar discovers the order hidden within adversity.

The Sage: Acceptance, Transcendence, and Compassionate Awareness

The Sage, embodying Shen, transforms suffering into wisdom and compassion. This does not deny pain; it expands consciousness to hold pain within a larger field of meaning.

Sage qualities include:

- deep acceptance
- emotional spaciousness
- compassion for self and others
- non-attachment to outcomes
- willingness to feel without resistance
- intuition about deeper purpose

Spiritual traditions describe this as "the cleansing of the heart" or "illumination through grief." Modern neuroscience shows that compassion-based practices restructure neural pathways, increasing emotional regulation and resilience (Siegel, 2012). The Sage turns suffering into connection, insight, and purpose.

Suffering as the Catalyst of Identity Transformation

In Hermeticism, suffering often initiates *identity transitions*, or developmental thresholds where old patterns dissolve and new forms emerge. This mirrors psychological models of adult development, which emphasize that growth often follows disruption, disillusionment, or crisis (Kegan, 1994).

These thresholds include:

- the collapse of previously held beliefs
- the recognition of shadow
- the loss of egoic self-images
- the confrontation with mortality
- the disintegration of unhealthy relationships
- the revelation of false identity structures

Suffering destabilizes the old self so that a deeper, more integrated self may emerge. This reflects the alchemical stage of **Nigredo** (Jung, 1968), or the darkening before transformation.

The Principle of Rhythm: The Cycles of Pain and Healing

Suffering follows rhythmic cycles:

- contraction (pain)

- stabilization
- reflection
- expansion (insight)
- integration
- rest

These cycles mirror emotional waves, trauma recovery stages, and neurobiological rhythms of repair. Healing is not linear; it oscillates. Progress may be followed by regression, clarity by confusion, strength by fatigue. The adept navigates these cycles with patience, regulating breath, grounding the body, and trusting the rhythm of healing.

The Principle of Polarity: Pain and Meaning as Complementary Forces

The Principle of Polarity teaches that opposites are part of a continuum. Pain and meaning exist on the same spectrum:

- pain without meaning becomes suffering
- meaning without adversity becomes abstraction
- adversity infused with meaning becomes transformation

This is why spiritual and psychological development often follows hardship. Pain deepens awareness; awareness transforms pain.

Suffering as a Teacher: Lessons of the Great Work

Adversity teaches the adept:

1. Impermanence

All states pass, including pain.

2. Humility

Suffering dissolves arrogance and superficial identity.

3. Compassion

Shared pain connects people more profoundly than shared pleasure.

4. Boundaries

Hardship clarifies what can and cannot be tolerated.

5. Strength

Resilience develops only through challenge.

6. Self-awareness

Pain reveals unconscious patterns.

7. Purpose

Adversity often points toward one's calling.

The adept does not seek suffering but does not waste it when it comes.

Trauma, Abuse, and the Limits of Spiritualizing Pain

Hermeticism rejects the distortion that all suffering is "meant to be" or inherently "good." Trauma inflicted by cruelty, neglect, exploitation, or unethical authority must be confronted, not glorified.

The adept must distinguish between:

- suffering that leads to growth
- suffering that requires intervention
- suffering that signals boundary violation
- suffering that reflects systemic harm

Spiritual bypassing or minimizing trauma through metaphysical rationalizations, is antithetical to the Great Work (Cashwell et al., 2007). Ethical discernment must guide the transmutation of suffering.

Resilience: The Hermetic Path Through Hardship

Resilience is the ability to:

- remain grounded under stress
- adapt to adversity
- recover from setbacks
- learn from hardship
- maintain virtue in difficulty

Hermetic resilience draws on all three archetypes:

- the **Warrior** stabilizes the body
- the **Scholar** reframes the story
- the **Sage** expands consciousness

This triad allows the adept to transform adversity without collapsing into victimhood or bypassing pain.

The Alchemy of Meaning: Transforming Pain Into Purpose

Meaning is the final stage of the alchemy of suffering. It arises when adversity becomes part of a coherent narrative, one that empowers rather than diminishes. Meaning-making involves:

- integrating lessons
- realigning values
- strengthening purpose
- cultivating compassion
- deepening presence
- expanding identity
- refining virtue

When meaning emerges, suffering transforms into fuel for the Great Work.

Suffering as the Crucible of the Adept

Suffering is not a deviation from the Hermetic path. It is woven into it. Through adversity, the adept learns:

- resilience (Warrior)
- understanding (Scholar)
- compassion (Sage)
- virtue (Eighth Principle)
- discernment
- inner peace
- deeper purpose

Adversity becomes the furnace in which the self is purified. Meaning becomes the gold extracted from the ore of hardship.

The next chapter extends this exploration by examining **how the adept integrates wisdom from suffering into service, leadership, and the embodiment of inner light.**

23. Becoming a Luminous Presence

Integrating Wisdom into Service, Leadership and Daily Life

As individuals progress through the Great Work, suffering is transformed into insight, fear into courage, confusion into clarity, and fragmentation into integration. The culmination of this inner alchemy is not separation from the world but deeper participation within it. The adept becomes a **luminous presence,** a stabilizing, clarifying, compassionate influence that uplifts relationships, communities, and collective consciousness.

Hermetic texts describe this transformation as the "illumination of the soul," where inner light radiates outward, influencing the world through virtue, integrity, and wisdom (Copenhaver, 1992). Taoist philosophy captures this idea through the concept of *De* (moral character; virtue; morality), the moral radiance that emerges naturally when a person lives in harmony with the Tao (Kohn, 2009). Modern neuroscience and interpersonal neurobiology reveal that individuals with high integration, emotional regulation, and compassion measurably calm the nervous systems of those around them (Siegel, 2012; Cozolino, 2014).

de = virtue. morality

This chapter explores how an adept becomes a luminous presence, how inner transformation becomes outer influence, how virtue becomes leadership, and how wisdom integrates into the mundane flow of daily life.

The Emergence of Luminous Presence

Luminosity is not charisma, performance, or spiritual façade. Instead, it arises from:

- nervous system coherence
- emotional maturity
- ethical clarity
- integrated shadow
- authentic humility
- compassion paired with boundaries
- alignment with the Eight Principles

A luminous presence is felt before it is seen or heard.
It manifests as:

- calm in chaos
- clarity in confusion
- kindness without weakness
- strength without aggression
- honesty without cruelty
- openness without naivety

This presence is what Hermeticism calls the radiance of the "reborn soul."

The Science of Presence: Nervous System Regulation and Social Resonance

Modern psychology confirms that humans influence each other through nonverbal channels, including:

- microexpressions
- tone of voice
- facial musculature
- posture
- breath rhythm
- heart rate variability
- mirror neuron activation

These physiological cues create interpersonal "fields" of safety or threat (Porges, 2011). Individuals who have integrated trauma, stabilized emotion, and cultivated inner coherence naturally:

- calm conflict
- reduce social anxiety in others
- increase cooperation
- improve communication
- encourage authenticity

This is the biological basis of Hermetic luminosity.

The Warrior: Luminosity Through Stability

The Warrior contributes to luminous presence through grounded embodiment:

- steady breath
- relaxed posture
- calm eye contact
- firm but non-threatening boundaries
- physical presence that exudes safety rather than dominance

The Warrior's luminosity comes from **presence**, not performance. People feel safer simply by being near someone whose nervous system is not chaotic. This makes the Warrior essential in environments of conflict, instability, or emotional turbulence.

The Scholar: Luminosity Through Clarity

The Scholar radiates luminosity through intellectual and emotional clarity:

- clear communication
- balanced judgment
- accurate interpretation of events
- emotional attunement
- capacity to articulate truth gently
- curiosity without defensiveness

The Scholar's clarity dissolves confusion and misinformation, acting as a cognitive anchor for others. Luminosity here is not brilliance or superiority, it is the ability to remain mentally *unentangled* even when others are overwhelmed.

The Sage: Luminosity Through Compassion, Virtue, and Wisdom

The Sage embodies the highest expression of luminosity through:

- compassionate awareness
- intuitive insight
- ethical alignment
- acceptance without passivity
- forgiveness without self-abandonment

- deep presence
- effortless influence

The Sage transforms environments not by instruction but by *being*. Shen radiates through subtle interpersonal channels, creating a sense of spaciousness, dignity, and trust. This presence is what ancient traditions referred to as "the halo," "the aura," or "the field."

Integrating Luminosity into Service

Service arises naturally from luminosity. It is not driven by saviorism or ego but by:

- empathy
- humility
- moral responsibility
- understanding of human suffering
- respect for autonomy

Luminous service takes the form of:

1. Stabilizing Others

Through calm presence, grounding, and emotional containment.

2. Offering Insight Without Control

Sharing knowledge only when useful, without imposing.

3. Setting Ethical Boundaries

Protecting oneself and others from harm.

4. Modeling Healthy Behavior

Letting others witness integration rather than hear lectures.

5. Encouraging Growth

Removing obstacles but not carrying others' burdens.

6. Cultivating Community

Fostering cooperation, safety, and authenticity.

Service is the outward expression of inner luminosity.

Leadership as Ethical Radiance

Hermetic leadership is not authoritarian or hierarchical. It emerges naturally from:
- lived integrity
- emotional regulation
- clear communication
- relational attunement
- moral courage
- wisdom in action

Modern leadership studies refer to this as *transformational leadership*, leadership through inspiration, model behavior, and moral example (Bass & Riggio, 2006).

A luminous leader:
- unifies opposing viewpoints
- diffuses tensions
- acts with fairness
- communicates transparently
- protects the vulnerable
- challenges unethical behavior
- inspires virtue

Leadership becomes the social expression of Hermetic ethics.

Living as a Beacon: How Luminosity Transforms Daily Life

Luminous presence is not reserved for special moments. It expresses itself in daily interactions:

- listening without distraction
- speaking truthfully and kindly
- respecting boundaries
- managing irritability and reactivity
- treating others with dignity
- maintaining calm amidst crisis
- choosing virtue over convenience
- uplifting through example rather than instruction

Daily luminosity is subtle but powerful. It is felt by family, friends, coworkers, strangers, and communities. It is not grand; it is consistent.

Shadow Integration and the Avoidance of False Luminosity

Luminosity is not spiritual performance. False luminosity occurs when:

- the ego masquerades as wisdom
- harmony is posed while truth is avoided
- kindness substitutes for boundaries
- compassion masks enabling behavior
- calmness is used to suppress emotion
- spiritual identity replaces real integration

Hermeticism rejects false luminosity. True luminosity requires:

- acknowledging shadow
- healing trauma
- integrating anger and grief
- maintaining humility
- taking responsibility for harm

- practicing forgiveness with boundaries

Illumination requires honesty, not perfection.

The Cycle of Luminosity: Expansion, Withdrawal, Renewal

Just as the Principle of Rhythm governs all things, luminosity waxes and wanes:

- periods of service followed by solitude
- periods of clarity followed by introspection
- periods of influence followed by retreat

This cycle ensures that luminosity does not become exhaustion or depletion. The Sage knows when to withdraw not from avoidance but from alignment with natural cycles. The luminous adept serves the world while honoring inner rhythm.

Luminosity and Collective Evolution

A luminous presence contributes to collective evolution by:

- reducing societal reactivity
- strengthening interpersonal trust
- inspiring ethical behavior
- modeling secure attachment
- fostering community resilience
- countering disinformation and fear
- elevating moral and emotional culture

Social networks amplify luminosity. Psychological research demonstrates that emotional states, ethical behavior, and even physiological conditions spread through communities like contagions (Christakis & Fowler, 2009). Thus, one luminous individual can influence hundreds or thousands through direct and indirect pathways. Luminosity becomes a force multiplier for the Great Work.

The Adept as Light-Bearer

Becoming a luminous presence does not mean transcending humanity. It means embodying humanity in its integrated, compassionate, courageous form.

Luminosity arises when:

- the Warrior stabilizes
- the Scholar clarifies
- the Sage illuminates
- Virtue guides every action

This radiance uplifts others not through pressure or instruction but through authenticity, integrity, and presence.

The next chapter will explore the final stage of the adept's journey: **integration, completion, and the embodiment of the Great Work in every dimension of life.**

24. Integration and Completion

Living the Great Work

The Hermetic path begins with curiosity and ends with integration. Between the two lies transformation of perception, emotion, identity, relationships, purpose, and consciousness. The culmination of this process is what the Hermetic tradition calls **the Great Work**, the lifelong journey of refining the self until it becomes a vessel of clarity, compassion, and wisdom.

Unlike mystical systems that emphasize escape from the world or withdrawal into ascetic isolation, Hermeticism teaches that the completion of the Great Work is found within everyday life. The *Corpus Hermeticum* makes this clear: the enlightened soul does not flee the world, but returns to it with renewed purpose, illuminating it through presence, virtue, and service (Copenhaver, 1992).

Modern psychology affirms this insight. Integration is the highest developmental achievement, defined as the capacity to maintain coherence between thought, feeling, and behavior while navigating life's complexity (Siegel, 2012). This coherence resembles the alchemical union of opposites, the merging of shadow and light, ego and essence, body and spirit, Warrior–Scholar–Sage.

This chapter explores the final stage of the path: the embodiment of integration, the maintenance of balance, and the lived expression of the Great Work.

Integration as Wholeness: The Return of the Fragmented Self

To integrate is to return home to reclaim every part of the self once lost to trauma, fear, shame, or confusion. Integration does not erase wounds; it incorporates them into a coherent narrative, transforming them into sources of wisdom.

Integration includes:

- unity of body, mind, and spirit
- alignment between values and action
- acceptance of imperfection
- recognition of shadow without judgment
- stable emotional regulation
- coherent identity
- a sense of existential purpose

This mirrors the alchemical stage of rubedo, where the purified matter acquires a deep, inner radiance. Integration is not the elimination of conflict, but the capacity to hold complexity with equanimity.

The Warrior, Scholar, and Sage as a Unified Trinity

Throughout the journey, the adept developed these three archetypes:

The Warrior (Jing)

Stabilizes the body, regulates the nervous system, asserts boundaries, and anchors presence.

The Scholar (Qi)

Clarifies perception, interprets meaning, reframes suffering, and discerns truth from illusion.

The Sage (Shen)

Illuminates the path, embodies compassion, acts ethically, and aligns the self with virtue.

In the final stage of the Great Work, these three archetypes cease functioning as separate modes. Instead, they merge into a cohesive internal unity.

- Courage without wisdom becomes recklessness.
- Wisdom without courage becomes passivity.
- Insight without compassion becomes arrogance.
- Compassion without boundaries becomes self-neglect.
- Knowledge without virtue becomes manipulation.
- Virtue without clarity becomes naivety.

The integrated adept embodies all three simultaneously, creating a stable, luminous identity capable of navigating life without fragmentation.

The Principle of Correspondence: Inner Coherence Creates Outer Coherence

The integrated adept experiences a profound shift: *as within, so without* becomes a lived reality.

- Internal coherence generates coherent relationships.
- Emotional regulation creates relational safety.
- Clarity of values shapes ethical choices.
- Stability of presence transforms environments.
- Virtue inspires trust and cooperation.
- Integration minimizes projection and conflict.

This is not metaphysics but interpersonal neurobiology: coherent minds generate coherent relationships (Cozolino, 2014). The fully integrated adept becomes a microcosm of harmony within a complex world.

Living the Great Work Through Rhythm

Integration is not a static achievement; it is a dynamic process that follows the **Principle of Rhythm**. The adept:

- works and rests
- engages and withdraws
- serves and renews
- expands and consolidates
- acts and reflects

Completion of the Great Work is not the elimination of cycles; it is the mastery of them. Just as the breath oscillates between inhalation and exhalation, the integrated adept moves fluidly between phases without fear, resistance, or confusion.

Shadow as Ally: The End of Inner War

At earlier stages, the shadow was a source of fear, conflict, or denial. With integration, the shadow becomes:

- an advisor
- a teacher
- a reminder of humility

- a reservoir of emotional power
- a source of compassion

Jung (1959) described this as the reconciliation of the ego and the unconscious, where previously rejected traits become integrated strengths. The end of inner war marks the completion of the Hermetic process of *Solve et Coagula,* dissolve and recombine.

Ethical Discernment as a Way of Life

Integration requires continuous ethical awareness, guided by the **Eighth Principle of Virtue.**

The integrated adept:

- chooses truth over convenience
- compassion over ego
- boundaries over resentment
- humility over superiority
- accountability over blame
- courage over avoidance

Virtue becomes not a performance but a reflex. Ethics are no longer deliberated; they emerge naturally from an aligned nervous system and coherent identity.

Relationships as Mirrors and Arenas of Practice

Just as suffering is a crucible for transformation, relationships are the laboratories of integration. The integrated adept navigates relationships through:

- clear communication
- tempered honesty
- grounded boundaries
- compassionate presence
- non-reactivity
- awareness of projection
- acceptance of imperfection
- mutual accountability

Relationships no longer serve to complete the self, but to express the self. Integration allows the adept to sustain meaningful, mature, and healthy connections.

Purpose: The Expression of Integrated Identity

Purpose emerges naturally from integration. It is no longer a search, but a recognition of one's:

- strengths
- limitations
- values
- calling
- lived wisdom
- capacity to contribute

Purpose becomes the expression of the integrated self acting in alignment with destiny and free will. This is what Hermeticism describes as *the divine spark fulfilling its nature.*

Service as Completion: The Adept's Gift to the World

As explored in earlier chapters, service arises organically from integration. The adept no longer serves out of obligation, guilt, or ego, but out of:

- compassion
- wisdom
- resonance
- ethical alignment
- the desire to uplift others

Service becomes the natural overflow of inner coherence. In Hermeticism, the final stage of the Great Work is **returning to the world as a light-bearer,** not to dominate or convert, but to illuminate.

Integration in Daily Life: The Mundane as Sacred

The integrated adept discovers the sacred within ordinary life:

- breath

- meals
- conversations
- walking
- resting
- listening
- conflict resolution
- work
- solitude

Spirituality is no longer something separate from daily existence; it permeates daily existence. This is the *philosopher's stone*, not a magical object but the capacity to transmute daily experiences into meaning, presence, and virtue.

Completion as Beginning: The Cyclical Nature of the Great Work

The completion of the Great Work is not final. Hermeticism teaches that the path loops back upon itself:

- each insight reveals deeper layers
- each integration opens new possibilities
- each cycle leads to higher refinement

The adept becomes a perpetual student of life, cycling through the Hermetic principles with increasing subtlety and mastery. Completion is a threshold, not an endpoint.

The Lived Hermetic Path

Living the Great Work means embodying:

- the Warrior's stability
- the Scholar's clarity
- the Sage's compassion
- the **Eighth Principle's virtue**

Integration allows the adept to walk through the world with:

- inner peace
- ethical courage

- luminous presence
- emotional resilience
- spiritual depth
- clarity of purpose
- commitment to service

The Great Work is not a philosophy to be studied but a life to be lived. The adept becomes what the ancient Hermeticists called *a living temple of the divine,* a being who illuminates the world not through rhetoric or ritual, but through presence, character, and compassionate action.

The next section will provide the **Epilogue**, offering a final reflection to the reader about the path ahead.

Part VII – Appendices & Resources

Appendix A – Concept of Kan and Li

Kan & Li (water on top, fire below)

Traditional Chinese medicine and Eastern philosophy states that fire rises and water sinks within the body. Fire resides in the heart. It is inevitable that it will move upwards, fuelled by the emotional state. This causes fire to move away from the water energy, residing in the kidneys. Water sinks downwards as the essence (Jing) is not adequately preserved throughout our lives. This causes the energy of fire and water to move away from the lower energy center (DanTien) and in this way divides these two forces even more.

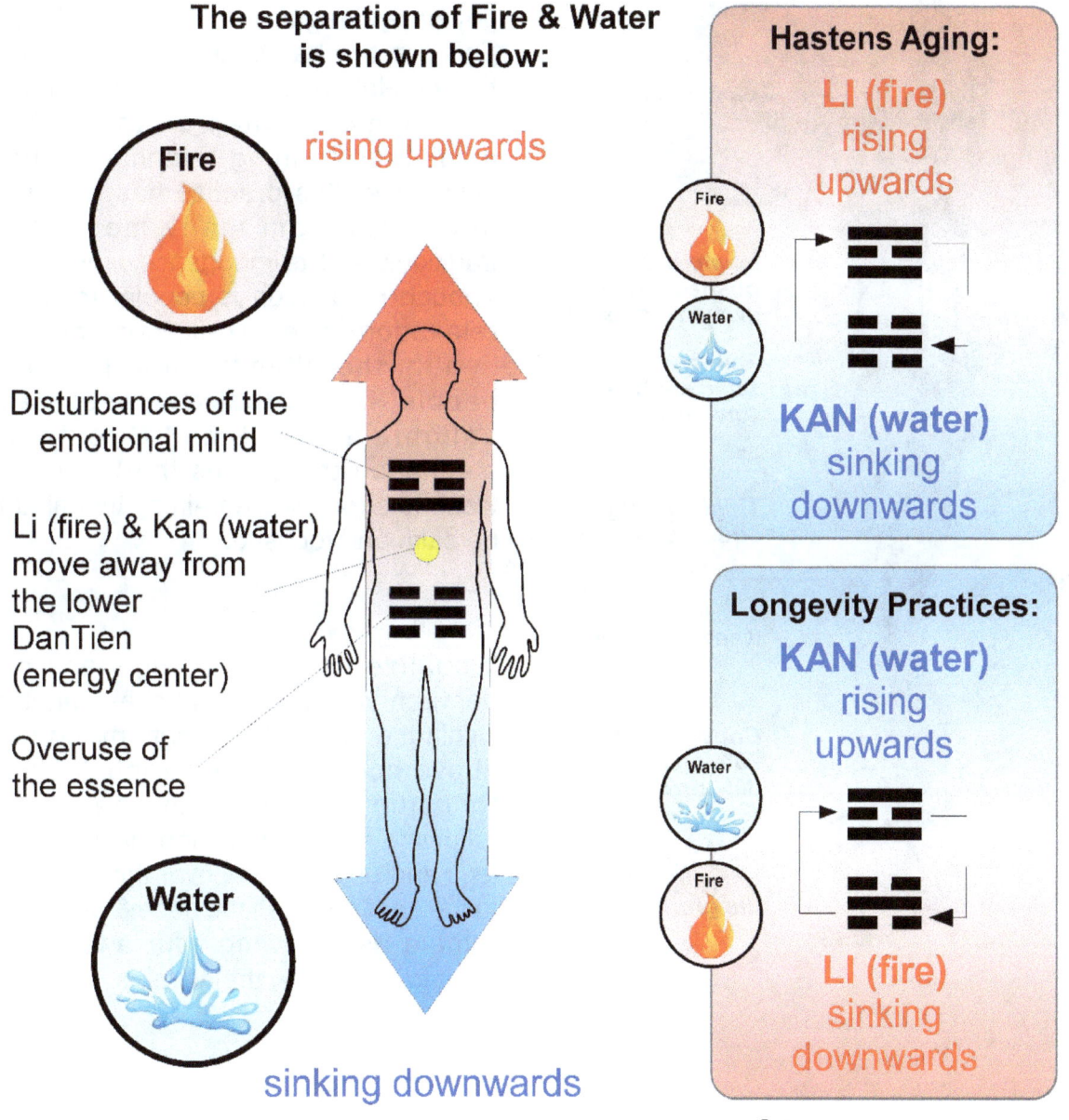

© Copyright 2019 - CAD Graphics, Inc.

Opening the Small Circulation (Kan & Li - water over fire)

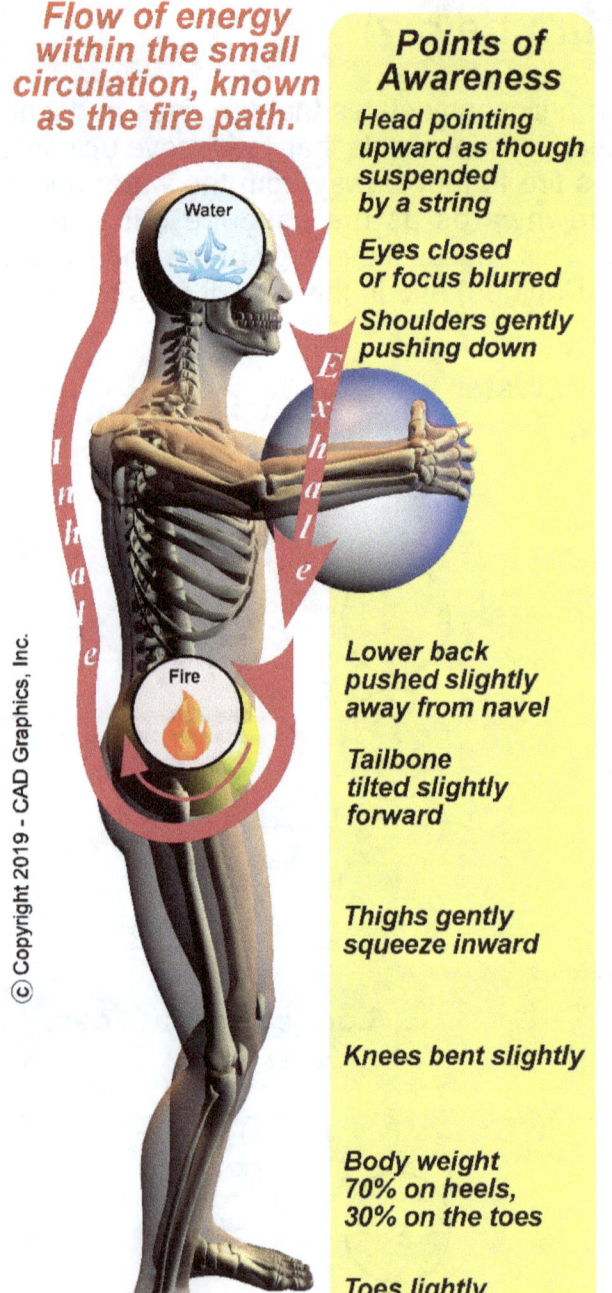

Flow of energy within the small circulation, known as the fire path.

Points of Awareness

Head pointing upward as though suspended by a string

Eyes closed or focus blurred

Shoulders gently pushing down

Lower back pushed slightly away from navel

Tailbone tilted slightly forward

Thighs gently squeeze inward

Knees bent slightly

Body weight 70% on heels, 30% on the toes

Toes lightly gripping into the ground

The Small Circulation, Small Circle, or the Microcosmic Orbit, is the practice of circulating one's internal energy (Qi or chi), within the human body. The illustration to the left represents the awareness of energy flow throughout the Governing and Conception meridians; in this case, the fire path. These meridians are located on the center line of the body and in turn govern and regulate the other meridians. This practice has been considered to be the foundation of Internal Qigong. It was a fundamental step on the path of meditation training in ancient times. Over time, this practice has gradually been lost from many meditation traditions, and its importance diminished. Though meditation is popular today for relaxation, stress relief and general health, the ultimate goal for some people, is spiritual awareness and enlightenment. Small Circulation Meditation transforms the body from weak to strong while training the mind to be calm and focused.

Visualize holding a weightless ball between your palms and chest, another within the pelvis. After conforming to the above body alignments, inhale while focusing just below the navel and following your center line between the legs and up the back, over the head and to the spot between the nose & upper lip. Exhale as following your awareness back to just below the navel.

Mundane thoughts and stress overtakes and affect our energies, increasing the divide causing the aging processes to hasten. Ideally, reversing fire on top to water on top, is an ancient Taoist practice of extending longevity. Practicing Fire Path breathing, Tai Chi, BaguaZhang and Qigong all offer methods of reversing this flow of energy. This is where the Wind (BaguaZhang practices) and Water (Tai Chi practices) makes Fire (internal energy-Qigong practices) terminology becomes apparent.

Fire Path Breathing of the Small Circulation:

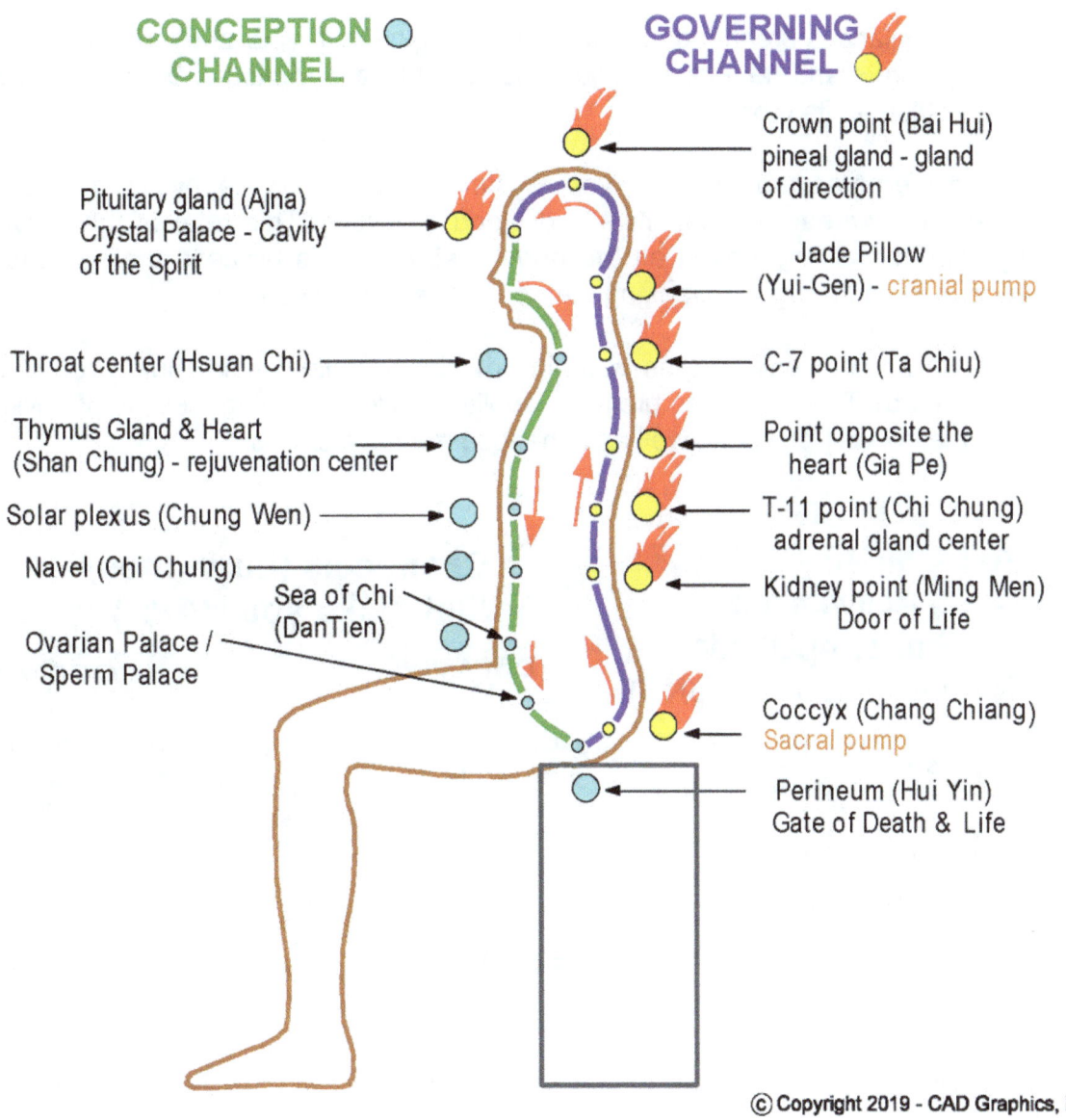

Appendix B – Nervous Systems

Parasympathetic & Sympathetic Nervous Systems

When respiration slows to 10 breaths per minute or slower, the parasympathetic nervous system is activated. Qigong, Tai Chi, BaguaZhang, yoga, etc. are all effective methods of exercise that activate this nervous system. These techniques have proven the test of time in being an option to remove or manage the inner critical dialogue and learn to regulate the fast paced modern existence we all experiencing.

Qigong balances breathing and promotes conditions in your body for it to be able to regenerate and heal itself. Qigong does not treat symptoms, but rather solves the problem at its root.

When the parasympathetic nervous system is activated, "happy" hormones are released, decreasing heart rate and blood pressure. This relaxes the nervous system, slows and calms all the body systems. This process then promotes regeneration through decreasing metabolic rate at all levels.

Deep breathing encourages pumping of cerebrospinal fluid (fluid around the spinal cord). This increases brain metabolism while promoting feelings of physical and mental well-being, as well as enhanced mental alertness.

NOTE: This study guide is a general reference for the exercises shown. Consult with your physician if you are uncertain of your physical ability to perform such exercises.

A ROOT SOLUTION to COMBAT DISEASE: Activate the Parasympathetic Nervous System (PSNS)

12-18 breaths per minute average keeps us in the Sympathetic Nervous System of "Fight or Flight"

10 BPM or less activates PSNS

Fight or flight response transitions to restore and regenerate

DOSE chemicals & hormones released instead of Cortisol
D - dopamine
O - oxytocin
S - seratonin
E - endorphins

www.MindAndBodyExercises.com

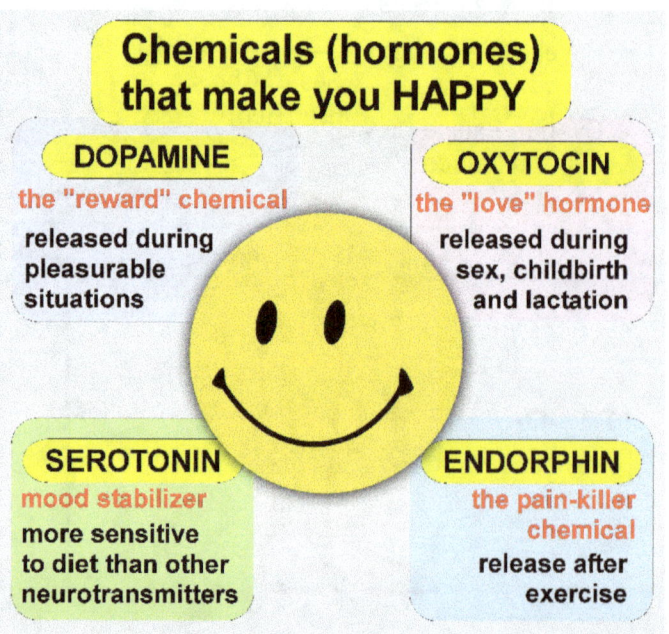

Chemicals (hormones) that make you HAPPY

DOPAMINE — the "reward" chemical — released during pleasurable situations

OXYTOCIN — the "love" hormone — released during sex, childbirth and lactation

SEROTONIN — mood stabilizer — more sensitive to diet than other neurotransmitters

ENDORPHIN — the pain-killer chemical — release after exercise

© Copyright 2018 - CAD Graphics, Inc.

Too much activity within the sympathetic nervous system causes the body to constantly respond as if in the "fight" or flight" mentally eventually deteriorating many body systems.

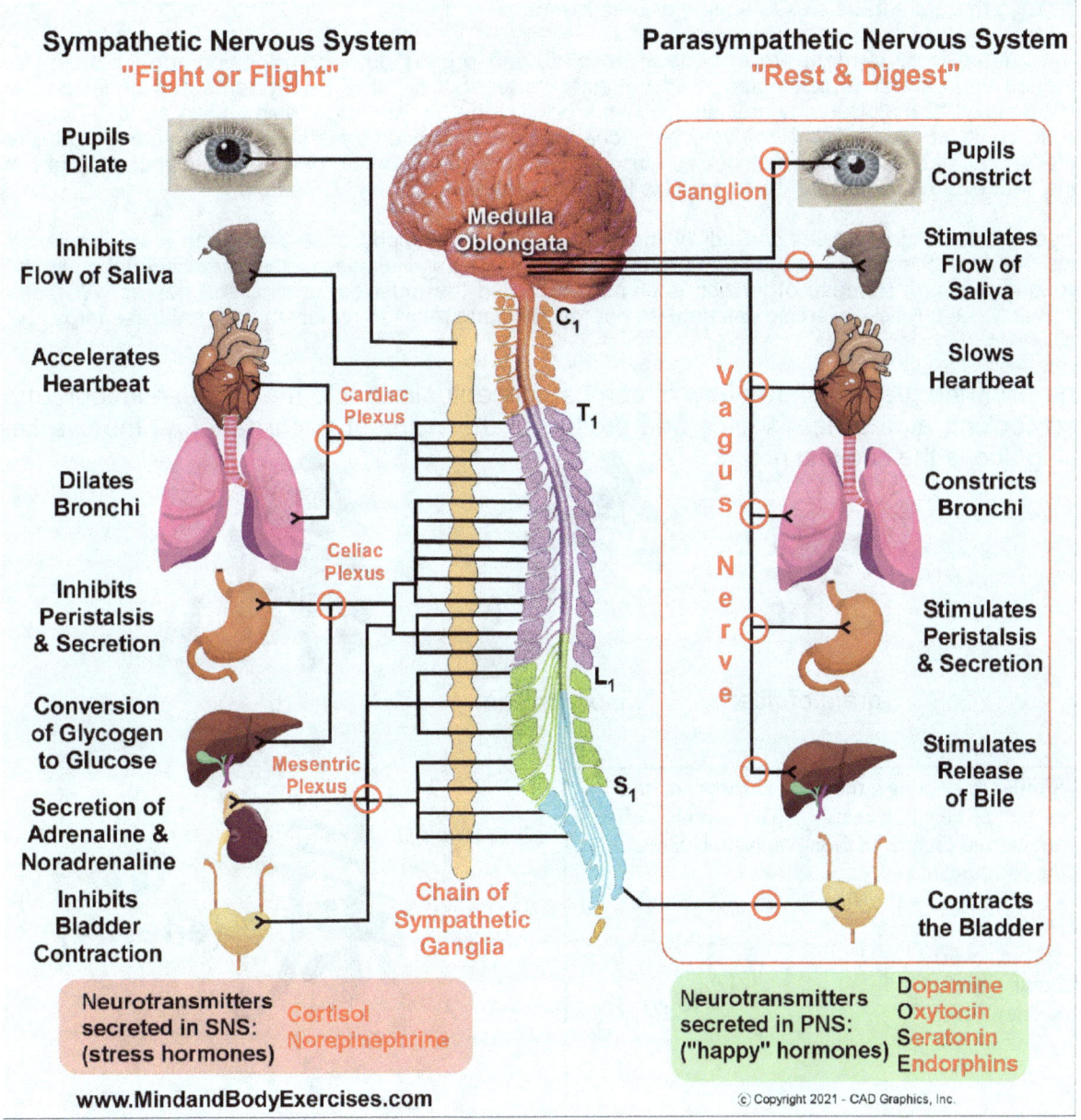

Appendix C - Qigong

Qigong, Chi Kung & Gi Gong www.MindAndBodyExercises.com

Qi, Chi or Gi means air, energy or breath in Chinese and Korean

Gong or Kung means work

Qi Gong therefore translates to energy or breath work

The human body is made up of bones, muscles, and organs amongst other components. Veins, arteries and capillaries carry blood and nutrients throughout to all of the systems and components. Additionally, 12 major energy medians carry the body's energy, "life force" also known as "qi". Ones qi is stored in the lower Dan Tien. Daily emotional imbalances accumulate tension and stress gradually affecting all of the body's systems. Each discomfort, nuisance, irritation or grudge continues to tighten and squeeze the flow of the life force. This is where "dis-case" claims its foothold.

Qigong breathing exercises can adjust the brainwaves to the Alpha state where the mind is relaxed and the body chemistry changes and promotes natural healing. Relaxing of the deep skeletal muscles, working outward. Release of tension accumulated within the muscles, organs and nerves. Whereas conventional physical exercise can deplete energy, Qi Gong helps to replenish your natural energy.

The following graphic shows how qi can be conceptualized into the Chinese ideogram of rice cooking atop a heat source and producing the wisps of vapor (energy) that we see rising above the cooking rice.

grain of rice   wisp of steam   qi

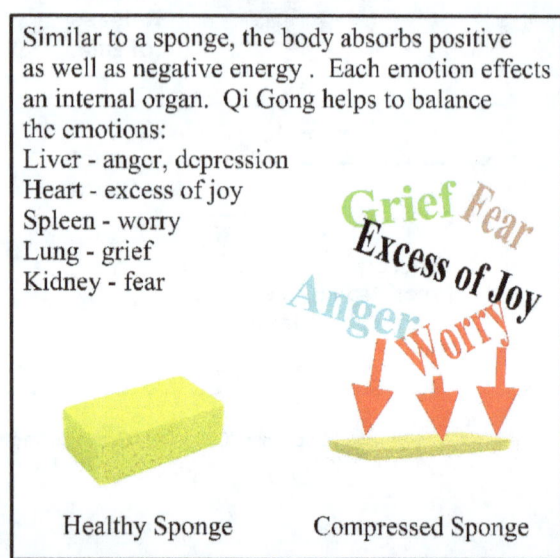

Similar to a sponge, the body absorbs positive as well as negative energy. Each emotion effects an internal organ. Qi Gong helps to balance the emotions:
Liver - anger, depression
Heart - excess of joy
Spleen - worry
Lung - grief
Kidney - fear

Healthy Sponge   Compressed Sponge

Qi (energy)

Gong (work) (cultivation)

© Copyright 2016 - CAD Graphics, Inc.

Qigong, Chi Kung & Gi Gong   www.MindAndBodyExercises.com

Neutral, horse-riding or "Wuji" stance and alignments

Head pointing skyward as though suspended by a string

Eyes closed or focus blurred

Shoulders gently pushing downwards

Lower back pushed slightly away from navel

Tailbone tilted slightly forward

Thighs gently squeeze inward

Knees slightly bent forward

Body weight 70% supported on heels, 30% on the toes

Toes lightly gripping into the ground

"Dan Tien" refers to the 3 energy centers of the body

- located at eyebrow level
- located at heart level
- located below the navel and inward

By relaxing the arches in the spine, bending the knees and tilting the tailbone forward, the spine is lengthened allowing for a release of tension and stream-lined flow of energy within the body. By aligning ones body as the figure on the left, this can be accomplished.

Lengthening of the spine

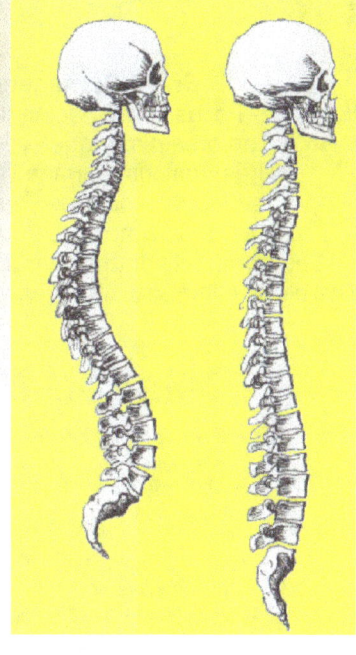

Qigong, Chi Kung & Gi Gong www.MindAndBodyExercises.com

Qi Gong exercise can change brainwaves to the Alpha state:
Alpha - relaxed concentration, creative sta
Beta - attentive, alert
Delta - unconscious
Theta - drowsy state of mind

Best Times:
- morning (calm, nature awakening)
- evenings (calm, tranquil)
- anytime (even a few minutes)

Best Locations:
- outside and peaceful
- inside and uncluttered
- anywhere possible

© Copyright 2016 - CAD Graphics, Inc.

Active Mind
Beta Brain Waves (14-30 Hz)
- State of brain most of our waking time
- Associated with stress, anxiety, fear
- Short term memory, logic
- Used for routine tasks, critical reasoning
- Stress hormone cortisol is released

go from here

Breath Management
- Focus on managing the breath
- The breath manages your emotions
- The emotions manage your thoughts
- The thoughts manage your brain waves
- The brain waves manage your hormone levels
- The hormones manage your blood chemistry
- The blood chemistry manages your heath or illness

to here

Relaxed Mind
Alpha Brain Waves (8-13.9 Hz)
- Relaxed focus
- Long term memory
- Creativity and visualization
- Light meditation, daydreaming
- Serotonin (happiness hormone) is released
- Accessed by focussing on your breathing, and quieting your mind

Basic Qi Gong exercise:
1) Stand, sit or lay in the position as shown to the right.

2) Try to align the body as listed in the steps on front side.

3) Inhale and exhale through the nose as the tongue gently touches the roof of the mouth behind the teeth.

4) Relax the forehead, eyebrows, eyelids, eyes, cheeks, lips and the jaw. close the mouth but don't clench your teeth. Close the eyes to take away the distractions of what your eyes see.

5) Try to picture your body in your thought as you begin a scan from the top of your head working downward towards the toes.

6) As you think of the different parts of the body, try to imagine the deep skeletal muscles releasing from the bones as if they were melting or dissolving away.

7) Continue to become more self-aware of where you are holding tension within the body. As you exhale, try to release any tension in those areas by "dissolving" it away.

8) Follow your breathe from the diagram as you fill the lungs from bottom to top.

9) Let the stomach muscles pull inward as exhaling and bringing your thought back downward to just below the navel to the "Lower Dan Tien".

10) Continue this process as long or little as you choose, mindful that longer periods of time don't neccessarily reflect increased benefits if not performed correctly. However, most benefits are arrived at over a period of time with consistent practice.

Qigong, Chi Kung & Gi Gong   www.MindAndBodyExercises.com

Breathe from the diaphragm by pulling the stomach muscles inwards during exhaling. Then relax the abdominal muscles as inhaling.

Try to imagine the muscles and the tension held within, dissolving away with each exhale.

Arm Variations:

Types:
- sitting
- standing
- lying
- moving

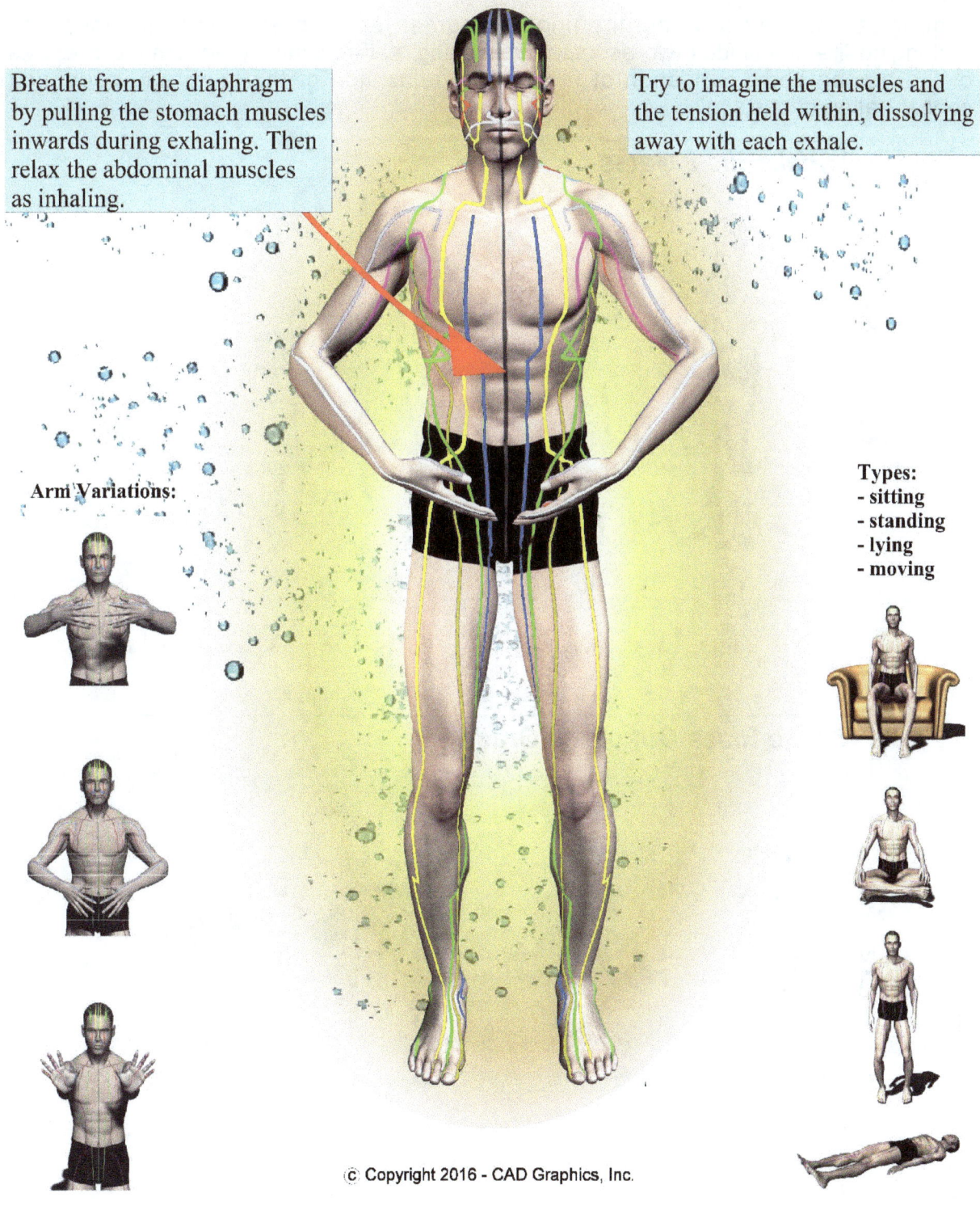

© Copyright 2016 - CAD Graphics, Inc.

Appendix D – Small Circulation Exercises

www.MindAndBodyExercises.com

Qigong is one way of strengthening the human body, preventing diseases and prolonging life. It includes two aspects. One being, self-training by performing postures of the human body, regulation of respiration, relaxation of the mind and body, and concentration of one's mind.

Exercise 1

Shake the 9 Gates

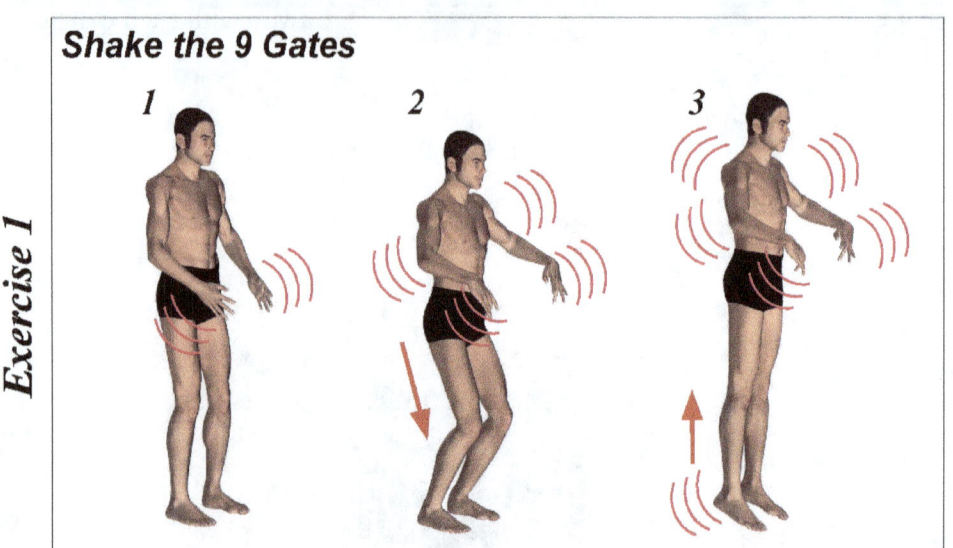

NOTES: 1- Loosely shake hands & fingers. **2-** Continue shaking hands working your way up to elbows & shoulders. Bend & straighten knees while shaking upper body. **3-** Same motion but add gentle bouncing forward on to the balls of the feet.

Exercise 2

Snake Rises Out of the Grass

NOTES: 1- Inhale as bending knees as arching back, chin up. **2-** Round back as chin dips forward. **3-** exhale as straightening legs, as spine lifts one vertebrae at a time. **4-** Inhale, straighten the head and repeat from neutral position.

Opening the Small Circulation (Kan & Li - water over fire)

This aspect is to regulate and strengthen the physical functions of the practitioner's own body. The second aspect is more advanced in that the specialist of Qigong can send out their Qi externally to particular areas of another person in order to treat or prevent illness.

Exercise 3

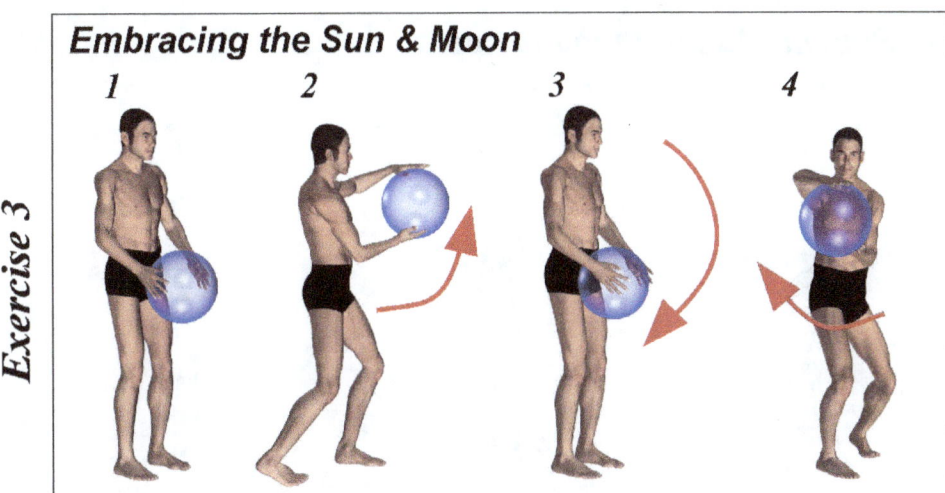

Embracing the Sun & Moon

NOTES: 1- Inhale as visualizing holding a weightless ball between the palms. **2-** Exhale as shifting weight to left leg as twisting the torso to the left & lifting the arms to shoulder height. **3-** Return to center position as inhaling. **4-** Repeat as twisting to the right side.

Exercise 4

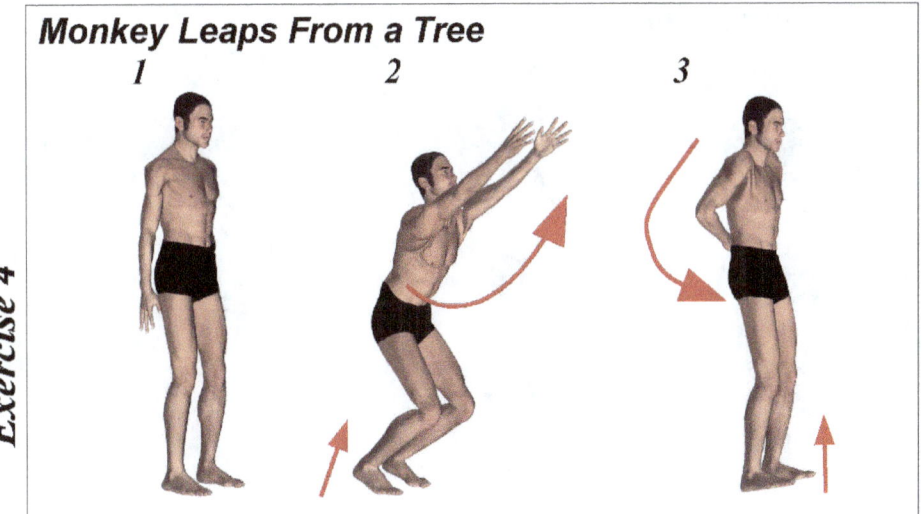

Monkey Leaps From a Tree

NOTES: 1- Start in a neutral position. **2-** Inhale as swinging arms forward, rock on to balls of feet. **3-** Exhale while bringing hands to lower back, round back & tuck tailbone forward, rock on to heels.

Opening the Small Circulation (Kan & Li - water over fire)

Basically, the small circulation refers to the practice of regulating and increasing the flow of one's internal energy throughout the conception and governing channels. This increase in energy throughout the body has been known for centuries to promote health and longevity.

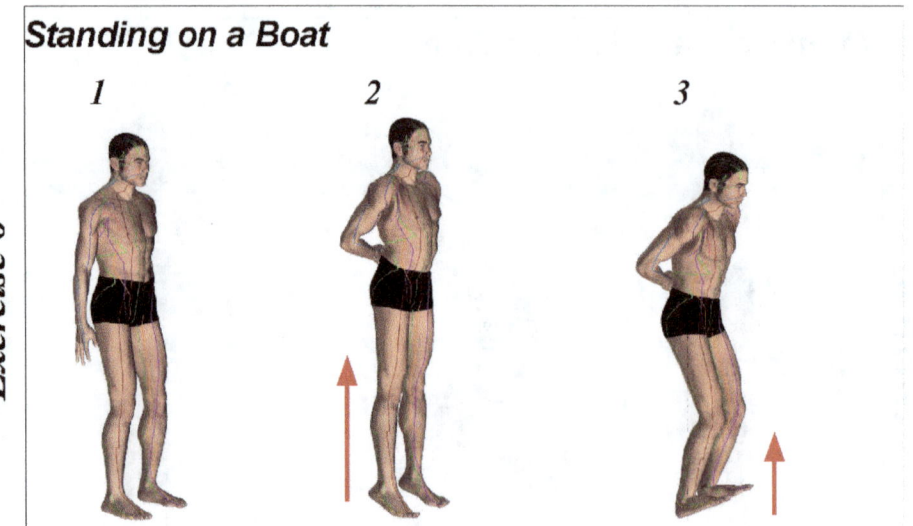

Exercise 5

Phoenix Ascend the Flames

NOTES: 1- Visualize holding a weightless ball between the palm, rock back on the heels of the feet. **2-** Inhale as extending arms upward to the sides, as rocking on to the balls of the feet. **3-** Exhale as returning arms to start position. **4-** Repeat.

Exercise 6

Standing on a Boat

NOTES: 1-Inhale as arching the lower back. **2-** Rock forward onto the balls of the feet. **3-** Exhale as rocking back onto the heels, while tucking the tailbone slightly forward.

Beginning meditation training can be started by practicing breathing deeply from the diaphragm or Abdominal Breathing. The Small Circulation can be the next stage of meditation training. Eventually, one can practice the Grand Circulation Meditation, which circulates Qi everywhere in the body.

Exercise 7: Gather the Clouds to Make a Pillow

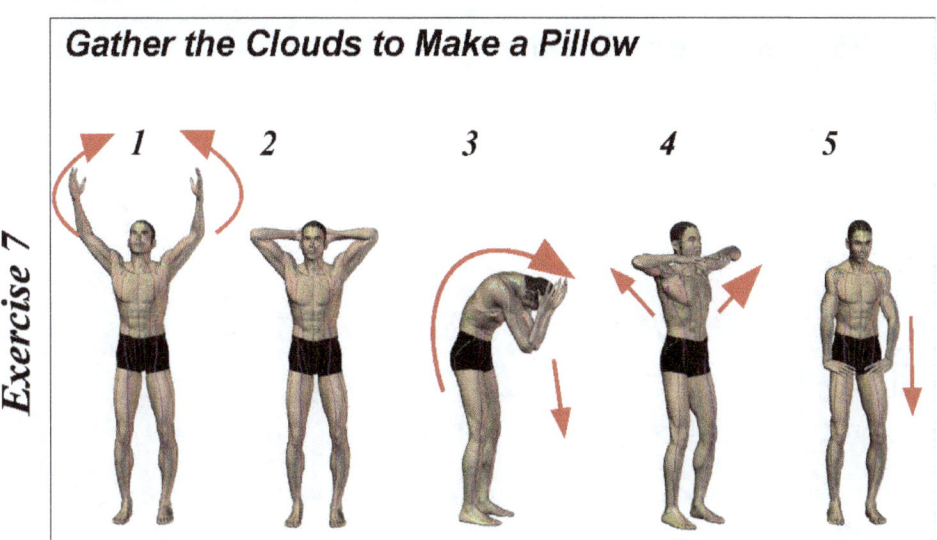

NOTES: 1- Stretch arms above the head as inhaling. **2-** Interlock fingers behind the head. **3-** Exhale as rounding spine & chin forward as bringing elbows together. **4-** Elbows & head up as inhaling. **5-** Arms push downward as exhaling.

Exercise 8: Clearing the Seven Energy Centers

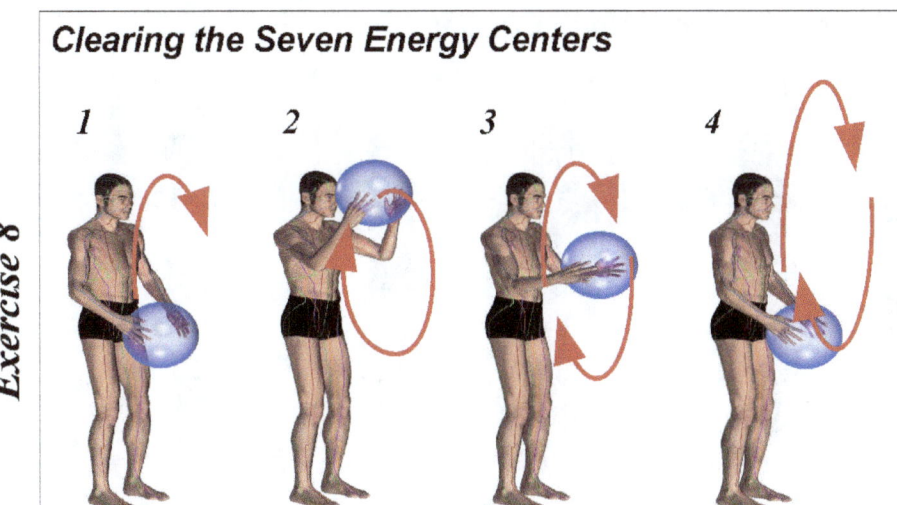

NOTES: 1- Position hands as if holding a light ball in front of the navel. **2-** Inhale as guiding the arms up the front of the body. **3-** Exhale as continuing to circle the arms forward & downward. **4-** Repeat the arm motion increasing the height of the oval each rep.

Opening the Small Circulation (Kan & Li - water over fire)

Qigong is interrelated to the energy meridians. When consistent practice reaches a certain level, the individual can feel the Qi and blood flow through the meridians. The paths of the meridians must be some-what familiar while practicing Qigong so as promote Qi to move along them.

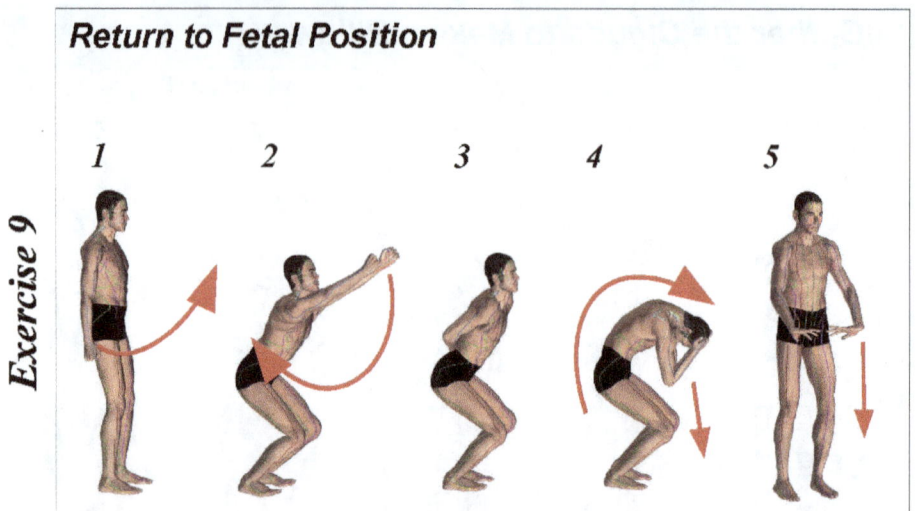

Return to Fetal Position — Exercise 9

NOTES: 1- Stand upright as swinging arms forward. **2&3-** Inhale as bending knees and swinging hands back to rest upon lower back. **4-** Round spine forward as elbows come together. **5-** Straighten spine, legs and arms downward as exhaling.

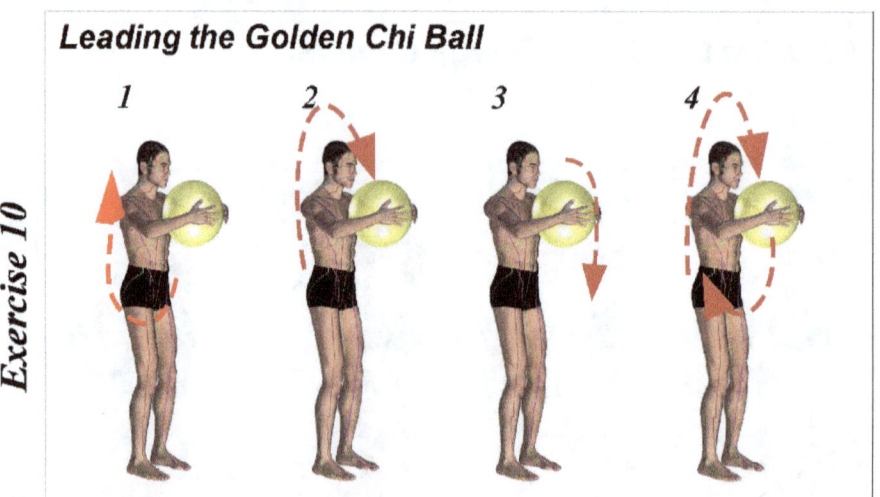

Leading the Golden Chi Ball — Exercise 10

NOTES: All of the previous 9 exercises, lead up to this one. Review left side of previous page for more detail. **1-** Inhale as focusing awareness to lower abdomen, through the legs and up the spine. **2-** Continue the breath as the awareness moves over the head to the upper lip. **3-** Exhale as following the awareness back down to the lower abdomen. **4-** Continue the circular breathing pattern.

Appendix E – Other Breathing Patterns

Advanced Breathing Patterns

Correct breathing is a key to a long and healthy life. Through focused thought and breathing (meditation), many positive mental and physical benefits can be achieved.

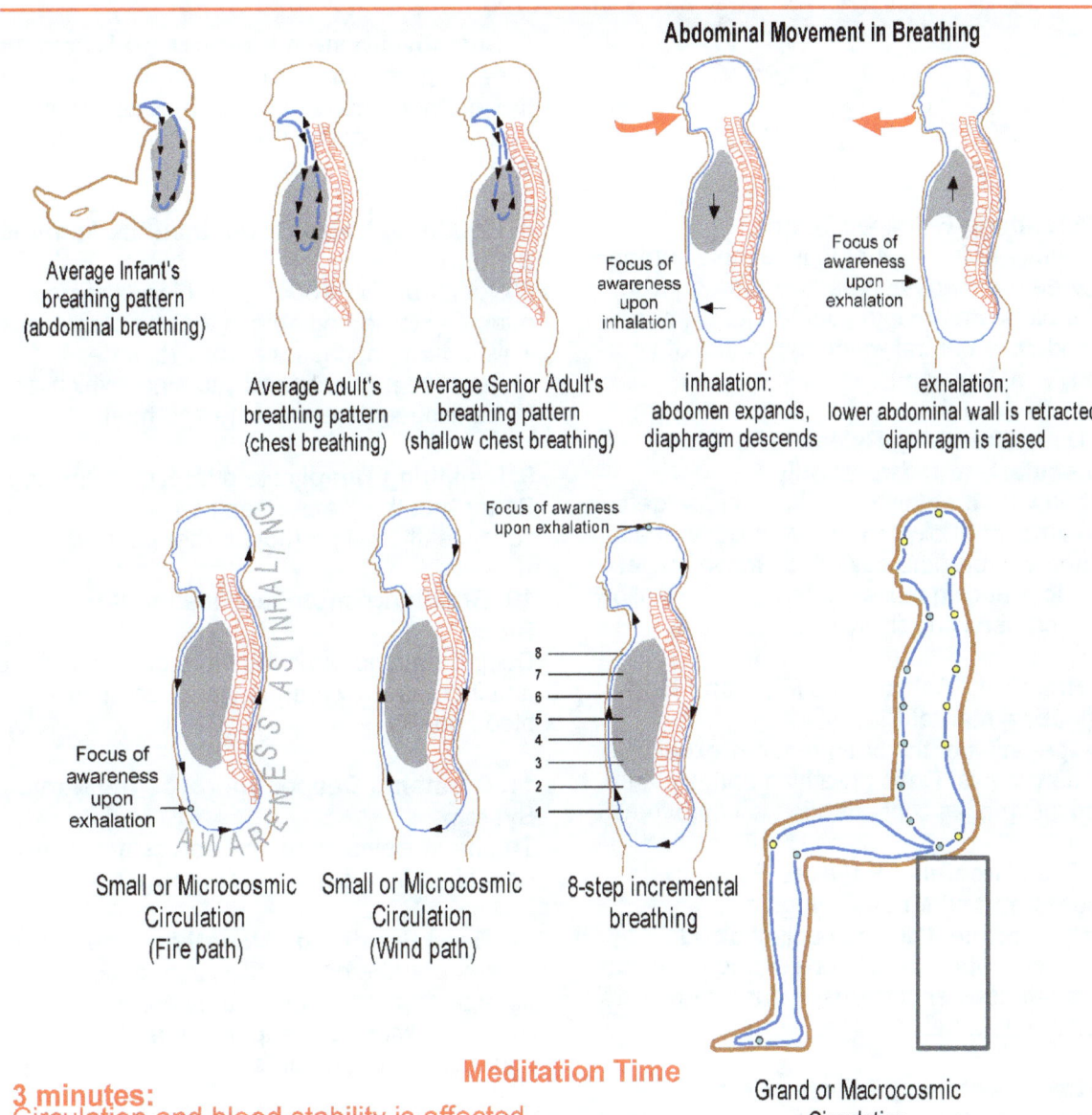

Meditation Time

3 minutes:
Circulation and blood stability is affected

11 minutes:
The pituitary and nerves begin to change

22 minutes:
The three minds (Negative, Positive and Neutral) balance and begin to work together

62 minutes:
Your subconscious (shadow mind) and your positive (outer) projection are integrated

2-1/2 hours:
Holds the change in the subconscious mind throughout the cycle of the day.

Other Benefits of Deep Breathing Practices

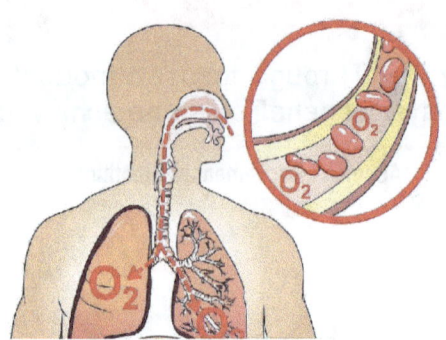

1. Breathing Releases Toxins
Exhaling air from your lungs, expels carbon dioxide that has been passed through from your bloodstream into your lungs. Carbon dioxide is a natural waste byproduct of your body's metabolism.

2. Deep Breathing Releases Tension Muscularly and Structurally
When your breathing is deep, you are getting the amount of oxygen that your body needs. When you breathe easier you move easier due to reducing muscular tension. This allows an increase in flexibility of joints.

3. Breathing Relaxes the Mind and Body, Affecting Mental Clarity
Oxygenation of the brain reduces excessive anxiety levels. Deep breathing brings clarity and insights as concentration is improved.

4. Deep Breathing Relieves Emotional Problems and Mood Swings
Regulated breathing can adjust blood chemistry which effects one's emotional state. This releases endorphins, natural painkillers that create a natural high.

5. Deep Breathing Relieves Pain
Studies show that breathing into your pain helps to ease it.

6. Breathing Massages Your Organs
Diaphragm movement during deep breathing massages the stomach, small intestine, liver and pancreas.

7. Digestive System Works More Efficiently
Breathing deep from the diaphragm massages the internal organs to function better. This regulates and calms the emotions, directly affecting the digestion system.

8. Breathing Helps Strengthen the Immune System
Oxygen travels through your bloodstream by attaching to hemoglobin in the red blood cells. This in turn enriches the body to better metabolize nutrients and vitamins. Which also helps tissues to regenerate and heal.

9. Breathing Deeply Help Improve Posture
Better breathing exercises practiced consistently, will promote better posture.

10. Breathing Improves Quality of the Blood
Deep breathing removes more carbon-dioxide and increases oxygen in the blood, increasing blood quality.

11. Breathing Deeper Improves the Nervous System
The brain, spinal cord and nerves are more nourished by receiving more oxygen.

12. Deep Breathing Strengthens the Lungs
As you breathe deeply the lungs become stronger and powerful as they are also exercised with more expansion and contracting of each breath.

© Copyright 2018 - CAD Graphics, Inc.

13. Breathing Deeper Makes the Heart Healthier.
Breathing exercises reduce the workload on the heart. Deep breathing promotes more efficient lungs, which distributes more oxygen into contact with blood sent to the lungs by the heart.

14. Blood Circulation Improves with Deep Breaths
Deep breathing leads to a greater pressure differential within the lungs, leading to an increase in the blood circulation, thereby resting the heart slightly.

15. Better Breathing Can Assist in Weight Loss
Extra oxygen throughout the body, burns up excess fat more efficiently.

16. Deep Breathing Boosts Energy levels and Improves Stamina

17. Breathing Improves Cellular Regeneration

18. The Lymphatic System Works Better with Deeper Breathing
Increased circulation of lymphatic fluid speeds recovery after illnesses, removing waste by-products more efficiently.

19. Elimination of Waste Through Exhaling Works Better
70% of the body's waste is eliminated through the breath.

20. Self-Awareness & Spirituality Can be Enhanced from Deep Breathing
Creativity and Intuition increases when you're relaxed.

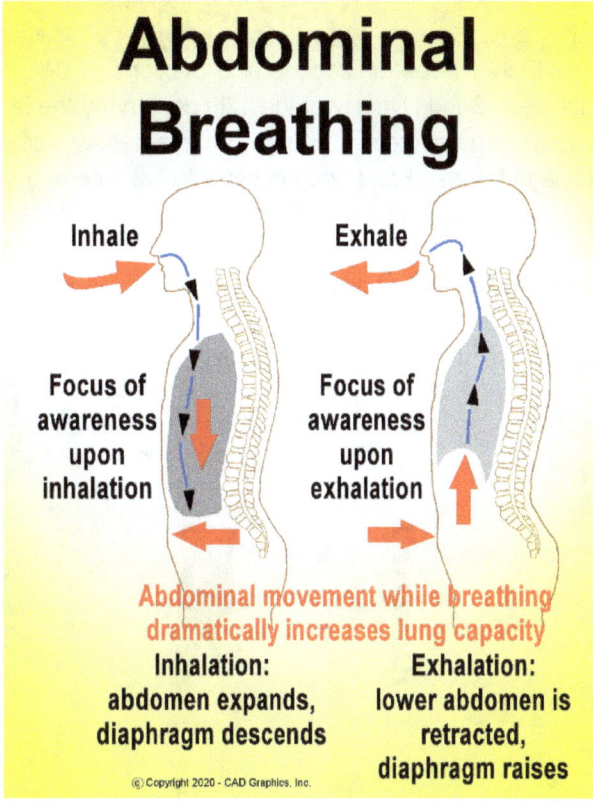

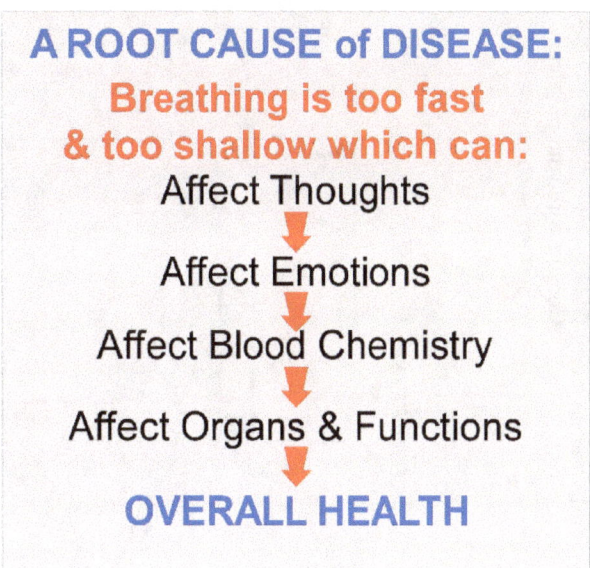

© Copyright 2018 - CAD Graphics, Inc.

Appendix F – 8 Pieces of Brocade

8 Pieces of Brocade - Opening the 9 Gates

The Eight Pieces of Brocade or 8 Sections of Silk, is said to have been composed sometime during the Southern Sung Dynasty of the 12th century by the famous Chinese general, Yueh Fei. Yueh Fei was also known to have created Hsing I, an internal style of martial arts. The purpose of these exercises was to engage the mind and body in order to balance and strengthen the body's vital functions, as well as purge stagnant energy and toxins from the body. If practiced as simple physical exercises, one can loosen their muscles, improve posture, increase blood circulation, and relax the body as well as the mind. These exercises and methods have been practiced and studied for hundreds of years to help maintain good health, prevent and sometimes cure diseases, to calm the mind, and uplift the spirit of the person performing them.

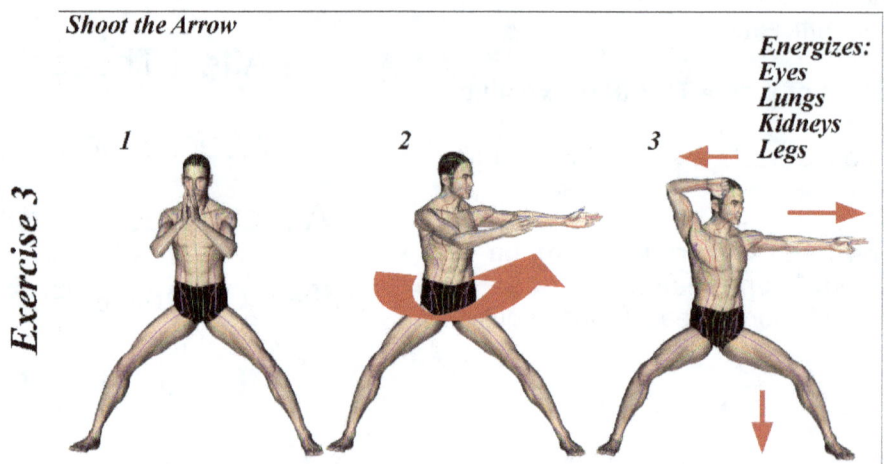

Exercise 1 — Push up the Heavens

Energizes: Heart, Lungs, Stomach, Liver

NOTES: 1- Interlace fingers and rest behind the head. **2-** Inhale as stretching arms & shoulders upward as balancing on the balls of the feet. **3-** Exhale with feet flat as leaning torso to the left side while still stretching shoulders outward. **4-** Repeat step **2**, then repeat leaning to right side.

Exercise 3 — Shoot the Arrow

Energizes: Eyes, Lungs, Kidneys, Legs

NOTES: 1- Palms press together as legs apart in a high horse-riding stance. **2-** Twist torso to the left as bringing right hand to left elbow. Inhale as drawing back right arm as if pulling back the string on a bow. **3-** Right hand in a fist, left hand has the index & middle fingers extended, while thumb, ring & little finger touch together. Exhale as sinking the hips downward.

NOTE: This study guide is a general reference for the exercises shown. Consult with your physician if you are uncertain of your physical ability to perform such exercises.

© Copyright 2016 - CAD Graphics, Inc.

www.MindAndBodyExercises.com

Ancient literature shows and explains body postures and exercise routines similar to the Eight Pieces of Brocade, but dating back roughly 2,100 years. This is important in establishing that these exercises and concepts are not a new fitness fad with little documented facts of actual benefits achieved. Some doctors throughout China, often prescribe exercises like these to prevent of heal injuries, cure illness or disease and improve overall health. This set is possibly the most popular and often practiced chi kung (energy exercises) routines practiced throughout the world, maybe my millions of people. It is just one of perhaps hundreds of different exercise sets in the vast chi kung category. To achieve optimal health benefits, these exercises should be practiced every day. Use a pace and amount of repetitions that are appropriate for your overall physical and mental condition.

NOTE: This study guide is a general reference for the exercises shown. Consult with your physician if you are uncertain of your physical ability to perform such exercises.

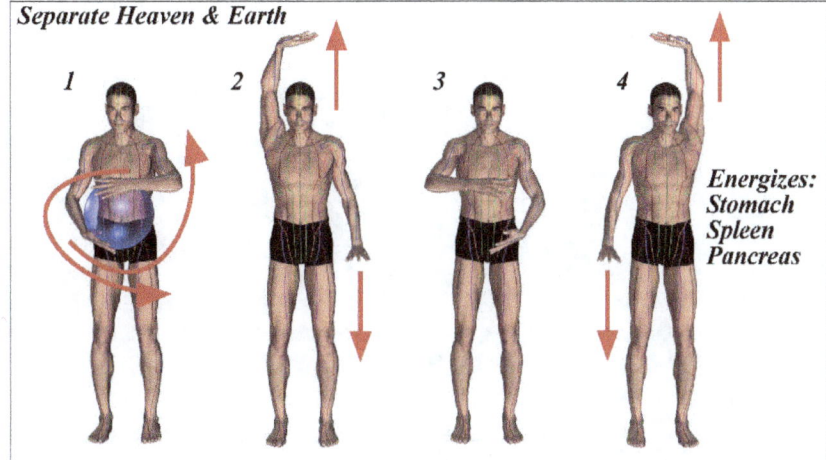

Exercise 2 — *Separate Heaven & Earth*

Energizes:
Stomach
Spleen
Pancreas

NOTES: 1- *Place hands as if holding a beach ball.* **2-** *Inhale as bottom hand continues to rise upward as opposite hand pushes downward from near the left hip.* **3-** *Exhale as returning the hands to the ball holding position with the hands now opposite.* **4-** *Repeat step* **2** *with arms opposite as to alternate sides.*

Exercise 4 — *Looking Side to Side*

Energizes:
Eyes
Spleen
Immunity

NOTES: 1- *Interlock fingers behind the head and inhale.* **2-** *Reposition back of left hand onto lower back as turning head to the left & exhaling.* **3-** *Turn head to the right as switching the arms to the opposite position.*

© Copyright 2016 - CAD Graphics, Inc.

8 Pieces of Brocade - Opening the 9 Gates

Focusing of the mind and one's intention are key in accessing the advanced benefits available from this set. Utilizing the concept of "where thought goes, energy follows", can enhance the movement of "chi" or life force within the body. Slower and deliberate movements will greatly help improve your focus by paying attention to the body as moving exactly how and where you want to. Some traditional practitioners share the view that 100 days of consecutive practice will provide noticeable benefits well beyond the basic benefits of increased strength, flexibility and balance. Cultivating internal wellness requires some consistent effort.

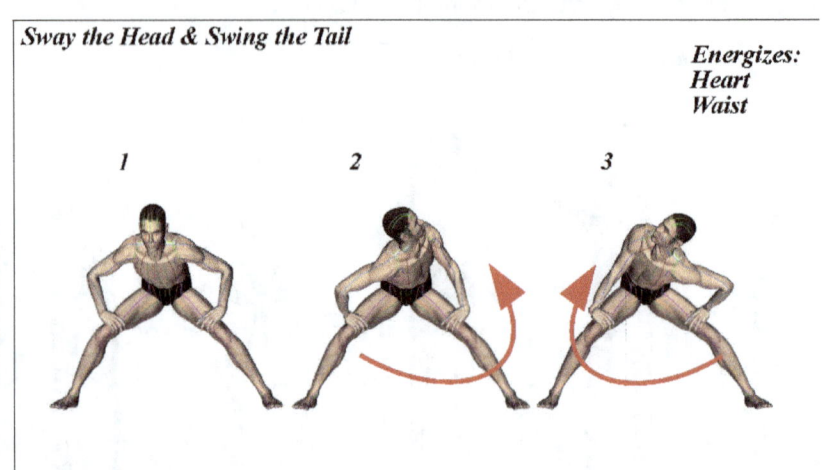

NOTES: 1- Wide horse stance with hands on thighs and torso leaning forward as inhaling. **2-** Exhale as twisting the head and torso to the left while keeping hands on thighs. **3-** Alternate twisting from left to right.

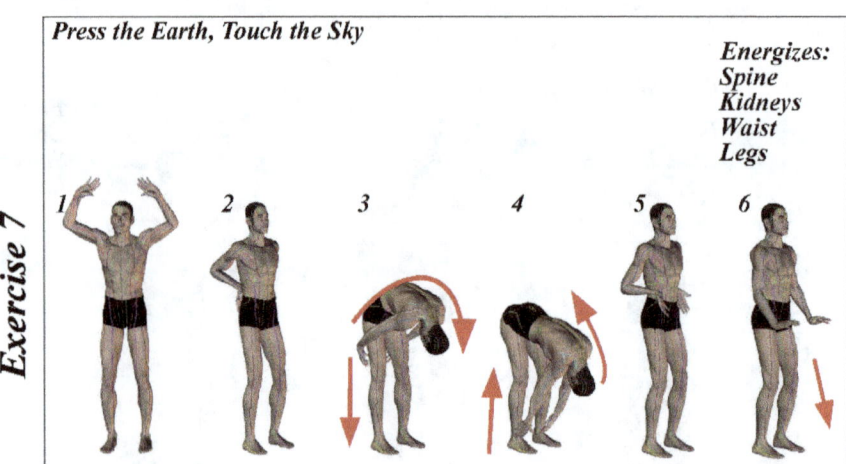

NOTES: 1- Arms make a heart shape motion as inhaling. **2-** Hands come to rest on the lower back. **3-** Exhale as bending spine forward as hands glide down back of legs to the heels. **4-** Inhale as straightening the spine as hands glide up the front of the legs. **5&6-** Exhale as straightening arms downward.

Anything of value worth achieving, will take some time and effort. One cannot grow a garden in one day and expect to reap the fruit without some time and nurturing. Relax as breathing deeply and naturally while doing the 8 Brocades. Sink your weight into the earth as becoming fully aware of your body and the surroundings. Relax the facial muscles and blur the vision. Perform 10 or more repetitions before advancing to the next exercise in this series.

NOTE: This study guide is a general reference for the exercises shown. Consult with your physician if you are uncertain of your physical ability to perform such exercises.

Exercise 6

Punching the Fist with Fiery Eyes

Energizes:
Eyes
Heart
Liver

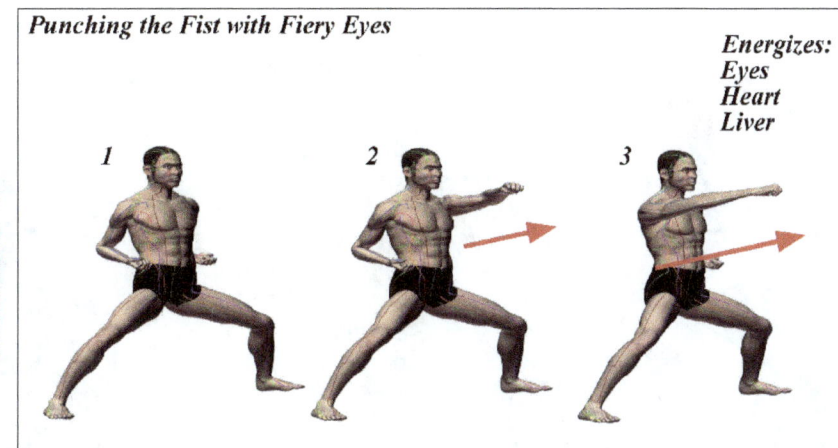

NOTES: 1- Wide horse stance with arms back and fists palm up on hips. **2-** Exhale as extending left fist forward as turning fist to have palm facing down-ward. **3-** Inhale as pulling left fist back to hip as right fist repeats step **2**. Alternate from left to right arms.

Exercise 8

Lifting Up the Heels

Energizes:
Immunity
All Organs

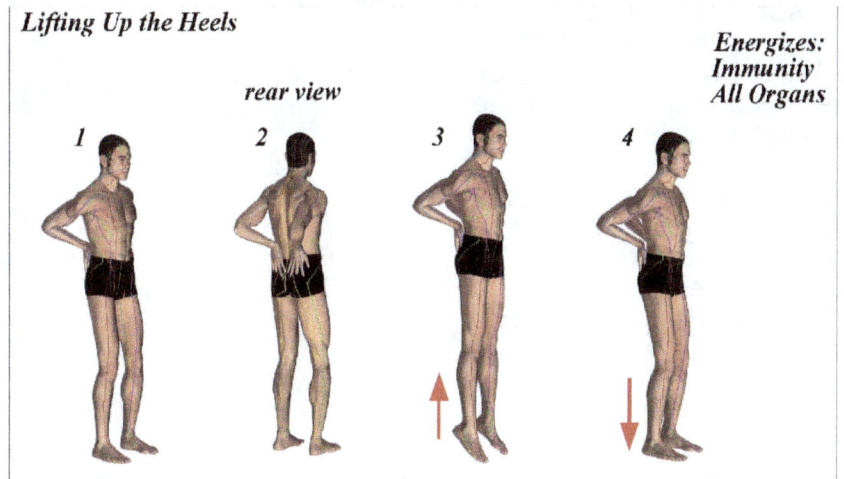

NOTES: 1- Stand with palms on lower back. **2-** Rear view. **3-** Inhale as lifting up heels and balancing on the balls of the feet. **4-** Gently drop down to feet flat as exhaling. Repeat.

Appendix G – 5 Element Qigong

5 Element Qigong - Chi Kung

The 5 element theory is a major component of thought within TCM or traditional Chinese medicine. Each element represents natural aspects with-in our world. Natural cycles and interrelationships between these elements, is the basic for this theory. These elements have corresponding relationships within our environment as well as within our own being.

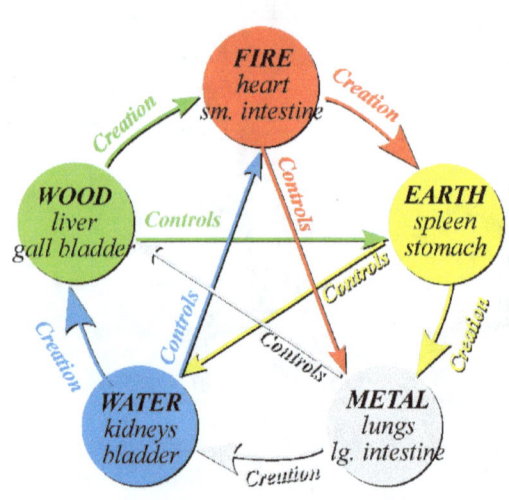

Points of Awareness

- Head pointing upward as though suspended by a string
- Eyes closed or focus blurred
- Shoulders gently pushing downwards
- Lower back pushed slightly away from navel
- Tailbone tilted slightly forward
- Thighs gently squeeze inward
- Knees bent slightly
- Body weight 70% on heels, 30% on the toes
- Toes lightly gripping into the ground

→ Breathe in
→ Breathe out

In the creation cycle, as shown above, each organ provides energy for the next in the sequence. The control cycle represents the regulation of energy, relative to excess or lack thereof energy corresponding to the next element in the cycle.

Basically, the organs are not only responsible in providing energy to one another, but additionally regulating that energy in order to provide balance throughout the human body.

These exercises are designed with enhancing balance within the organs, utilizing the theory of the 5 elements. Try each body position and breathing pattern for 1 minute before advancing to the the next. Gradually add time as you are able working up to 5-10 minutes for each position. These exercises can also be practiced while sitting.

NOTE: This study guide is a general reference for the exercise shown. Consult with your physician if you are uncertain of your physical ability to perform such exercises.

© Copyright 2016 - CAD Graphics, Inc.

www.MindandBodyExercises.com

There are twelve main medians and 8 other special meridians within the human body. Meridians are similar to electrical wires or nerves. They run from the top of the head to the tips of the toes and fingers. Each meridian is associated with an internal organ. When there is a lack of energy flow or blockage within the meridians, health problems can arise. Through proper diet, exercises and life style, it is possible to keep the chi (energy or life force) flowing through the meridians. These exercises help to increase this flow in addition to enhancing strength and balance. The illustration to the left represents the awareness of energy flow from one organ and/or meridian to the next.

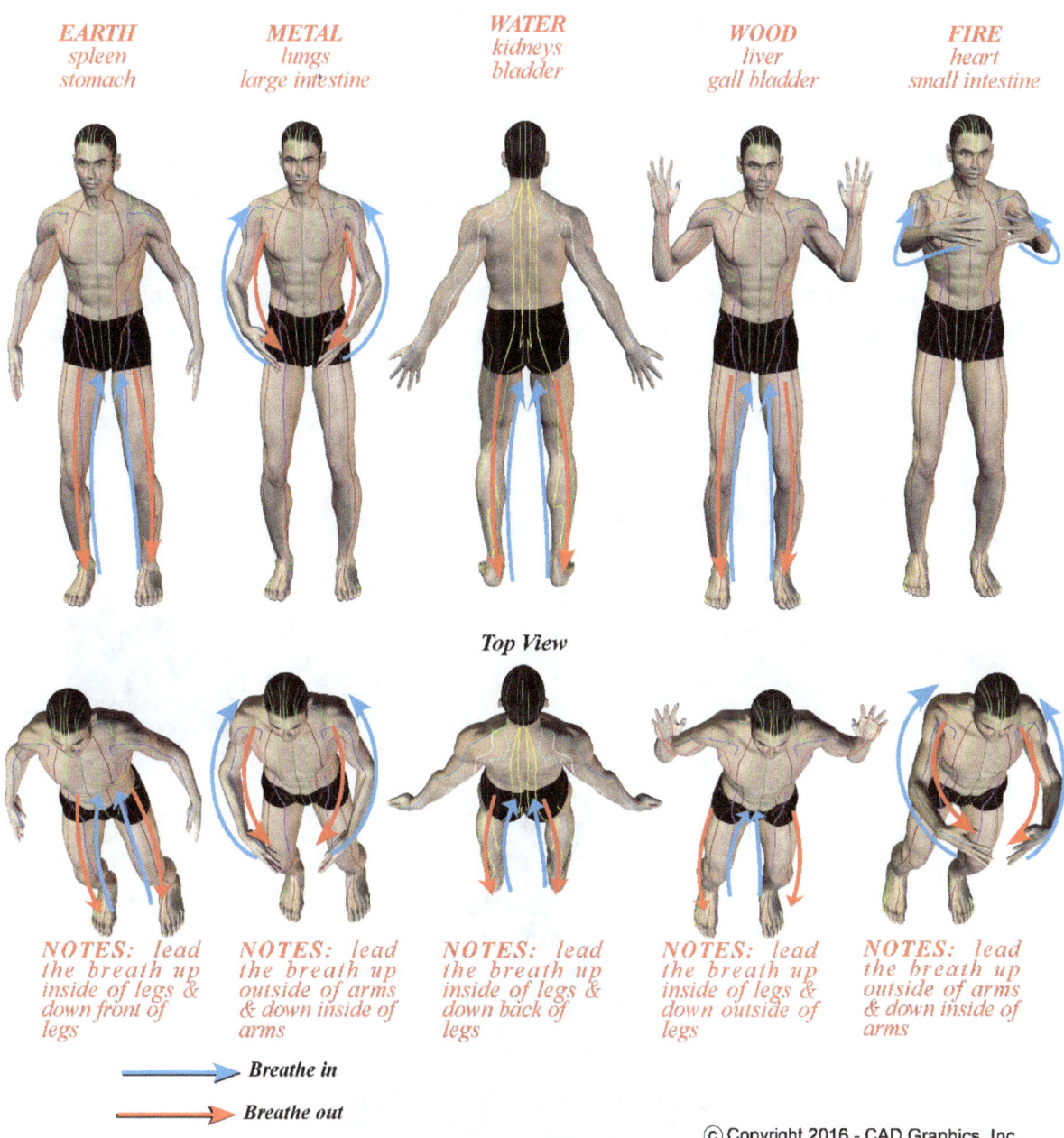

EARTH
spleen
stomach

METAL
lungs
large intestine

WATER
kidneys
bladder

WOOD
liver
gall bladder

FIRE
heart
small intestine

Top View

NOTES: lead the breath up inside of legs & down front of legs

NOTES: lead the breath up outside of arms & down inside of arms

NOTES: lead the breath up inside of legs & down back of legs

NOTES: lead the breath up inside of legs & down outside of legs

NOTES: lead the breath up outside of arms & down inside of arms

→ Breathe in
→ Breathe out

© Copyright 2016 - CAD Graphics, Inc.

Appendix H – Chamsa Meditation

Inner Vision, Pre-Birth Awareness, and the Mirror of Enlightenment

A Korean-Taoist Path of Self-Inquiry and Spiritual Return

Introduction

Within the quiet intersections of Korean martial arts, Seon Buddhism, Taoist inner alchemy, and indigenous contemplative practice, there exists a lesser-known meditative path called **Chamsa (참사)**. Translated loosely as "true reflection" or "sincere contemplation," this practice involves a series of inner visualizations that begin with the face and end with formless awareness. It guides the practitioner from physical identity, through spiritual regression, and into the vast, unconditioned presence that many traditions call enlightenment, *nirvana*, or union with the *Tao*.

Chamsa serves not only as a vehicle of personal transformation but also as a symbolic journey through layers of ego, memory, and form, toward a realization of the true self that was never born and never dies.

I. Origins and Conceptual Foundations

1. Linguistic Meaning

In Korean, **Cham (참)** means "true" or "authentic," while **Sa (사)** may refer to "thought," "contemplation," or "reflection" (Kim, 2018). Thus, Chamsa points to a practice of authentic inward reflection, aligned with the spiritual aim of uncovering the nature of self and reality.

2. Syncretic Influences

The practice bridges three major influences:

- **Seon (Zen) Buddhism**: Emphasizes *hwadu* (Kōan-style inquiry), non-dual awareness, and meditation as a route to awakening (Aitken, 1990; Dumoulin, 2005).

- **Taoist Neidan (inner alchemy)**: Employs visualizations, energy return, and prenatal regression to restore original spirit (Komjathy, 2013; Yang, 1997).

- **Korean shamanic mysticism**: Embraces spiritual vision, ancestral awareness, and altered states as portals to insight (Kim, 2018).

II. The Stages of Chamsa Practice

Chamsa is typically taught as a stage-based meditation, though advanced practitioners may cycle through its phases in a single session. Each stage builds upon the last, guiding the practitioner from concrete visualization to subtle realization.

Stage 1: Face Visualization

- **Description**: Eyes closed, visualize your own face in full, accurate detail, every wrinkle, mole, and asymmetry. Include features such as the slope of the nose, eyebrow placement, asymmetries, scars, skin texture, color, and even the micro-expressions of your resting face. The image should be as vivid and lifelike as if one were looking into a mirror with eyes open.

- **Purpose**: Strengthen *shen* (spirit), develop internal focus, and anchor awareness in the "mind mirror." This aligns with Taoist inner vision practices (nèishì), projecting awareness from the third eye center or upper dantian (Kohn, 1993; Yang, 1997).

Stage 2: Dissolution of the Face

- **Description**: Allow the mental image of the face to gradually blur, dissolve, or melt away without force. Observe any resistance or attachment as the image fades.

- **Purpose**: Cultivate detachment from personal identity and begin breaking down the egoic image of the self. This mirrors both Zen and Taoist instructions for letting go of attachment to form (Dumoulin, 2005).

Stage 3: Witness Inquiry

- **Description**: With the face gone, turn awareness inward and ask: *"Who is seeing this image?"* or *"What remains when the face disappears?"*

- **Purpose**: This self-inquiry parallels Seon (Zen) Buddhism's hwadu method and Taoist "reflection on the void." It shifts attention to the formless witness, revealing the distinction between perception and identification (Aitken, 1990).

Stage 4: Womb Regression

- **Description**: Begin to visualize yourself in the womb. Sense the floating, fluid warmth of the pre-birth state. This visualization is not merely symbolic; it is a meditative immersion into pre-verbal, pre-identity awareness.

- **Purpose**: Return to the state of *yuan qi* and *yuan shen* (original energy and spirit), reconnecting with the undisturbed potential of consciousness prior to conditioning. This corresponds to Taoist embryonic breathing, and the process of returning to the origin (Komjathy, 2013).

Stage 5: Original Face

- **Description**: Let go of all visualizations. Abide in spacious presence. Ask: *"What was my original face before my parents were born?"*

- **Purpose**: This stage reflects the heart of Zen realization. All form, memory, and thought dissolve, revealing emptiness and unconditioned awareness (Aitken, 1990).

Stage 6: Return and Integration

- **Description**: Slowly bring awareness back to the breath, body, and senses. Open the eyes and re-engage with the outer world from this clarified state.

- **Purpose**: To integrate realization into daily life. The clarity cultivated through chamsa should inform one's behavior, relationships, and presence, aligning with both Taoist spontaneity and the Zen Ox-herding picture of reentering the world with open hands (Dumoulin, 2005; Yang, 1997).

Chamsa Meditation Progression

Face Visualization — Eyes closed, visualize your own face in full detail

Dissolution of the Face — Allow the face image to blur, dissolve, fade

Witness Inquiry — Ask, "Who is seeing this image?" or "Who am I?"

Womb Regression — Visualize within your mother's womb

Original Face — Ask, "What was your original face before your parents were born?"

Return & Integration — Gently return to your body and the external world

III. Practice Progression: Gradual vs. Cyclical

Progressive Practice (for most practitioners)

Stage	Timeframe	Developmental Aim
Face Visualization	1–2 weeks	Image clarity, stillness
Dissolution	1–2 weeks	Letting go, self-inquiry begins
Inquiry	2+ weeks	Direct experience of the observer
Womb Regression	Variable	Comfort with silence and non-conceptual being
Original Face	Ongoing	Insight into emptiness and non-duality

This mirrors the traditional model used in both Zen training and Taoist alchemical refinement (Komjathy, 2013; Dumoulin, 2005).

Cyclical Practice (for advanced practitioners)

Experienced meditators may move through all stages in a single sitting. This is often employed in advanced *neigong, zazen,* or during spiritual retreats (Yang, 1997).

IV. Chamsa and Enlightenment

1. As a Route to Enlightenment

Chamsa progressively dismantles the layers of self-identity. It leads to *direct realization* of formless presence, making it consistent with both Zen's gradual approach and Taoism's return to source (Aitken,1990; Komjathy, 2013).

2. As an Expression of Enlightenment

At deeper levels, the practice becomes a *reflection of the awakened state*. It is used not to attain enlightenment, but to maintain presence and live from insight (Dumoulin, 2005).

"The enlightened one returns to the marketplace with open hands." — Zen Ox-Herding Picture #10

V. Comparative Models of Enlightenment

Aspect	Chamsa	Zen Buddhism	Taoist Alchemy	Tibetan Dzogchen
Starting Point	Visualization of face	Hwadu or breath focus	Jing → Qi → Shen transmutation	Rigpa recognition
Key Turning Point	Dissolution and womb regression	"Great doubt" or koan resolution	Return to origin	Breakthrough to spontaneous presence
Final Aim	Witnessing the "original face"	Satori, then integration	Unity with Tao	Recognition of non-dual awareness
Method	Visual inquiry & regression	Self-inquiry & zazen	Breath, energy, visualization	Direct pointing-out instruction
Expression	Calm presence, embodied wisdom	Actionless action, compassion	Spontaneity, longevity, clarity	Effortless awareness, freedom

VI. Conclusion: Returning to the Formless Mirror

Chamsa meditation is both a method and a metaphor: a way of seeing the self by watching it dissolve. It begins with the familiar image of the face and guides the practitioner back to the unconditioned awareness before identity, thought, and time.

Whether used as a route to insight or a means of stabilization, Chamsa bridges Korean, Taoist, and Buddhist traditions. It reveals that the journey inward is not a retreat, but a return to that which has always been present.

"To know the self is to forget the self. To forget the self is to be enlightened by all things."
— Dōgen Zenji, *Genjōkōan*

References:

Aitken, R. (1990). *The Gateless Barrier: The Wu-Men Kuan (Mumonkan)*. North Point Press. https://archive.org/details/gatelessbarrierw0000aitk

Dumoulin, H. (2005). *Zen Buddhism: A History (Vol. 2: Japan)*. World Wisdom. Zen Buddhism : a history : Dumoulin, Heinrich : Free Download, Borrow, and Streaming : Internet Archive

Kim, C. (2018). Korean shamanism. In *Routledge eBooks*. https://doi.org/10.4324/9781315198156

Kohn, L. (1993). *The Taoist Experience: An Anthology*. SUNY Press. https://archive.org/details/thetaoistexperienceliviakohn

Komjathy, L. (2013). *The Daoist Tradition: An Introduction*. Bloomsbury Academic. https://www.bloomsbury.com/us/daoist-tradition-9781441168733/

Yang, J. (1997). *The Root of Chinese Qigong: Secrets of Health, Longevity, and Enlightenment*. YMAA. https://archive.org/details/therootofchineseqigongbyyangjwingming1997

Appendix I – 8 Vessels Matrix of Exercises

8 Vessels Ship Pal Gye Qigong Sets	Posture 1	Posture 2	Posture 3
Set #1 - introduction to basic stances and hand positions. Focus on proper body alignments.			
Set #2 - Various hand positions with more concern towards the wrists			
Set #3 - Combination of sets 1 & 2, requiring more thought and coordination			
Set #4 - Increased focus on wrist, elbow & shoulder			
Set #5 - Increased focus on fingers, wrist, elbow, shoulder and the meridians that they effect			
Set #6 - Similar benefits as all previous with more attention to the spine			
Set #7 - Extra attention to the spine and fingers			
Set #8 - Most strenuous with added focus to all joints & muscles.			

Appendix J – Emotional Energetics: Energy Vampires & Energy Suns

A Research-Supported Perspective on Human Energetic Influence

Human beings continuously influence one another through subtle behavioral, emotional, and physiological exchanges. Although the phrases "energy vampire" and "energy sun" originate from popular psychology, research from social neuroscience, organizational studies, and communication science supports the underlying concepts. These metaphors capture two recognizable interpersonal patterns. Some individuals leave others feeling depleted, tense, or emotionally burdened. Others create an atmosphere of ease, motivation, and uplift. Scientific findings show that these effects are not imagined. The emotional tone of individuals spreads through groups, shapes perceptions of social environments, influences health, and even alters network-level performance.

Emotional Contagion as the Foundation of Energetic Influence

One of the most robust frameworks supporting these ideas is **emotional contagion**, the automatic transmission of mood between individuals. Hatfield, Cacioppo, and Rapson (1994) demonstrated that people unconsciously mimic facial expressions, posture, vocal tone, and behavioral cues. These physical micro-responses alter the observer's own emotional state. When someone with chronic negativity enters a room, others may mirror their tension or irritability. When someone with warmth or enthusiasm enters, others tend to "catch" that energy instead.

Laboratory and field studies confirm this spreading effect. Group emotional tone shifts in measurable ways based on the mood of a single individual (Barsade, 2002). Even incidental exposure to positive or negative emotional expressions influences subsequent behavior. For instance, Kramer et al. (2014) found that altering the emotional content of social media feeds changed the emotional tone of users' own posts. This suggests that emotional contagion is so fundamental that it occurs in digital environments without direct face-to-face interaction.

These findings support the core distinction between "energy vampires" and "energy suns." The former transmits emotional states that narrow cognitive flexibility and elevate tension. The latter transmits states that promote openness, collaboration, and psychological ease.

Positive and Negative Energizers in Organizational Research

Within organizational psychology, there exists a well-developed framework that parallels this conceptual language. Researchers studying **positive relational energy** have identified individuals known as **positive energizers**. These people elevate motivation, creativity, and performance among peers (Cameron, 2012). Positive energizers are consistently described as supportive, trustworthy, solution oriented, and meaning oriented. They communicate hope, strength, and possibility. Teams with a high concentration of positive energizers demonstrate better job satisfaction, higher collaboration, and stronger organizational commitment.

Negative energizers are the opposite. They are sometimes referred to as "black holes" due to their draining effect (Baker, 2020). Their communication style often includes cynicism, complaint, emotional volatility, or self-focused interaction. Research mapping organizational networks shows that individuals who are widely perceived as negative energizers reduce the quality of teamwork and the performance of those around them. Notably, relational energy has been found to be more predictive of employee performance than information flow or hierarchical position (Cameron, 2012). In other words, how someone makes others feel is more important than how much technical authority they possess.

This research provides direct empirical support for distinguishing between "energy vampires" and "energy suns" in group dynamics.

Social Relationships, Stress Physiology, and Health

The effects of draining or nourishing individuals extend beyond mood. They influence physiology. Social isolation and chronically negative relationships are strongly associated with elevated stress hormones, heightened inflammation, and increased risk of depression and mortality (Holt-Lunstad et al., 2015). Conversely, emotionally supportive relationships act as buffers against stress. For example, women who received a brief supportive gesture from their romantic partners before a stressful task showed significantly reduced cortisol responses during the task (Grewen et al., 2003). Physiological synchrony also occurs within relationships. Partners' cortisol levels often rise and fall together, demonstrating a biochemical form of emotional contagion (Liu et al., 2013). A highly reactive or negative individual can elevate the stress physiology of those around them. A calm and emotionally regulated person can have the opposite effect.

These findings again support the idea that "energy vampires" consume psychological and physiological resources, while "energy suns" replenish them.

Social Networks and Life Satisfaction

Large-scale studies show that the structure and emotional quality of one's social network predict well-being. People with more positive, frequent social contacts report greater life satisfaction, better cognitive functioning, and healthier aging (Litwin & Shiovitz-Ezra, 2011). Negative social ties predict stress, emotional exhaustion, and lower resilience.

Energy Vampire vs. Energy Sun: Comparison

Category	Energy Vampire	Energy Sun
General Impact	Drains emotional resources; leaves others feeling heavy or tense	Replenishes emotional resources; leaves others feeling uplifted and clear
Emotional Contagion	Spreads negativity, irritability, or fear	Spreads calm, optimism, and emotional ease
Communication Style	Dominates conversations; complains; criticizes; focuses on problems	Communicates supportively; encourages; listens with presence; focuses on solutions
Effect on Group Dynamics	Reduces cohesion; causes withdrawal and decreased creativity	Increases cohesion; enhances engagement and creativity
Physiological Influence	Elevates stress responses; contributes to tension and emotional fatigue	Lowers stress; promotes relaxation and psychological safety
Behavioral Patterns	Seeks attention or validation; projects blame; emotionally reactive	Shares credit; takes responsibility; maintains emotional steadiness
Social Network Outcome	Creates toxic or draining relational patterns; weakens morale	Creates nourishing networks; strengthens morale and resilience
Resulting Environment	Heavy, tense, unmotivated atmosphere	Warm, collaborative, energized atmosphere

While the terminology of "energy vampire" is metaphorical, the pattern aligns with empirically observed **toxic social exchanges**, characterized by constant criticism, excessive neediness, hostility, or emotional unpredictability. These relationships create cognitive load and drain psychological resources. The opposite pattern, nourishing and emotionally attuned relationships, aligns with "energy sun" qualities that brighten and stabilize group interactions.

The metaphors of "energy vampires" and "energy suns" are vivid representations of patterns strongly supported by scientific research. Emotional contagion explains how individuals transmit their inner states to others. Organizational studies show that positive or negative energizers dramatically influence group performance and satisfaction. Social neuroscience demonstrates that supportive or hostile interactions directly influence stress physiology. Network studies confirm that emotionally nourishing relationships consistently predict well-being and resilience.

In holistic health, psychology, and social dynamics, these insights converge into a simple but powerful truth. Individuals who enter a room have the capacity to uplift or deplete the collective environment. Recognizing these patterns allows people to cultivate protective boundaries, encourage energizing relationships, and consciously embody the qualities that make them an "energy sun" in the lives of others.

References:

Baker, W., Cross, R., & Wooten, M. (2003). Positive organizational network analysis and energizing relationships. In K. S. Cameron, J. E. Dutton, & R. E. Quinn (Eds.), *Positive Organizational Scholarship: Foundations of a New Discipline* (pp. 328–342). San Francisco, CA: Berrett-Koehler.

Barsade, S. G. (2002). The ripple effect: Emotional contagion and its influence on group behavior. *Administrative Science Quarterly, 47*(4), 644–675. https://doi.org/10.2307/3094912

Cameron, K. S. (2012). *Positive leadership: Strategies for extraordinary performance.* Berrett-Koehler.

Grewen, K. M., Anderson, B. J., Girdler, S. S., & Light, K. C. (2003). Warm partner contact is related to lower cardiovascular reactivity. *Behavioral Medicine, 29*(3), 123–130. https://doi.org/10.1080/08964280309596065

Hatfield, E., Cacioppo, J. T., & Rapson, R. L. (1994). *Emotional contagion.* Cambridge University Press.

Holt-Lunstad, J., Smith, T., Baker, M., Harris, T., & Stephenson, D. (2015). Loneliness and social isolation as risk factors for mortality. *Perspectives on Psychological Science, 10*(2), 227–237. https://doi.org/10.1177/1745691614568352

Kramer, A. D. I., Guillory, J. E., & Hancock, J. T. (2014). Experimental evidence of massive-scale emotional contagion through social networks. *Proceedings of the National Academy of Sciences, 111*(24), 8788–8790. https://doi.org/10.1073/pnas.1320040111

Litwin, H., & Shiovitz-Ezra, S. (2011). Social network type and subjective well-being in later life. *The Gerontologist, 51*(3), 379–388. https://doi.org/10.1093/geront/gnq094

Liu, S., Rovine, M. J., Klein, L. C., & Almeida, D. M. (2013). Synchrony of diurnal cortisol pattern in couples. *Journal of Family Psychology, 27*(4), 579–588. https://doi.org/10.1037/a0033735

Epilogue - The Journey Continues

Embodying Hermetic Wisdom in a Changing World

Every journey eventually returns to its beginning, but with new eyes. This manuscript has traced the contours of Hermeticism through history, philosophy, psychology, alchemy, and lived human experience. It has explored the Seven Principles and the essential Eighth Principle of Virtue, not as abstract doctrines but as living dynamics within the body, mind, and spirit.

It has shown how the Warrior, Scholar, and Sage reflect the developmental arc of humankind; how trauma, suffering, and adversity become crucibles of transformation; and how service, ethics, and luminous presence arise as the natural expression of the matured soul. Yet despite the depth and breadth of these explorations, the Hermetic path remains fundamentally simple:

>*Know yourself.*
>*Refine yourself.*
>*Serve the world.*

This simple triad reflects the rhythm of the Great Work: inward, upward, outward.
A cycle as ancient as human consciousness itself.

The Adept's Work in a Fragmented Age

The world the reader inhabits is not the world of ancient Egypt, Greece, or early modern Europe. It is a world of rapid technological advancement, social fragmentation, chronic stress, emotional dysregulation, and an unprecedented collapse of meaning. In such an age, Hermetic principles are not relics, but they are necessities.

The Principle of Mentalism reminds individuals that perception shapes reality in a world overwhelmed by information.

The Principle of Correspondence offers coherence in a culture that feels increasingly incoherent.

The Principle of Vibration teaches regulation in an era dominated by anxiety and speed.

The Principle of Polarity brings nuance in a civilization caught in extremism.

The Principle of Rhythm restores balance in a society that has forgotten rest.

The Principle of Cause and Effect restores accountability within systems that reward impulsivity.

The Principle of Gender heals the split between action and receptivity, structure and empathy.

And **Virtue, the Eighth and balancing principle** anchors all of these in ethical coherence.

In this context, the Hermetic adept becomes not an esoteric mystic but a stabilizing force in a volatile world.

The Lived Path Beyond the Page

The Hermetic path cannot be mastered through reading alone. It is learned in:

- relationships
- breath
- conflict
- stillness
- decisions
- boundaries
- failures
- compassion
- grief
- joy
- solitude
- service

It is lived in the ordinary as much as in the extraordinary. It is expressed through small acts of courage, daily choices aligned with virtue, and the steady cultivation of emotional and ethical maturity.

The reader who has walked through the preceding chapters is now equipped not with final answers but with enduring principles, keys that unlock deeper understanding as life unfolds.

Hermeticism invites continual practice rather than attainment. Mastery is not a destination but a mode of being.

The Light Carried Forward

Every person who integrates Hermetic wisdom becomes a point of light, small at first, then brighter, eventually illuminating the lives of others. Not through force, persuasion, or spiritual performance, but through:

- steadiness in uncertainty
- kindness in conflict
- clarity amidst confusion
- integrity under pressure
- humility in accomplishment
- compassion toward suffering
- courage in ethical decisions

This light does not belong to the individual; it moves through them. It is the manifestation of the Great Work made visible. In this way, the Hermetic adept becomes a quiet but powerful influence on the social, relational, and moral fabric of the world. Collective evolution begins with individual coherence, and the reader now carrying the insights of Hermeticism contributes to that evolution simply by living with awareness, virtue, and depth.

The Invitation

The Great Work does not end with understanding. It begins with embodiment.

This book offers a framework, a mirror, and a set of tools, but the path itself unfolds in the reader's breath, relationships, challenges, and choices. The invitation of Hermeticism is ongoing: to return again and again to the principles, to refine perception, to cultivate presence, and to act with courage and compassion.

There will be moments of clarity and moments of confusion. Times of expansion and times of contraction. Periods of service and periods of retreat. Phases of insight and phases of integration. This is not failure. It is Rhythm. It is life. And throughout these cycles, the adept returns to the center, the still axis around which experience turns.

A Final Word

The world does not need more information, more dogma, or more division. It needs individuals of depth, coherence, character, and compassion.

Individuals who embody the truths they aspire to.

Individuals who refine their inner world before attempting to influence the outer one.

Individuals who carry light without arrogance.

Individuals who understand that wisdom is service.

Individuals who cultivate the Warrior's stability, the Scholar's clarity, and the Sage's compassion until these three become one.

This is the Great Work. This is the path of the Hermetic adept. And this journey, subtle, profound, and lifelong, now continues in the hands of the reader.

Chart of the Hermetic Principles and Relevance to the I Ching

Hermetic Principle	I Ching / Bagua Equivalent	Relevance
1. Mentalism "The All is Mind."	The Tao / Wu Ji	*Divergence.* Hermeticism views the source as an active "Mind." Taoism views it as an ineffable "Void" or flow. They agree on a non-material source, but the "flavor" is different (Active Thought vs. Passive Begetting).
2. Correspondence "As above, so below."	Heaven, Earth, Man (San Cai)	*High Relevance.* The I Ching is based on the idea that the microcosm (a coin toss or a hexagram) perfectly reflects the macrocosm (the universe's current state).
3. Vibration "Everything moves."	Qi (Chi)	*High Relevance.* Trigrams represent different "frequencies" or elemental states of Qi (e.g., Fire moves upward/rapidly; Mountain is still/slow vibration).
4. Polarity "Everything has opposites."	Yin / Yang	*Direct Relevance.* The fundamental binary code of the I Ching.
5. Rhythm "Everything flows, out and in."	The Cycles of Change	*High Relevance.* The I Ching is the "Book of Changes." It tracks the rhythmic shift from one state to another (e.g., Night to Day, Winter to Spring).
6. Cause and Effect "Every cause has its effect."	Karma / Yuan	*Moderate Relevance.* The I Ching teaches that a specific action (cause) in a specific moment leads to a specific outcome (fortune/misfortune), though it focuses more on *timing* than mechanical causality.
7. Gender "Gender is in everything."	Qian (Male) / Kun (Female)	*Direct Relevance.* As noted above, the Trigrams are explicitly categorized as a family unit of father, mother, and children.

References

Barrett, L. F. (2017). *How emotions are made: The secret life of the brain*. Houghton Mifflin Harcourt.

Bargh, J. A., & Chartrand, T. L. (1999). The unbearable automaticity of being. *American Psychologist, 54*(7), 462–479. https://doi.org/10.1037/0003-066X.54.7.462

Bass, B.M., & Riggio, R.E. (2006). Transformational Leadership (2nd ed.). Psychology Press. https://doi.org/10.4324/9781410617095

Bass, B. M., & Riggio, R. E. (2006). *Transformational leadership* (2nd ed.). Lawrence Erlbaum Associates Publishers. https://doi.org/10.4324/9781410617095

Beck, A. T. (1976). *Cognitive therapy and the emotional disorders*. International Universities Press.

Brewer, J. A., Worhunsky, P. D., Gray, J. R., Tang, Y., Weber, J., & Kober, H. (2011). Meditation experience is associated with differences in default mode network activity and connectivity. *Proceedings of the National Academy of Sciences, 108*(50), 20254–20259. https://doi.org/10.1073/pnas.1112029108

Campion, N. (2008). A history of western astrology: Volume II. Continuum.

Cashwell, C. S., Bentley, P. B., & Yarborough, J. P. (2007). The only way out is through: the peril of spiritual bypass. *Counseling and Values, 51*(2), 139–148. https://doi.org/10.1002/j.2161-007x.2007.tb00071.x

Christakis, N. A., & Fowler, J. H. (2009). *Connected: The surprising power of our social networks and how they shape our lives*. Little, Brown.

Clark, A. (2013). *Whatever next? Predictive brains, situated agents, and the future of cognitive science. Behavioral and Brain Sciences, 36*(3), 181–204. https://doi.org/10.1017/S0140525X12000477

Clear, J. (2018). *Atomic habits: An easy & proven way to build good habits and break bad ones*. Avery.

Copenhaver, B. P. (1992). Hermetica: The Greek Corpus Hermeticum and the Latin Asclepius in a new English translation. Cambridge University Press.

Cozolino, L. (2014). *The neuroscience of human relationships: Attachment and the developing social brain* (2nd ed.). W. W. Norton & Company.

Craig, A. D. (2008). How do you feel — now? The anterior insula and human awareness. *Nature Reviews. Neuroscience, 10*(1), 59–70. https://doi.org/10.1038/nrn2555

Crum, A. J., Salovey, P., & Achor, S. (2013). Rethinking stress: The role of mindsets in determining the stress response. *Journal of Personality and Social Psychology, 104*(4), 716–733. https://doi.org/10.1037/a0031201

Czeisler, C. A. (1999). Stability, precision, and near-24-hour period of the human circadian pacemaker. *Science, 284*(5423), 2177–2181. https://doi.org/10.1126/science.284.5423.2177

Damasio, A. (1999). *The feeling of what happens: Body and emotion in the making of consciousness*. Harcourt Brace.

Doidge, N. (2007). *The brain that changes itself: Stories of personal triumph from the frontiers of brain science*. Viking Press.

Duhigg, C. (2012). *The power of habit: Why we do what we do in life and business*. Random House. https://dn790007.ca.archive.org/0/items/CharlesDuhigg.ThePowerOfHabit_201808/Charles-Duhigg.The-Power-of-Habit.pdf

Foster, R. (2021). *Life time: The new science of the body clock, and how it can revolutionize your sleep and health*. Penguin Random House.

Fowden, G. (1993). The Egyptian Hermes: A historical approach to the late pagan mind. Princeton University Press. https://archive.org/details/egyptianhermeshi0000fowd

Frankl, V. E. (2006). *Man's search for meaning* (Revised and updated ed.). Beacon Press.

Gigerenzer, G. (2007). Gut feelings: The intelligence of the unconscious. Viking Press.

Godwin, J. (2017). The Hermetic tradition: Symbols and teachings of the Hermeticists. Inner Traditions.

Goleman, D. (2006). *Social intelligence: The revolutionary new science of human relationships*. Bantam Books. https://archive.org/details/socialintelligen0000gole_k0p5

Haidt, J. (2024). *The anxious generation: How the great rewiring of childhood is causing an epidemic of mental illness—and what we can do about it*. Penguin Press.

Herman, J. L. (1992). *Trauma and recovery: The aftermath of violence—from domestic abuse to political terror*. Basic Books. https://ia803207.us.archive.org/14/items/radfem-books/Trauma%20and%20Recovery_%20The%20Afterm%20-%20Judith%20L.%20Herman.pdf

Initiates, T., (1862–1932). (2013). *The Kybalion*. YOGeBooks: Hollister, MO. https://www.yogebooks.com/english/atkinson/1908kybalion.pdf

Jung, C.G. (1959). Aion: Researches Into the Phenomenology of the Self (1st ed.). Routledge. https://doi.org/10.4324/9781315725543

Jung, C. G. (1968). Alchemical studies (R. F. C. Hull, Trans.). Princeton University Press. https://www.jungiananalysts.org.uk/wp-content/uploads/2018/07/C.-G.-Jung-Collected-Works-Volume-13_-Alchemical-Studies.pdf

Kashdan, T. B., & Rottenberg, J. (2010). Psychological flexibility as a fundamental aspect of health. Clinical Psychology Review, 30(7), 865–878. https://doi.org/10.1016/j.cpr.2010.03.001

Kegan, R. (1994). *In Over Our Heads: The Mental Demands of Modern Life*. Harvard University Press. https://doi.org/10.2307/j.ctv1pncpfb

Keltner, D. (2009). *Born to be good: The science of a meaningful life*. W. W. Norton & Company.

Kohn, L. (2009). *The Taoist experience: An anthology*. SUNY Press. https://archive.org/details/thetaoistexperienceliviakohn

Kohlberg, L. (1981–1984). *Essays on moral development* (Vols. 1–2). Harper & Row.

Leiberg, S., Klimecki, O., & Singer, T. (2011). Short-Term compassion training increases prosocial behavior in a newly developed prosocial game. *PLOS One*. https://doi.org/10.1371/journal.pone.0017798

Lissak, G. (2018). Adverse physiological and psychological effects of screen time on children and adolescents: Literature review and case study. *Environmental Research, 164*, 149–157. https://doi.org/10.1016/j.envres.2018.01.015

Lutz, A., Dunne, J. D., & Davidson, R. J. (2007). Meditation and the neuroscience of consciousness: An introduction. In P. D. Zelazo, M. Moscovitch, & E. Thompson (Eds.), The Cambridge handbook of consciousness (pp. 499–551). Cambridge University Press. https://doi.org/10.1017/CBO9780511816789.020

Maslow, A. (1962). *Toward a psychology of being.* D Van Nostrand. https://doi.org/10.1037/10793-000

McEwen, B. S. (2011). The ever-changing brain: Cellular and molecular mechanisms for the effects of stressful experiences. Developmental Neurobiology, 72(6), 878–890. https://doi.org/10.1002/dneu.20968

McEwen B. S. (2012). The ever-changing brain: cellular and molecular mechanisms for the effects of stressful experiences. *Developmental neurobiology, 72*(6), 878–890. https://doi.org/10.1002/dneu.20968

McKnight, P. E., & Kashdan, T. B. (2009). Purpose in Life as a System that Creates and Sustains Health and Well-Being: An Integrative, Testable Theory. *Review of General Psychology, 13*(3), 242-251. https://doi.org/10.1037/a0017152

Miller, E. K., & Cohen, J. D. (2001). An integrative theory of prefrontal cortex function. *Annual Review of Neuroscience, 24*, 167–202. https://doi.org/10.1146/annurev.neuro.24.1.167

Park, C. L. (2010). Making sense of the meaning literature: An integrative review of meaning making and its effects on adjustment to stressful life events. *Psychological Bulletin, 136*(2), 257–301. https://doi.org/10.1037/a0018301

Pennebaker, J. W., & Chung, C. K. (2011). Expressive writing and its links to emotional and physical health. In H. S. Friedman (Ed.), *The Oxford handbook of health psychology* (pp. 417–437). Oxford University Press.

Peper, E., Harvey, R., Cuellar, Y., & Membrila, C. (2022). Reduce anxiety. *NeuroRegulation, 9*(2), 91–97. https://doi.org/10.15540/nr.9.2.91

Porges, S. W. (2011). *The polyvagal theory: Neurophysiological foundations of emotions, attachment, communication, and self-regulation.* W. W. Norton & Company.

Principe, L. M. (2013). The secrets of alchemy. University of Chicago Press.

Ratey, J. J., & Hagerman, E. (Collaborator). (2008). Spark: The revolutionary new science of exercise and the brain. Little, Brown and Co.

Rest, J. (1986). *Moral development: Advances in research and theory.* Praeger. https://archive.org/details/moraldevelopment0000rest

Richards, Ruth. (2018). Everyday Creativity and the Healthy Mind: Dynamic New Paths for Self and Society. 10.1057/978-1-137-55766-7.

Sapolsky, R. M. (2004). Why zebras don't get ulcers: The acclaimed guide to stress, stress-related diseases, and coping (3rd ed.). Henry Holt & Company

Seligman, M. E. P. (1975). *Helplessness: On depression, development, and death.* W H Freeman/Times Books/ Henry Holt & Co.

Siegel, D. J. (2012). *The developing mind: How relationships and the brain interact to shape who we are* (2nd ed.). Guilford Press.

Tedeschi, R. G., & Calhoun, L. G. (2004). Posttraumatic growth: Conceptual foundations and empirical evidence. *Psychological Inquiry, 15*(1), 1–18. https://doi.org/10.1207/s15327965pli1501_01

Tversky, A., & Kahneman, D. (1974). Judgment under uncertainty: Heuristics and biases. *Science, 185*(4157), 1124–1131. https://doi.org/10.1126/science.185.4157.1124

van der Kolk, B. A. (2014). *The body keeps the score: Brain, mind, and body in the healing of trauma*. Viking. https://ia601604.us.archive.org/35/items/the-body-keeps-the-score-pdf/The-Body-Keeps-the-Score-PDF.pdf

Teasdale, J. D., Segal, Z. V., Williams, J. M., Ridgeway, V. A., Soulsby, J. M., & Lau, M. A. (2000). Prevention of relapse/recurrence in major depression by mindfulness-based cognitive therapy. *Journal of consulting and clinical psychology, 68*(4), 615–623. https://doi.org/10.1037//0022-006x.68.4.615

Yates, F. A. (1964). Giordano Bruno and the Hermetic tradition. University of Chicago Press. https://archive.org/details/giordanobrunoher0000yate

Zaccaro, A., Piarulli, A., Laurino, M., Garbella, E., Menicucci, D., Neri, B., & Gemignani, A. (2018). How breath-control can change your life: A systematic review on psychophysiological correlates of slow breathing. *Frontiers in Human Neuroscience, 12*, 353. https://doi.org/10.3389/fnhum.2018.00353

Glossary of Terms

A

Activation Energy (Behavioral Science)

The initial mental effort required to begin an action or habit; lowering activation energy increases compliance and behavior change.

Adaptive Capacity (Psychology / Resilience)

The ability to adjust to stressors while maintaining psychological and physiological integrity.

Adept

An individual who has progressed significantly along the Hermetic path through study, practice, integration, and ethical development. Adepts embody the principles of the Great Work in thought, behavior, and presence.

Albedo (Alchemy)

The "whitening" phase following *nigredo*, representing purification, insight, and psychological clarity.

Alchemy

Originally referring to material and spiritual transmutation, alchemy symbolizes the inner work of transforming the raw material of human experience—suffering, shadow, ignorance—into wisdom, virtue, and illumination.

Allostatic Load (Neuroscience / Physiology)

The cumulative strain on bodily systems from repeated or chronic stress; central to trauma, burnout, and autonomic dysregulation.

Anxiety Response Loop (Neuroscience)

A self-reinforcing cycle of threat perception, autonomic activation, and cognitive interpretation.

Archetype (Jungian Psychology)

Universal symbolic patterns such as the Warrior, Scholar, Sage, Shadow, or Self that structure human behavior and meaning.

As Above, So Below (Hermeticism)

A central axiom of the Principle of Correspondence, asserting parallel dynamics between inner and outer realities.

B

Balance

The dynamic equilibrium between polar forces (e.g., masculine/feminine, action/rest, expansion/contraction). Balance is not static but rhythmic, responsive, and adaptive.

Boundary Formation (Psychology)

The internal and external limits that protect energy, safety, identity, and integrity.

Breathwork (Physiology / Trauma Science)

Intentional regulation of breathing to influence the autonomic nervous system, emotional state, and cognitive clarity.

Burning the Chong Mai (Daoist Cultivation)

A Taoist energetic method for strengthening the thrusting vessel to enhance vertical integration of Jing, Qi, and Shen.

Bounded Choice (Sociology / Coercive Systems)

A psychological state in which individuals appear to have autonomy but operate within tightly restricted options constructed by a high-control environment.

C

Cause and Effect, Principle of (Hermeticism)

The doctrine that nothing happens by chance and all events arise from prior causes—internal, external, or symbolic.

Central Nervous System (Neuroscience)

Composed of the brain and spinal cord; governs cognition, emotion, behavior, and perception.

Chong Mai (Traditional Chinese Medicine)

The thrusting vessel; a deep, central meridian associated with vitality, emotional grounding, and psycho-energetic stability.

Cognitive Dissonance (Psychology)

The discomfort caused by conflicting beliefs or behaviors, often resolved through rationalization or meaning-making—central to cult dynamics and trauma narratives.

Cognitive Reappraisal (Psychology)

A strategy that reframes an emotional event to alter its meaning and psychological impact.

Co-Regulation (Polyvagal Theory / Attachment Science)

The process by which the nervous systems of two individuals influence and stabilize each other through cues of safety, presence, and attunement. Essential for trauma recovery and relational healing.

Coniunctio (Jungian Alchemy)

The symbolic union of opposites—conscious/unconscious, masculine/feminine, light/shadow—representing mature individuation.

Conjunction

An alchemical term describing the fusion of opposites—masculine and feminine, conscious and unconscious—into a unified whole.

Correspondence, Principle of (Hermeticism)

The idea that patterns repeat across levels of reality (microcosm ↔ macrocosm), allowing spiritual, psychological, and physical systems to mirror one another.

Cortisol (Physiology)

A stress hormone regulating energy release, immune response, focus, and threat perception.

Critical Thinking (Psychology / Philosophy)

The disciplined process of evaluating information, assumptions, and beliefs—central to the Scholar archetype.

D

Dark Night of the Soul (Mystical Psychology)

A profound psychological descent characterized by disorientation, loss of meaning, and emotional collapse preceding transformation.

Default Mode Network (Neuroscience)

A brain system responsible for self-referential thinking, autobiographical memory, and rumination; modulated by meditation, breathwork, and trauma.

De (德)

A Taoist term meaning "virtue," "inner power," or "moral radiance." It reflects the luminous presence that emerges from inner alignment and ethical behavior.

Destiny

In Hermeticism, destiny is not predetermination, but a field of potential shaped by one's nature, environment, choices, and development. Destiny interacts with free will rather than negating it.

Dopamine (Neurochemistry)

A neurotransmitter involved in motivation, reward, curiosity, and goal-directed behavior; foundational to habit formation.

Dysregulation (Trauma Science)

Instability in autonomic arousal (sympathetic or parasympathetic), often resulting from trauma, chronic stress, or manipulation.

E

Ego Strength (Psychology)

Resilience, identity coherence, and the capacity to make grounded decisions under pressure.

Ego Death (Transpersonal Psychology)

Temporary dissolution of self-boundaries, often arising through meditation, trauma, or mystical states.

Eighth Principle (Virtue)

The ethical foundation that balances the seven Hermetic principles. Virtue ensures that knowledge and power are applied responsibly, compassionately, and wisely.

Emanation

The process through which higher principles or states of being unfold into lower or more material forms. Similar to the descent of consciousness into physical experience.

Emergence (Systems Theory)

Higher-order patterns or functions arising from interaction among simpler components; central to consciousness, social behavior, and Hermetic metaphysics.

Emotional Alchemy (Hermetic / Psychological)

The transformative process of converting primitive emotional reactions into clarity, insight, and constructive action.

Emotional Contagion (Social Psychology)

The automatic transmission of emotional states between individuals—relevant to leadership, manipulation, and group dynamics.

Equanimity (Contemplative Psychology)

A stable, balanced state of mind that maintains clarity in the presence of emotional intensity.

Entrainment (Physiology / Neuroscience)

The natural process by which one system's rhythm synchronizes with another, such as breath, emotion, or energy aligning with external or interpersonal cues.

Ethical Presence (Leadership / Hermetic Psychology)

Influence rooted in integrity, steadiness, coherence, and alignment—not authority or coercion.

F

Fight–Flight–Freeze–Fawn (Trauma Physiology)

Four instinctive survival responses mediated by the autonomic nervous system; highly relevant to manipulative group dynamics.

Flow State (Positive Psychology)

A highly focused, immersive state in which challenge and skill are balanced—representing the Scholar's refined engagement.

Frontal Cortex (Neuroscience)

The region responsible for executive function, decision-making, impulse control, and moral reasoning—often compromised under chronic stress or coercion.

Free Will

The capacity to act intentionally, ethically, and consciously within the structure of destiny. Free will influences how one interprets and responds to life events.

Frequency, Principle of (Hermeticism)

Also known as the Principle of Vibration: all things exist in states of motion or oscillation; emotional and mental states can be intentionally shifted.

G

Gamma Waves (Neurophysiology)

High-frequency brainwaves associated with insight, integration, and moments of holistic understanding; often elevated during meditative clarity.

Gender, Principle of (Hermeticism)

The Hermetic principle describing the interplay of active (masculine) and receptive (feminine) forces present in all things, not limited to biological sex.

Gestalt (Psychology)

A holistic perspective emphasizing that the whole is greater than the sum of its parts—relevant to identity, trauma integration, and Hermetic unity.

Great Work

The central pursuit of Hermeticism: the lifelong refinement of the self through understanding, integration, and ethical action. The Great Work culminates in luminous presence and service to others.

Grounding (Somatic Psychology)

Regulating the nervous system by orienting attention to physical sensation, breath, or present-moment stability.

Groupthink (Social Psychology)

A cognitive bias in which group cohesion suppresses dissent and critical thinking—characteristic of high-control environments.

H

Habituation (Neuroscience)

A decrease in response to repeated stimuli; relevant to trauma desensitization, meditation, and habit formation.

Hawthorne Effect (Social Psychology)

The alteration of behavior when individuals know they are being observed; relevant to manipulation and self-awareness.

Heart Rate Variability (HRV) (Physiology)

A measure of autonomic flexibility and resilience; higher HRV corresponds with emotional regulation and parasympathetic activation.

Hemispheric Integration (Neuroscience)

Communication between the brain's left and right hemispheres, supporting emotional balance, creativity, and cognitive flexibility.

Hermes Trismegistus

A legendary syncretic figure combining elements of the Greek god Hermes and the Egyptian god Thoth. Considered the founder of Hermetic philosophy.

Hermetic Adept (Hermeticism)

One who embodies the principles of the Great Work through virtue, awareness, and refined action.

Hermetica

The body of ancient texts attributed to Hermes Trismegistus, containing philosophical, mystical, and cosmological teachings foundational to Hermeticism.

Homeostasis (Physiology)

The body's ability to maintain internal equilibrium; disrupted by chronic stress or trauma and restored through self-regulation practices.

I

Identity Reconstruction (Trauma Recovery / Psychology)

The rebuilding of a coherent self-concept after manipulation, trauma, or ideological dissolution.

Illumination

A heightened state of clarity, insight, and moral awareness resulting from integration, shadow work, and lived experience.

Individuation (Jungian Psychology)

The developmental process of integrating unconscious and conscious elements of the psyche to achieve wholeness.

Inflammatory Cascade (Physiology)

A chain reaction in the immune system triggered by stress, injury, or chronic dysregulation—central to mind–body interaction.

Inner Alchemy (Taoist / Hermetic)

The refinement of Jing, Qi, and Shen—or body, energy, and spirit—into higher consciousness through disciplined practice.

Inner Narrative (Psychology / Neuroscience)

The ongoing internal monologue that shapes identity, meaning, and emotional interpretation.

Interoception (Neuroscience)

The perception of internal bodily sensations (breath, heart rate, visceral states); essential for emotional awareness and self-regulation.

Integration

The unification of the personality—body, mind, emotions, shadow, and spirit—into a coherent whole. Integration is the culmination of the Great Work.

Internal Working Model (Attachment Theory)

Deep, unconscious templates formed early in life that shape expectations in relationships.

Iterative Self-Cultivation (Hermetic / Psychological)

The process of continual refinement through small, repeated actions, aligning with both Hermetic rhythm and modern habit science.

J

Jing (Daoist Physiology)

In Taoist internal alchemy, Jing is "essence"—the physical foundation of vitality. It corresponds to the Warrior archetype (stability, strength, grounding).

Judgment, Ethical (Moral Psychology)

The capacity to discern right action is based on principles rather than fear, impulse, or external pressure.

K

Kairos (Philosophy)

A moment of significance or "right timing," contrasted with chronological time (*chronos*); central to insight and transformation.

Kundalini (Yogic Psychology)

A symbolic representation of latent spiritual energy rising along the spine; parallels Daoist inner fire and Hermetic ascent.

Kybalion

A modern (1908) text distilling key Hermetic principles. Not historically ancient but influential in Western esoteric thought.

L

Lateral Prefrontal Cortex (Neuroscience)

A region associated with planning, discernment, impulse control, and rational thought—strengthened through meditation and weakened by coercion.

Learned Helplessness (Psychology)

A state in which individuals believe they have no control over outcomes, often resulting from trauma or coercive group environments.

Light (Inner Light)

The symbolic and experiential illumination that arises from integration, wisdom, compassion, and ethical alignment. Often referred to as "luminous presence."

Limiting Beliefs (Cognitive Psychology)

Deeply ingrained assumptions that constrain perception or behavior; central to personal transformation work.

Limbic System (Neuroscience)

The emotional center of the brain, mediating fear, attachment, desire, and memory—often dysregulated in trauma.

Logos (Philosophy / Hermeticism)

The underlying order, rational structure, or divine intelligence that manifests through nature and psyche.

M

Macrocosm (Hermeticism)

The larger universe; reflects and interacts with the microcosm of the individual.

Meaning-Making (Psychology)

The process of interpreting life events in ways that support coherence, identity, and growth.

Meditative Absorption (Contemplative Science)

Deep, stable states of attention where sensory noise diminishes and clarity increases.

Mentalism (Principle of)

The principle stating that "The All is Mind." Reality is shaped by consciousness, perception, and thought.

Metacognition (Psychology)

Awareness of one's own thought processes; crucial for discernment and psychological freedom.

Microcosm (Hermeticism)

The individual human being, seen as a miniature reflection of the cosmos.

Moral Injury (Trauma Studies)

Psychological harm resulting from betrayal, unethical environments, or actions that violate one's core values.

Myelination (Neuroscience)

The process of insulating neural pathways for faster conduction; strengthened through repetition and practice.

N

Neuroception (Polyvagal Theory)

The unconscious detection of safety or threat through cues in the environment, shaping autonomic responses.

Neuroplasticity (Neuroscience)

The brain's ability to reorganize and form new neural connections through experience and practice.

Nigredo (Alchemy / Depth Psychology)

The "blackening" phase of dissolution, chaos, and psychic disorientation that precedes purification and renewal.

Nominalization (Psycholinguistics)

Turning dynamic processes into static nouns (e.g., "failure," "weakness"), often obscuring complexity or agency.

Nervous System Regulation (Trauma Science)

The intentional modulation of sympathetic and parasympathetic activation to restore balance and resilience.

Nondual Awareness (Contemplative Psychology)

A state of consciousness in which the perceived boundary between self and world temporarily dissolves.

O

Observer Consciousness (Contemplative Psychology)

The capacity to witness thoughts, emotions, and bodily sensations without identification; foundational to self-regulation and Hermetic mentalism.

Oxytocin (Neurochemistry)

A hormone associated with bonding, trust, social connection, and co-regulation; suppressed by chronic stress or coercive environments.

Ontological Security (Philosophy / Sociology)

A sense of stable identity and worldview; destabilized by trauma, indoctrination, or manipulation.

P

Parasympathetic Nervous System (Physiology)

The "rest-and-digest" branch of the autonomic nervous system responsible for recovery, calmness, and social engagement.

Perception, Principle of (Hermetic / Psychological)

A Hermetic insight that reality is shaped by mental interpretation; mirrors modern predictive processing models in neuroscience.

Personal Agency (Psychology)

The belief that one can act intentionally to influence outcomes; restored through autonomy and individuation.

Pineal Symbolism (Hermetic / Esoteric)

A symbol of spiritual insight, higher perception, and inner illumination; metaphorically connected to awakening or expanded consciousness.

Plasticity, Synaptic (Neuroscience)

Changes in the strength of connections between neurons; the biological basis of learning and habit transformation.

Polarity (Principle of)

The principle that opposites are identical in nature but differ in degree. Applied psychologically, this includes emotional spectrums, cognitive biases, and relational dynamics.

Polyvagal Theory (Neuroscience / Trauma Science)

Stephen Porges' model describing how the vagus nerve mediates safety, connection, and threat responses through three hierarchical states.

Post-Traumatic Growth (Psychology)

Positive transformation emerging from the struggle with significant adversity, leading to deeper meaning, strength, and insight.

Predictive Processing (Neuroscience)

The brain's ongoing attempt to guess incoming sensory information based on past experience; heavily influenced by trauma or conditioning.

Principle of Mentalism (Hermeticism)

The Hermetic doctrine stating "All is Mind," emphasizing consciousness as the underlying substance of reality.

Principle of Rhythm (Hermeticism)

The observation that all phenomena cycle, rise, fall, and oscillate—mirrored in emotional waves, seasons, circadian rhythms, and habit loops.

Principle of Polarity (Hermeticism)

The law that opposites are the same in nature but different in degree, and can transmute into one another.

Projection (Psychology)

Attributing one's disowned emotions, motives, or beliefs onto others; central to shadow dynamics.

Q

Qi (Traditional Chinese Medicine)

Vital energy or life force in Taoist internal cultivation. Qi corresponds to the Scholar archetype (clarity, thought, insight, emotional regulation)

Quieting the Mind (Contemplative Psychology)

Practices that reduce cognitive noise and rumination, allowing greater clarity and equanimity.

R

Reappraisal (Cognitive Psychology)

A cognitive strategy that alters emotional responses by reframing the meaning of a situation.

Resonance (Somatic / Relational Science)

The energetic and physiological synchronization between individuals during safe, attuned connection.

Rhythm (Principle of)

The Hermetic principle stating that all things rise and fall, expand and contract, in predictable cycles. Emotion, motivation, seasons of life, and spiritual growth all follow rhythmic patterns.

Rubedo (Alchemy)

The final red stage of alchemical transformation, representing integration, embodiment, and the completion of the Great Work.

Rumination (Psychology)

Repetitive, passive focus on distress; associated with sympathetic activation and DMN overactivity.

S

Sacred Geometry (Hermetic / Esoteric)

Symbolic mathematical patterns are seen as foundational to nature, consciousness, and the structure of reality.

Sage

The Hermetic archetype representing Shen (spirit). The Sage embodies wisdom, compassion, intuition, and ethical clarity.

Scholar Archetype (Developmental Psychology / Hermetic)

The aspect of the psyche seeking truth, clarity, knowledge, and discernment; associated with Qi.

Self-Actualization (Humanistic Psychology)

The realization of one's potential through authenticity, integration, and meaning-making.

Self-Regulation (Neuroscience / Trauma Science)

The capacity to manage emotional arousal, impulses, and autonomic states through conscious strategies.

Service

The natural outflow of the Great Work. Service arises not from obligation but from overflowing presence, compassion, and virtue.

Shadow (Jungian Psychology)

The unconscious, unintegrated aspects of personality—fears, instincts, and desires disowned or repressed.

Shen (Daoist Psychology)

Spirit or consciousness in Taoist alchemy. Shen corresponds to the Sage archetype (wisdom, compassion, luminous awareness).

Solve et Coagula

An alchemical maxim meaning "dissolve and recombine." It symbolizes breaking down old patterns and integrating them into a higher order.

Somatic Marker (Neuroscience)

Damasio's theory that bodily sensations guide decision-making and intuition.

Somatic Calibration (Psychological / Embodiment)

The alignment of bodily, emotional, and cognitive systems through awareness, breath, posture, and movement.

Somatic Memory (Trauma Science)

The imprint of past experiences held in bodily sensations and autonomic patterns rather than verbal narrative.

Sympathetic Nervous System (Physiology)

The "fight-or-flight" branch of the autonomic system responsible for mobilization, vigilance, and stress responses.

T

Tao (Eastern Philosophy)

The natural flow of existence, fundamental principle of Taoism. Aligning with the Tao corresponds to aligning with the rhythms of nature, self, and destiny.

Theta Waves (Neurophysiology)

Brainwaves associated with deep relaxation, meditation, creativity, and early-phase learning.

Transference (Psychology)

The projection of past relational patterns onto current relationships, often unconsciously.

Transmutation (Alchemy / Hermeticism)

The process of converting lower or chaotic states into refined, integrated consciousness.

Trauma Response Loop (Neurobiology)

A self-reinforcing pattern where past threat imprints generate present autonomic activation.

Triune Brain Model (Neuroscience — Metaphorical)

A conceptual model dividing the brain into reptilian, limbic, and neocortical systems to explain behavior and emotion.

U

Unconscious Bias (Cognitive Psychology)

Automatic mental shortcuts or associations influencing perception and behavior outside of awareness.

Unconscious Competence (Learning Theory)

The stage in which skills or behaviors become automatic and integrated.

Unity

The final stage of integration where body, mind, and spirit—Warrior, Scholar, Sage—operate as one coherent whole.

Unity Consciousness (Hermetic / Spiritual)

The perception of interconnectedness between self, others, and the cosmos.

V

Vagal Tone (Neuroscience / Physiology)

An indicator of vagus nerve function related to emotional regulation and social engagement.

Values Clarification (Psychology)

Identifying principles that guide choices and ethical alignment; central to the Sage's path.

Vibration, Principle of (Hermeticism)

The assertion that all things are in motion and can shift their frequency, including emotional and mental states.

Virtue (Ethics / Hermeticism)

The ethical foundation of Hermetic practice — including integrity, compassion, honesty, courage, humility, and responsibility. Virtue directs power toward constructive ends.

W

Warrior Archetype (Jungian / Hermetic)

The aspect of the psyche that embodies strength, discipline, boundaries, and unwavering presence; associated with Jing.

Working Memory (Neuroscience)

Short-term mental workspace used for holding and manipulating information.

Wounded Healer (Jungian / Mythological)

A figure who transforms personal suffering into wisdom, service, and compassionate presence.

Y

Yang (Daoism)

Active, outward, dynamic energy; complements Yin.

Yin (Daoism)

Receptive, inward, still energy; complements Yang.

Z

Zenith Experience (Contemplative Psychology)

A peak state of expanded insight, clarity, and coherence; may follow periods of struggle, practice, or dissolution.

Be the Warrior, the Scholar, the Sage - a Blueprint to Happiness & Purpose

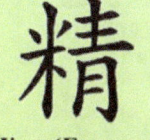

Jing (Essence)

Warrior Phase

Through practicing physical movements (Jing - essence), one can better develop:

1) Awareness – realization, perception or knowledge

2) Memory – the process of reproducing or recalling what has been learned or experienced

3) Coordination – bring actions together into a smooth concerted way

4) Control – skill in the use of restraint, direction and coordination

5) Endurance – ability to tolerate stress or hardship

6) Strength – power to resist or exert force

7) Stamina – combination of endurance and strength

8) Speed – rate of motion

9) Power – might or influence

10) Reflex – end result of reception, transmission and reaction

11) Strategy – a careful plan or method to achieve a goal

Mentally, these character traits are nurtured & refined:

Respect

Discipline

Self Esteem

Confidence

Determination to Achieve Goals

Qi (Energy)

Scholar Phase

Through practicing mental exercises (Qigong - vitality), one can better develop:

1) Relaxation of the muscles

2) Building of internal power

3) Strengthening of the organs

4) Improving the cardiopulmonary function

5) Strengthening the nerves

6) Improving vascular function

7) Can be practiced by the seriously ill

8) Help prevent injury to joints, ligaments & bones

9) Quicken recovery time from injuries & surgery

10) Building of athletic & martial arts power

11) Lessening of stress & balances emotions

12) Benefits sedentary individuals

Mentally, these concepts are comprehended & assimilated:

Human anatomy & physiology

Energy flow (Qi) with the energy meridians

Structural alignment of the skeletal & muscular systems

Shen (Spirit)

Sage Phase

Through practicing mediation exercises (Shen - consciousness), one can develop better understanding of:

1) The origin, nature, and character of things and beings

2) The human condition - study of human nature and conditions of life

3) The importance of communication on many different levels in order to share and disseminate wisdom

4) Sense of purpose

5) Making a difference

6) Self-less service to others

7) The inter-relationship between one another and how that can determine cause and effect

8) Our interaction between humans and the world (universe) we exist in

www.MindandBodyExercises.com

© Copyright 2023 - CAD Graphics, Inc.

Glossary - Graphic

Abdominal breathing – effective, diaphragmatic breathing that fills your lungs fully, reaches all the way down to your abdomen, slows your breathing rate, and helps you relax.

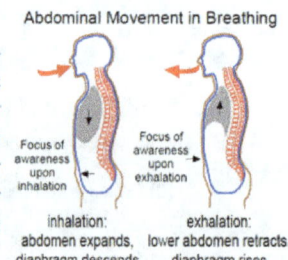

Bagua (or Pa Kua) / 8-trigrams - eight symbols used in Daoist philosophy to represent the fundamental principles of reality, seen as a range of eight interrelated concepts. Each consists of three lines, each line either "broken" or "unbroken," respectively representing yin or yang.

The Brass Basin – sits within the lower abdomen, touching at the navel in the front, between L2 & L3 vertebrae in the back and the perineum at the base.

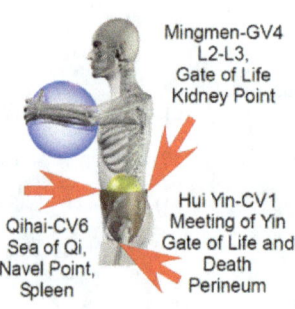

Bubbling Well - an energetic point located in the sole of the foot, slightly in front of the arch between the 2nd and 3rd toe. In the meridian system it is the same as the Kidney 1 point.

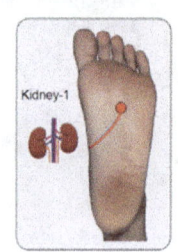

Dan Tian - 3 energy centers Lower Dan Tian (1 of 3) - also known as the "sea of qi," is positioned below and behind the naval encompassing your lower bowl and is closely related to jing (or physical essence).

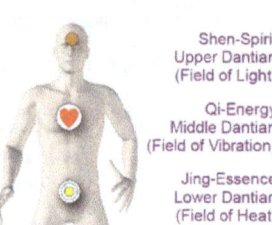

Daoyin, DaoYi, Daoist Yoga, Qigong – all names for energy exercises, with specific postures, little or no physical body movement and mindful regulated breathing patterns.

Feng Shui – translated into 'wind and water'; it is a Chinese philosophical system that teaches how to balance the energies in any given space.

Conception Vessel (Ren Mai) – flows up the midline of the front of the body and governs all of the yin channels. The Conception Vessel is connected to the Thrusting and Yin Linking vessels.

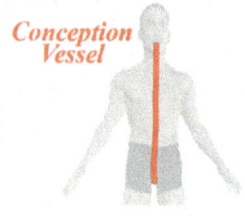

Governing Vessel (Du Mai) - flows up the midline of the back and governs all the Yang channels.

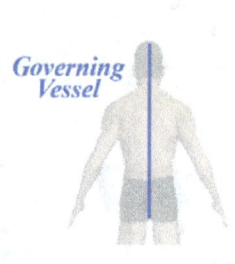

General Yu Fei – creator of the 8 Pieces of Brocade set.

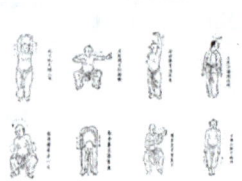

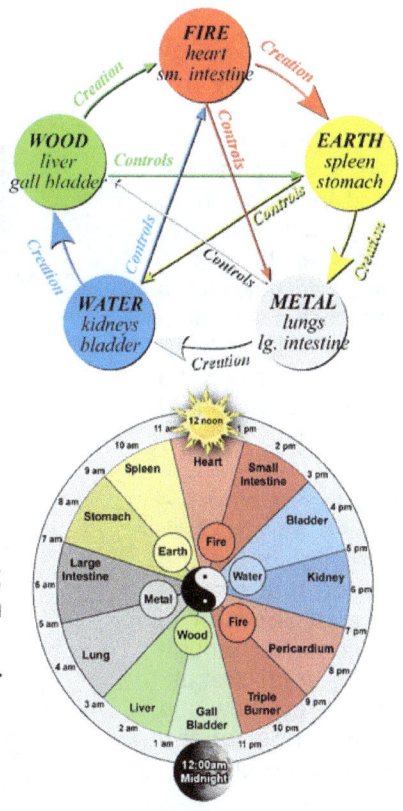

Controlling Cycle – the controlling or regulating sequence of the 5 element cycle. Wood controls Earth; Earth controls Water; Water controls Fire; Fire controls Metal; Metal controls Wood

Generating Cycle – the creative sequence of the 5 element cycle. Wood generates Fire; Fire generates Earth; Earth generates Metal; Metal generates Water; Water generates Wood.

Horary Cycle - 24 Hour Qi Flow Though the Meridians; This cycle is known as the Horary cycle or the Circadian Clock. As Qi (energy) makes its way through the meridians, each meridian in turn with its associated organ, has a two-hour period during which it is at maximum energy.

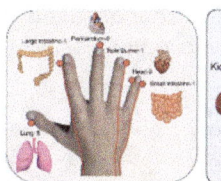 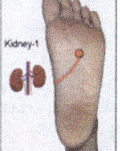 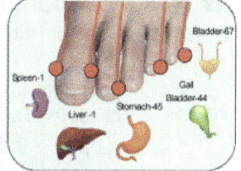

Jing Well - The Jing (Well) points are 1 of 5 of The Five Element Points (shu) of the 12 energy meridians. They are located on the fingers and toes of the four extremities. These points are thought to be where the Qi of the meridians emerges and begins moving towards the trunk of the body. These are of upmost importance in that these points can help restore balance within the energy flow throughout the human body.

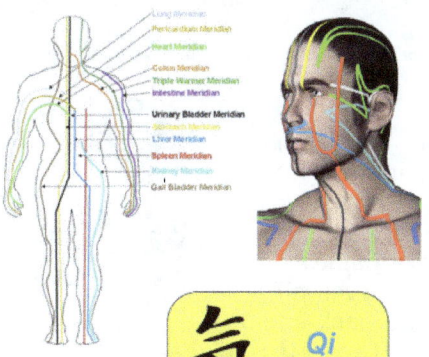

Meridians - a meridian is an 'energy highway' in the human body. There are 12 meridians and each is paired with an organ. Qi energy flows through these meridians or energy highways.

Qigong - or Chi Kung, is breathing exercises, with little or no body movement, that can adjust the brain waves to the Alpha state. When the mind is relaxed, the body chemistry changes and promotes natural healing.

San Jiao (Triple Burner/Heater) – is a meridian line that regulates respiration, digestion and elimination. It is responsible for the movement and transformation of various solids and fluids throughout the system, as well as for the production and circulation of nourishing and protective energy.

Upper Burner	WEI QI
Middle Burner	YING QI
Lower Burner	YUAN QI

Nine Gates - the energy gates in your body are major relay stations where the strength of your Qi are regulated. These gates are located at joints or, more precisely, in the actual space between the bones of a joint. The nine gates are located at the shoulder, elbow and wrists, hip, knee and ankles, and along the cervical, the thoracic, and the lumbar spine.

Seven Energy Centers – also known as chakras, are energy points in the subtle body that start at the base of the spinal column, continue through the sacral, solar plexus, heart, throat, eyebrow and end in the midst of the head vertex at the crown.

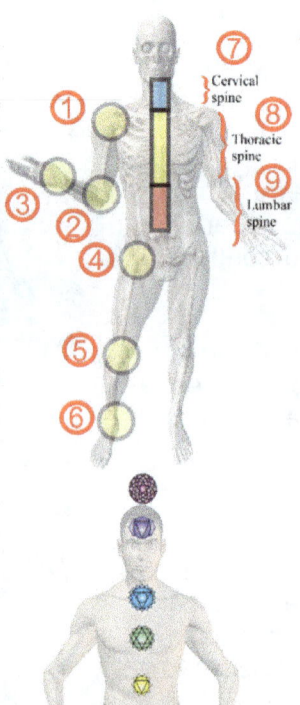

Three Treasures – Jing, Qi & Shen

Jing – (essence) the physical, yin and most dense of the Three Treasures. Think of Jing as a candle, specifically the quality and quantity of the wax.

Qi, chi or ki - (energy/breath) the energetic, vital force within all living things and it the most refined Treasure. Think of Qi as the burning flame of the candle.

Shen – (consciousness or spirit, is the most subtle of the Three Treasures and is the vitality behind Jing and Qi. Think of Shen as the light or illumination produced from the flame.

Six Healing Sounds – auditory sounds used for clearing internal (yin) organs and other tissues of stagnant Qi.

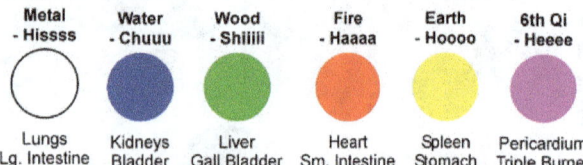

The 3 Hearts – Heart, abdomen, calves: The first heart is the heart in your chest for the oxygenation of the blood. Lower abdominal breathing is considered the second heart for circulation of fluid, Qi and digestion. The third heart is the calf muscles for re-circulation of the blood.

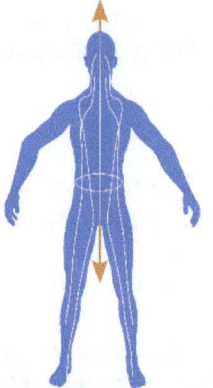

Small Circuit – the linking two energy pathways that run along the midline of the body into a cycling loop. The "fire pathway", Du Mai (Governing Vessel), extends up the back and the other, Ren Mai (Conception Vessel), down the front of the body.

Vessels – there are 8 extraordinary vessels that function as reservoirs of Qi for the Twelve Regular Meridians.

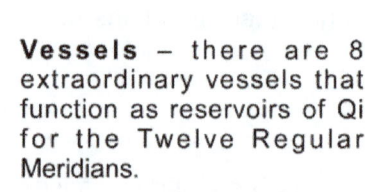

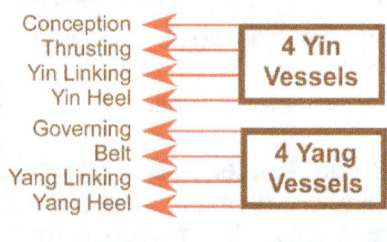

Taoism - (sometimes Daoism) is a philosophical or ethical tradition of Chinese origin, or faith of Chinese exemplification, that emphasizes living in harmony with the Tao (or Dao). The term Tao means "way", "path", or the "principle".

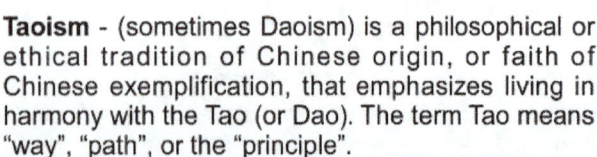

The Void (Supreme Mystery)

Wuji – ultimate stillness, the beginning of creation.

Yang Qi - yang refers to aspects or manifestations of Qi that are relatively positive: Also - immaterial, amorphous, expanding, hollow, light, ascending, hot, dry, warming, bright, aggressive, masculine and active.

Yin Qi - yin refers to aspects or manifestations of Qi that are relatively negative: Also - material, substantial, condensing, solid, heavy, descending, cold, moist, cooling, dark, female, passive and quiescent.

Taijitu - The term taijitu in modern Chinese is commonly used to mean the simple "divided circle" form (), but it may refer to any of several schematic diagrams that contain at least one circle with an inner pattern of symmetry representing yin and yang.

Yi – intellect, manifests as spirit-infused intelligence and understanding.

Baihui point - Governing Vessel 20 (GV 20). Sits on the crown of the head.

Jade Pillow – located at the top of the cervical vertebrae (C1).

Great Hammer – located on the midline at the base of the neck, between seventh cervical vertebra and first thoracic vertebra.

Mingmen point – Conception Vessel 6 (CV6), the 'Sea of Qi' located on the lower abdomen.

Qihai point – Conception Vessel 6 (CV6), the 'Sea of Qi' located on the lower abdomen.

Hui Yin point – Conception Vessel 1 (CV1), also known as the base chakra, is located between the genitals and the anus; the part of the body called the perineum.

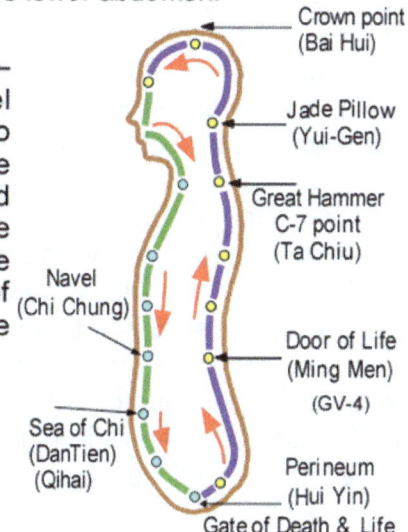

Wu Xing or 5 Elements - The 5 Element theory is a major component of thought within Traditional Chinese Medicine (TCM). Each element represents natural aspects within our world. Natural cycles and interrelationships between these elements, is the basis for this theory. These elements have corresponding relationships within our environment as well as within our own being.

Zang-Fu organs – solid, yin organs are Zang – yang and hollow organs are Fu.

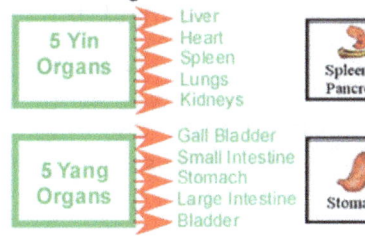
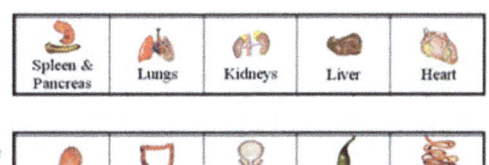
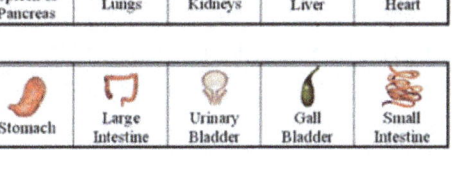

265

About the Instructor, Author & Artist - Jim Moltzan

My fitness training started at the age of 16 and has continued for almost 45 years. During that time, I attended high school, then college, and worked 2 jobs all while pursuing further training in martial arts and other fitness methods. Many years ago, I started up an additional business to help finance my next goal of owning my own school. I moved to Florida from the Midwest to make this goal a reality. Having owned two wellness and martial arts schools, I have surpassed what I once believed to be my potential. At this stage in my life, I have chosen not to open any more schools, as I found the business aspects took too much focus away from my true passion: training and teaching others.

Beyond my professional endeavors, I am also a husband and father of two grown children. I believe that we must be prepared to work hard mentally, physically and financially to earn our good health and well-being. Not only for ourselves but for our families as well. Good health always comes at a cost whether in time, effort, cost, sacrifice or some combination of the previous.

I returned to college in my later 50's, to pursue my BS in Holistic Health (wellness and alternative medicine). My degree program covered many wide-ranging topics such as anatomy and physiology, meditation, massage, nutrition, herbology, chemistry, biology, history and basis of various medical modalities such as allopathic, Traditional Chinese Medicine, Ayurveda/yoga, naturopathy, chiropractic, and complimentary alternative methods. I also studied religion, mythology of the world, stress relief/management as well as sociology, psychology (human behavior) and cultural issues associated with better health and wellness.

Most of the movements I teach and write about originate from Chinese martial arts. The Qigong (breathing work) is from Chinese Kung Fu and the Korean Dong Han medical Qigong lineage. I have also gained much knowledge of Traditional Chinese Medicine (TCM) from many TCM practitioners, martial arts masters, teachers and peers. This includes many techniques and practices of acupressure (reflexology, auricular, Jing Well, etc.), acupuncture, moxibustion as well as preparation of some herbal remedies and extracts for conditioning and injuries. I have been studying for over 20 years with Zen Wellness, learning medical Qigong as well as other Eastern methods of fitness, philosophy and self-cultivation. I have been recognized as a "Gold Coin" master instructor having trained and taught others for at least 10000 hours or roughly over 35 years. The core fitness movements are from Kung Fu and its forms in Tai Chi, Baguazhang, Dao Yin and Ship Pal Gi (Korean Kung Fu and weapons training). Each martial art has mental, physical and spiritual aspects that can complement and enhance one another. The more ways that you can move your body and engage your mind, the better it is for your overall health.

Physical health, mental well-being and the relationships within our lives; are these the most cherished aspects of our existence? Yet, how much effort do we put towards improving these areas on a daily basis?

Many have used martial arts and other mind-body methods of training as methods of learning to see one's character as others see them. I feel that I can offer the priceless qualities of truth, honor and integrity with my instruction. You must seek the right teacher for you, because in time a student can become similar to their teacher. Through the training that I have experienced and offer to others, an individual can understand and hopefully reach their full potential.

By developing self-discipline to continuously execute and perfect sets of movements, an individual can start to understand not only how they work physically but also mentally and emotionally. You can find your strengths and your weaknesses and improve them both. Through disciplined training, one not only enhances physical abilities but also cultivates mental resilience, allowing them to achieve their fullest potential in all areas of life.

I have co-authored a book, produced numerous other books and journals, graphic charts and study guides related to the mind and body connection and how it relates to martial arts, fitness, and self-improvement. A few hundred of my classes and lectures are viewable on YouTube.com.

Lineage

- Recognized as a 1000 and 10,000-hour student and teacher
- Earned gold coins through the Doh Yi Masters and Zen Wellness program
- Earned a 5th degree in Korean Kung Fu through the Dong Han lineage

Education

Bachelor of Science in Holistic Medicine - Vermont State University

Books Available Through Amazon

Book Titles by Jim Moltzan

Book 1 - Alternative Exercises

Book 2 - Core Training

Book 3 - Strength Training

Book 4 - Combo of 1-3

Book 5 - Energizing Your Inner Strength

Book 6 - Methods to Achieve Better Wellness

Book 7 - Coaching & Instructor Training Guide

Book 8 - The 5 Elements & the Cycles of Change

Book 9 - Opening the 9 Gates & Filling 8 Vessels-Intro Set 1

Book 10 - Opening the 9 Gates & Filling 8 Vessels-sets 1 to 8

Book 11 - Meridians, Reflexology & Acupressure

Book 12 - Herbal Extracts, Dit Da Jow & Iron Palm Liniments

Book 13 - Deep Breathing Benefits for the Blood, Oxygen & Qi

Book 14 - Reflexology for Stroke Side Effects:

Book 15 - Iron Body & Iron Palm

Book 17 - Fascial Train Stretches & Chronic Pain Management

Book 18 - BaguaZhang

Book 19 - Tai Chi Fundamentals

Book 20 - Qigong (breath-work)

Book 21 - Wind & Water Make Fire

Book 22 - Back Pain Management

Book 23 - Journey Around the Sun-2nd Edition

Book 24 - Graphic Reference Book

Book 25 - Pulling Back the Curtain

Book 26 - Whole Health Wisdom: Navigating Holistic Wellness

Book 27 - The Wellness Chronicles (volume 1)

Book 28 - The Wellness Chronicles (volume 2)

Book 29 - The Wellness Chronicles (volume 3)

Book 30 - The Wellness Chronicles (complete edition, volumes 1-3)

Book 31 - Warrior, Scholar, Sage

Book 32 - The Wellness Chronicles (volume 4)

Book 33 - The Wellness Chronicles (volume 5)

Book 34 - Blindfolded Discipline

Book 35 - The Path of Integrity

Book 36 - Spiritual Enlightenment Across Traditions

Contacts

For more information regarding charts, products, classes and instruction:

www.MindAndBodyExercises.com
info@MindAndBodyExercises.com

www.youtube.com/c/MindandBodyExercises
www.MindAndBodyExercises.wordpress.com

407-234-0119

Social Media:

Facebook:	MindAndBodyExercises
Instagram:	MindAndBodyExercises
Twitter:	MindAndBodyExercise

Jim Moltzan - Mind and Body Exercises
522 Hunt Club Blvd. #305
Apopka, FL 32703

Website

Blog

YouTube Channel

www.ingramcontent.com/pod-product-compliance
Lightning Source LLC
Chambersburg PA
CBHW080731300426
44114CB00019B/2549